ROUTLEDGE LIBR[illegible]
ACCOUN[illegible]

Volume 43

UNDERSTANDING ACCOUNTING IN ITS SOCIAL AND HISTORICAL CONTEXT

UNDERSTANDING ACCOUNTING IN ITS SOCIAL AND HISTORICAL CONTEXT

The Case of Cost Accounting in Britain, 1914–1925

ANNE LOFT

Routledge
Taylor & Francis Group
LONDON AND NEW YORK

First published in 1988 by Garland Publishing, Inc.

This edition first published in 2021
by Routledge
2 Park Square, Milton Park, Abingdon, Oxon OX14 4RN

and by Routledge
52 Vanderbilt Avenue, New York, NY 10017

Routledge is an imprint of the Taylor & Francis Group, an informa business

British Library Cataloguing in Publication Data
A catalogue record for this book is available from the British Library

ISBN: 978-0-367-33564-9 (Set)
ISBN: 978-1-00-304636-3 (Set) (ebk)
ISBN: 978-0-367-51115-9 (Volume 43) (hbk)
ISBN: 978-0-367-51124-1 (Volume 43) (pbk)
ISBN: 978-1-00-305249-4 (Volume 43) (ebk)

Publisher's Note
The publisher has gone to great lengths to ensure the quality of this reprint but points out that some imperfections in the original copies may be apparent.

Understanding Accounting in Its Social and Historical Context

The Case of Cost Accounting in Britain
1914 - 1925

ANNE LOFT

GARLAND PUBLISHING, INC.

NEW YORK & LONDON 1988

For a list of Garland's publications in accounting, see the final pages of this volume.

Library of Congress Cataloging in Publication Data

Loft, Anne.
Understanding accounting in its social and historical context: the case of cost accounting in Britain, 1914-1925 / Anne Loft.
p. cm. — (Foundations of accounting)
Bibliography : p.
ISBN 0-8240-6116-0 (alk paper) :
1. Cost accounting—Great Britain—History—20th century. 2. Managerial accounting—Grat Britain—History—20th century. 3. Cost accounting—Social aspects—Great Britain—History—20th century. I. Title II. Series.
HF5686.C8L56 1988
657' .42'0941—dc19 88-18798

Design by Renata Gomes

The volumes in this series are printed on acid-free, 250-year-life paper.

Printed in the United States of America

DEDICATED

WITH LOVE

TO

MY PARENTS

BARBARA & VERNON

CRAWFORD

AND

MY GRANDMOTHER

MARY CRAWFORD

Costing is the 'X-ray' of commerce.
Properly employed, it will penetrate the externals, reveal obstructions and irregularities, focus on danger-points, and provide a permanent evidence of unquestionable fact.

E. Miles Taylor, speaking at The Conference on Scientific Costing, June 1919.

ACKNOWLEDGEMENTS

The presentation of this book represents the fulfilment of a personal ambition, but would never have been completed but for the kind help and support that I have received from the many people who have also been involved in one way or another. The concept of this particular research has developed through my many discussions with Professor Anthony Hopwood, whose patient help and support has been invaluable, and I am pleased to have this opportunity of expressing my appreciation to him.

I also have an obligation for academic support and inspiration to colleagues working at other institutions, many of whom have been kind enough to read and comment upon my work. These include Ted O'Leary (University of Cork), Trevor Hopper (University of Manchester), Hugh Wilmott (Aston Management Centre), Peter Tetley (Birmingham Polytechnic), Derek Bailey (University of Birmingham), Simon Pitt (London Business School), Peter Miller (University of Sheffield), Peter Armstrong (Huddersfield Polytechnic), Tony Puxty (University of Sheffield) and Sten Jönsson (University of Göteborg). A general appreciation must also go to the members of the Management Control Workshop Group and the Doctoral Research Colloquia of the European Accounting Association.

Staff of many libraries have helped, those of the British Library at Bloomsbury and the Newspaper Library at Collingdale, the London Business School, Birkbeck College, University College, and the Institute of Chartered Accountants in England and Wales, have all done so at various times. Most of all, though, I must thank Ng Soot Hong and Jackie Solomon of the Institute of Cost and Management Accountants.

My greatest obligation, is, however, to my husband Mark, who has waited so long and patiently for its completion.

CONTENTS

CHAPTER 1

INTRODUCTION

1st Gent. Where lies the power, there let the blame lie too.

2nd Gent. Nay, power is relative; you cannot fright
The coming pest with border fortresses,
Or catch your carp with subtle argument.
All force is twain one: cause is not cause
Unless effect be there; and action's self
Must needs contain a passive. So command
Exists but with obedience.

George Eliot

Accounting has come to play an important role in the working of modern society. Along with this goes a portrayal of accounting as a merely technical matter; as a factual and objective form of knowledge untainted by social values or ideology. Accounting data are apparently asocial products almost untouched by human hand. Such a conception is reflected in popular definitions: in the Little Collins Dictionary, for instance, 'accountancy' is described as the "profession, duties, of accountant", an 'accountant' is a "keeper or inspector of accounts" and an 'account', in this context, a "statement of money received or paid"[1]. The role of the accountant is, it seems, to collect, keep and inspect a particular variety of facts about the world.

This general view of accounting as a purely technical matter is reflected in the writings and activities of practitioners and academics working in the area usually described today as 'management accounting'[2]. In a dictionary of business terminology the entry for management accounting reads: "a resource of management that supplies financial information at all levels to be used in the planning and administering of business" (Giordano, 1981). Management accountants' own understanding of the function and role of their work similarly relies upon the notion that it is 'information for management' that they are providing. They apparently perform a sophisticated service function in taking the raw facts of organisational life and converting them into a form which enables managers to make efficient decisions (see, for instance, Horngren, 1984, p.3).

Underlying this thesis is the belief that it is both interesting and insightful to examine accounting not as merely a technical process, nor as a technical process with social and political consequences, but as an activity which is both social and political *in itself*.[3] The accounting information which results from the use of accounting systems is, after all, a social product; it only has meaning in the context and culture in which is is produced. To the untutored eye of an Azande tribesman an accounting statement would have no meaning other than a random pattern upon paper, just as a religious artifact from that culture would have no significance to us beyond its immediate physical and aesthetic appearance.

One way of illuminating the social nature of accounting is through studying its cultural variations, for although accounting is a feature of modern industrial society the extent of its use varies across cultures. For example, it appears that the success of Japanese industry has occured without the same massive commitment to management accounting that has been made in the US (Hopwood, 1985). Even between Western European countries there are differences: Horowitz (1980) found that British management control practices had more of a financial emphasis than those prevalent in Germany. Hopwood remarks that in the Atlantic fringe countries of the USA, the UK and possibly the Netherlands, accountants have a level of influence in corporate management which they do not attain elsewhere (1985).

Here it is the examination of the history of accounting which provides a means to explore the complicated relationship between accounting and society. Traditionally the history of accounting has been regarded from a technical perspective. As Johnson (1986) writes, a school of management accounting has been dominant whose main concern was with the mechanical, procedural, and technical aspects of accounting. The past marches purposively toward the present in this scheme and cost accountancy practices appear to have necessarily and inevitably evolved into their present shape. Alongside this, although much more clearly developed in the case of financial accounting and auditing than management accounting, have developed histories of professional associations [for instance, ICAEW (1966), ICWA (1969), Banyard (1985), Garrett (1961), AAA (1966)]. These histories tend to assume not only that accountants are supremely necessary to society but also that the major factor enabling their current success has been their form of professional association. Dingwall (1976) christens such works 'official history', referring to the way in which they implicitly seek in their explanations of the past to further the use of the techniques and the social status of the practitioners in the present.

Recently, in the wake of the work of the business historian Alfred Chandler (1962, 1977), there has emerged a more sophisticated school of management accounting history. In this work the development of cost and management accounting is related to the emergence and growth of the large business enterprise (see Johnson, 1972, 1975, 1981; Kaplan, 1984). Although this is an interesting line of research, from the perspective being taken here it does not go far enough for the writers tend to concentrate on the accounting-organisation relationship and pay only scant attention to the broader social context. In addition, the knotty question of the relationship between the practising of the techniques and the emergence of a specialised occupation whose members claim special skills in the area tends to be sidestepped. It is precisely these wider accounting-society relationships which are to be focused upon here.

The inspiration for the method of study of the history of accounting adopted here comes from the work of Michel Foucault, in particular the history, described as 'genealogical' in form, *Discipline and Punish* (1977a). Although it is sub-titled *The Birth of the Prison*, the book is far more general in scope than this title suggests. Prisons are used as an exemplar of a wider phenomenon: the growth in society, rapid from the late eighteenth century onwards, of disciplinary institutions dedicated to the detailed surveillance and control of the everyday life of those within them. The prison becomes merely one site of the exercising of a disciplinary technology to be found emerging through the nineteenth century in armies, hospitals, schools, factories and other institutions. In the case of manufacturing, for instance, "great manufacturing spaces" were created where production could be organised on a much more systematic basis than when conducted by outworkers, or in cramped and dark workshops. As part of the control of activity in such 'spaces' individual workers could be assigned positions arranged to facilitate their surveillance and the creation of records about their work. These records in turn could enable the comparison of workers and the detailed assessment of their use to the business (ibid., Chap. 4). The genealogical perspective which Foucault advances is one which provides a meticulous and patiently documented account of the social and historical conditions under which developed both these institutions and the techniques which they use to discipline those who are subject to their influence. Foucault derived such a concept of genealogy from Nietzsche (see Foucault, 1977b), and given this it is apposite to note Nietzsche's suggestion to Dr Ree on reviewing his book *On the Origin of Moral Sensations*. He wrote that on seeking the origin of morals we should not do as Ree does and gaze around "haphazardly in the blue" but should look in the direction of an actual history of morality:

> For it must be obvious which colour is a hundred times more vital for a genealogist of morals than blue: namely grey, that which is documented, what can actually be confirmed and what has actually existed, in short the entire long hieroglyphic record, so hard to decipher, of the moral past of mankind! (1969, p.21)

Applied to management accounting, the questions which such a genealogical history address concern the conditions under which the accounting techniques for *knowing* the business organisation emerged and spread. Recognising that the surveillance and detailed control of individuals in a business organisation can be achieved in a number of different ways, of which cost and management accounting is only one, insights into the particular contribution of accounting can be gained by building on Braverman's (1974) analysis of how the concept of control adopted by modern management requires that every activity in production must have its several parallel activities in the management centre. These parallel activities result in a replication of the process of production in paper form before, as, and after it takes place in physical form (ibid., p.125). The resultant paper replication of the production processes provides knowledge in a permanent form of what should have happened and what did happen as regards production during a period of time. When seen in such terms, the characteristic feature of cost and management accounting is that it contributes to this replication of production by providing a record translated into monetary terms. Through this translation objects and events as diverse as wasted raw materials, a strike by lathe operators and the sales managers' business lunch can be linked. The cost and management accounting systems create a quite specific knowledge about the activities of the organisation; they make it 'visible' (Burchell et al, 1980, p.17) in terms of monetary values.

The knowledge which such systems produce may appear, at first sight, to be an inanimate one- of prices, costs, profits etc.- but this is a misleading impression. The knowledge only has meaning in its relationship to the activities and actions of human individuals. It is intimately related to power. Just as the records can be aggregated to provide an overall representation of the diverse activities of the organisation in financial terms, so that representation can be disaggregated to relate it to the actions and responsibilities of particular individuals or groups. The financial record is closely bound up with the functioning of the human organisation.

Foucault emphasises the ways in which knowledge and power are closely linked. He considers not only how knowledge enables the exercising of power but also how power itself tends to generate systems which produce knowledge. From such a perspective, 'knowledge' and 'truth' are part of the effects of power. However such a productive relationship needs to be seen in terms wider than knowledge being simply an ideology which legitimates power. For Foucault, the "methods of observation, techniques of registration, procedures for investigation and research. apparatuses of control" are in fact very effective instruments for producing power and when power is "exercised through these subtle mechanisms it cannot but evolve, organise and put into circulation a knowledge, or rather an apparatus of knowledge" (1980, p.102).

The emergence and functioning of management accounting systems are intimately bound up with the operation of such a power/knowledge relationship. On the one hand, they produce a knowledge which can be used to discipline individuals. Activities incorporated into the account can more readily be made subject to the exercising of power. On the other hand, the system of accounting which produces the knowledge is itself a product of the operation of power. Probing, investigation, questioning and requests for explanation are all implicated in the production of a system which creates a quite specific 'truth'. The exercising of power produces a 'reality' where the value of activities and events is of a carefully measured significance- a significance proportionate to their monetary value. Through cost and management accounting a 'regime of truth' (Foucault, 1980, p.133) is formed about events. The very positivity of the highly specific knowledge produced by accounting tends to exclude attention from a whole range of other issues. Not given prominence through the accounting system, they can often be ignored as they do not enter into the sanctioned conceptions of the real and the true.

The genealogical perspective seeks to illuminate the rich detail of the relationship between the development of cost and management accounting as a technique of knowledge and the exercising of power within both the disciplinary institutions of the factory and the wider social context. Compared with the official history of accounting which traces a path of evolution to the present with few hiccups having apparently disturbed its smooth progress, such an unofficial history seeks to explore the many 'small' ways in which this technique of knowledge emerged and spread. Through its patiently documentary methods a genealogy aims to consider the emergence of the techniques of accounting, their institutionalisation, and the formation of a discourse about them. A discourse which explains what it is and how it should be done- a discourse where the status of 'fact' and 'truth' is claimed.

The aspect of the emergence of management accounting that is the focus of the present study is its professionalisation. For accounting in business enterprises in the United Kingdom is not simply carried on by a hierarchy of bureaucratic functionaries but by professional accountants with allegiances to their professional associations as well as to the organisations in which they work. Through their publications, meetings, examination syllabi and other activities these associations play a role in defining and furthering the techniques of accounting, deciding who is competent to practise and in elaborating the discourse. They are clearly closely involved with the creation of management accounting as it can be seen operating in organisations.

Interestingly, however, in the literature of the sociology of professions the intellectual core, the knowledge base of the professions, is as Goldstein (1984, p.175) points out, taken as a given factor around which professionalisation takes place. The dependence of the intellectual core upon the social process of professionalisation has been ignored. Even Foucault's genealogies of disciplinary technologies did not explore explicitly the complex relationship between a body of knowledge and the social organisation of its practitioners.

Recognising the importance of this neglected area of investigation, the present study aims to explore one aspect of it. However the tracing of a genealogy is a task of immense proportions, not least because the details of the interrelationship between the techniques, the knowledge and the practitioners must be grounded in the social and organisational contexts in which they took place. For this reason one particular period in British history is the focus of the investigation- the period from 1914 to 1925.

The taking of this period is not meant to imply that it was the seminal period for cost accounting in the United Kingdom. It was, however, a very interesting period. During the First World War cost accounting, as a contemporary observer put it, "came into the light" (*The Cost Accountant*, December 1922, p.216), almost one could say as an unintended consequence of the way in which the Government attempted to prevent profiteering and to price their contracts with manufacturers in the absence of a free market. Manufacturers had costing forcibly brought to their attention through Government measures and, as a result, the institution of cost accounting systems in manufacturing industry seems to have proceeded quickly. Cost accounting and cost clerks thereby gained greater recognition for their activity and their numbers grew. Not only did professional accountants become far more involved with cost accounting during the war but also, in the politically and socially turbulent year of 1919, the Institute of Cost and Works Accountants [now called the Institute of Cost and Management Accountants(ICMA)] was formed to advance the interests of, and claim professional status for, cost accountants themselves. This new association began to act as a focal point for the growth of discussion about the nature of cost accounting knowledge and technique, and the role which cost accountants should play in society.

What precisely cost accounting was, how it should be done, what purposes it could serve and who (at both a professional and at an individual level) would be responsible for it were in a state of debate and flux in the period. Such a period of uncertainty provides an ideal context for considering one part of the genealogy of management accounting. Through a detailed examination of the active interplay between issues, institutions, occupational claims, knowledge and techniques an 'unofficial' history can begin.

NOTES

(1) This opening paragraph was inspired by the Introduction to Irvine et al (1979).

(2) The change which has occured during the last present century, from something called 'cost accounting' to something called 'management accounting' is a fascinating one, for as Heidegger comments, words and language are not just simply "wrapping in which things are packed for the commerce of those who write and speak" (quoted in Steiner, 1978, p.41). Writing in 1921, Howard Hazell summed up what was then known by a variety of names, amongst them 'industrial accounting' and 'cost accounting', as an "examination and collection of the facts and figures in a business or trade, in order to find the total cost of producing the commodities or of rendering the services by which the business or trade exists" (Hazell, 1921, pp.17-18); the aim being to obtain "the truth, the whole truth, and nothing but the truth about the costs and the production ... " (ibid., p.36). In contrast, writing in 1984, Charles Horngren declares: "Management accounting is the process of identification, measurement, accumulation, analysis, preparation, interpretation, and communication of information that assists executives in fulfilling organisational objectives (Horngren, 1984, p.3). Whereas Hazell's 'truth' is unconditional and stands aloof and independent from any use to which it might be put, the information which Horngren writes of gathering is collected with the purpose in mind of assisting the individual executive and depends on the needs of that executive. It seems that different information will be needed by the executive for different purposes, and thus it is an important part of the management accountants' task to select the relevant parts of the 'truth' for the executive.

Horngren's *Introduction to Management Accounting* is an American textbook aimed at college students, Hazell's *Costing for Manufacturers*, was a manual written and published in Britain, describing to manufacturers the virtues of installing a costing system and how to go about doing it in practice. In their own ways both are typical of the times in which they were written and provide an illustration of the changes which the last seventy years have brought.

In the United Kingdom in 1921, cost accounting was only just 'coming into the light'. Within the following thirty years cost accounting systems were installed, of various degrees of sophistication, in most medium and large sized companies. Some larger companies imported techniques, usually through the use of consultancy firms, from the United States. However, it was not until the 1950s that American accounting ideas and techniques began to obtain a wider press in

Britain. This was probably associated to some degree with the visit to the United States in 1950 of a specialist team, under the auspices of the Anglo-American Council on Productivity, to "find out what accounting, costing and statistical information is provided for American management at different levels: by what methods it is obtained and how it is used". Their report, entitled "Productivity Report: Management Accounting" (Anglo-American Council on Productivity, 1950), appears to have brought the term into general use to describe the internal accounting of an organisation. It appeared modern, and linked the activity with the new management literature, in a a way in which the old term 'cost accounting' did not.

The Institute of Cost and Works Accountants (ICWA) explicitly recognised this change by altering the name of their journal from *The Cost Accountant* to *Management Accounting* in 1965. The shift in title was indicative of a subtle change in the express purposes to which the activity was apparently directed. The president of the ICWA at this time, addressed the issue as follows:

> ... cost and works accountancy, as practised by the members of the Institute with their practical experience of costing in industry and their ability to see figures in terms of real things and real happenings, is the very stuff of management accounting" (*Management Accounting*, January 1965, p.1).

In 1972 the name of the ICWA itself was changed to the Institute of Cost and Management Accountants (ICMA).

An interesting further development on this question of name, is the outlining by the ICMA, in a recent strategy review, of their intention to try to change the institute's name to the Chartered Institute of Management Accountants. This would mean dropping the word 'cost' from their title altogether (reported in *Accountancy Age*, 7 November 1985, p.1).

(3) Critical perspectives have been developed regarding other (apparently) technical and scientific practices, for example, social statistics (Irvine et al, 1975; Hacking, 1981); law (Cain, 1983); the measurement of IQ (Gould, 1981; Sutherland, 1977); psychological testing (Rose, 1979); and the production of scientific knowledge in the laboratory (Woolgar, 1982), to give but a few examples.

CHAPTER 2

UNDERSTANDING COST AND MANAGEMENT ACCOUNTING IN ITS SOCIAL AND ORGANISATIONAL CONTEXT

> The technique of accountancy is of extreme importance because it works in the most nearly universal medium available for the expression of facts, so that facts of great diversity can be represented in the same picture. It is not the production of these pictures that is a function of management, but the use of them.
>
> *Productivity Report: Management Accounting*
>
> Anglo-American Council on Productivity: report of a specialist team which visited the USA (1950).

Introduction

In this theoretical chapter some of the ideas introduced in Chapter 1 are considered further. Cost and management accounting is a technique which produces, in monetary terms, a visible record of events which happened in an organisation- a 'regime of truth' about work there. The nature of this disciplinary technique is explored through the use of an architectural metaphor: Jeremy Bentham's panopticon, a building whose design rendered all actions of the inmates visible to those watching from a central inspection tower. Extending Michel Foucault's use of this metaphor, the discussion proceeds to consider Bentham's panopticon book-keeping system as an illustration of the way in which record-keeping systems create knowledge which is intimately linked with the operation of power. Translation of different forms of records into the common terminology of money renders them comparable with each other and in a form which makes it possible to aggregate them. This enabling of aggregation (and disaggregation) means that all the 'small' events of individuals going about their jobs in the organisation can be identified as part of a greater whole: the functioning of the entire organisation.

Cost and management accounting systems create part of what is counted as 'true' in the present, in that they create a socially accepted 'truth' about work. What counts in society as 'the truth' changes, and to understand the present it is necessary to ask where this truth came from and what influenced its form. One factor which must be considered is the practitioners themselves; the extent of usage of a disciplinary technique and the social organisation of its practitioners are inevitably related to one another. Widespread use, and high regard for the efficacy of the techniques will facilitate the formation of a closed occupational order of specialists demanding high monetary remuneration. Vice versa: if those in practice are well organised, and obtain high status, they will be more likely to be able to persuade those in authority of the efficacy of their techniques. They may also influence the knowledge base of the occupation itself-promoting and developing certain areas of knowledge and practice through their examinations, meetings and publications.

Whilst it is important to examine the social organisation of practitioners in shaping knowledge and practice, this influence should not be overestimated, however, for such a social organisation exists within a socio-economic framework which severely limits the forms of knowledge and action which exist. This cultural context not only forms the 'backdrop' to the emergence and institutionalisation of disciplinary techniques, such as cost accounting, but is inextricably linked to them- for these techniques themselves help to shape the cultural context. This chapter considers at a theoretical level the intimate linking of knowledge, practice and society; relationships to be explored in later chapters at a practical one in the context of the years 1914 to 1925.

Genealogical History[1]

Foucault writes that the purpose of his work is a "history of the present"; in contrast to those who write a "history of the past in terms of the present" (1977a, p.31). This latter form of history is characterised by the way in which the past is written about using the terms and perspectives of the present. The entire focus of such work tends to be on the way in which the 'truth' of the present smoothly emerged, in an evolutionary fashion, from the past. Collingwood succinctly criticises this form of history:

> If you allow yourself to think for a moment about the tactics of Trafalgar as if the ships were driven by steam and armed with long-range breech-loading guns you have for that moment allowed yourself to drift outside the region of history altogether (1970, p.58)

Even the more sensitive writers of accounting history tend to fall into this style. Pollard writes, for instance:

> The practice of using accounts as direct aids to management was not one of the achievements of the British industrial revolution; in a sense it does not belong to the later nineteenth century but to the twentieth (1968, p.288).

As Williams notes, the use of the term 'management' in a general sense to mean the administration of business is a twentieth century development (1983, pp.156-158) associated with the emergence of 'management' as a distinct occupational grouping in industrial nations. Pollard makes the error of trying to give nineteenth century accounting twentieth century aims- this is a 'history of the past in terms of the present'.

In contrast, Foucault's 'history of the present' is directed towards understanding how what now counts as being 'true' came to be regarded as so. The title of his chair at the Collége de France: the History of Systems of Thought, expresses this idea. The 'history of the past in terms of the present' takes the truths which are accepted in the present and explains their gradual emergence from the apparent sea of falsities erroneously taken for 'the truth' in the past. Foucault steps back from this, he gives no priority to the truth of the present above that of the past. Truth is a "thing of this world" and each society has its own "regime of truth" (1980, p.131). The 'truth' at a particular time is something to be understood in relation to the society within which it is accepted. The changing of what is accepted as 'the true' involves the study of the rich detail of history, of the discontinuities and unintended consequences of actions and events. In an interview entitled "Questions of Method" (1981), Foucault expressed these ideas as involving, firstly:

> Making visible *a singularity* at places where there is a temptation to invoke a historical constant, an immediate anthropological trait, or an obviousness which imposes itself uniformly on all. To show that things 'weren't as necessary as all that': it wasn't as a matter of course that mad people came to be regarded as mentally ill; it wasn't self-evident the only thing to be done with a criminal was to lock him up; it wasn't self-evident that the causes of illness were to be sought through the individual examination of bodies; and so on ...

secondly:

> ... rediscovering the connections, encounters, supports, blockages, plays of forces, strategies and so on which at a given moment establish what subsequently counts as being self-evident, universal and necessary (ibid, p.6).

The history which results from the application of such principles is very different, both in form and substance, from traditional history. Taking the example of the prison; in the past, histories have emphasised conscience as the motor of institutional change, and assume that the reformative practice of punishment proposed by the reformers was in intention, and in result, more humane than the harsh practices of the eighteenth century. The world outside the prison walls rarely features in these accounts (Ignatieff, 1981, p.154). In Foucault's account in *Discipline and Punish* (1977a) the prison becomes merely one site of the exercising of a disciplinary technology to be found developing rapidly, from the late eighteenth century onwards, in the army, hospitals, schools, asylums and other institutions. These developments reflect the application of a new philosophy of order and of sovereignty. In this the inmates of these institutions are no longer perceived of as part of the vast undifferentiated mass of humanity but as individual subjects to be known and understood.

The subject matter upon which Foucault has used this methodology, or perhaps it would be more accurate to say the history through which this methodology has emerged, is that of the 'human sciences'. This is the name he has given to the intellectual disciplines which concern themselves with the creation and application of knowledge about 'man'. Thus the first of Foucault's major works, *Madness and Civilisation: A History of Insanity in the Age of Reason* (1967), is concerned with changing concepts of madness, and its distinction from reason; the second, *The Birth of the Clinic* (1973), is about the emergence of modern medicine. In the latter work he describes the research he is undertaking as involving:

> ... a project that is deliberately both historical and critical, in that it is concerned- outside all prescriptive intent- with determining the conditions of possibility of medical experience in modern times (ibid., p.xix).

The human sciences require for their emergence and application a huge body of detailed knowledge about humans. This knowledge is not only created through the functioning of disciplinary institutions and technologies but provides, in itself, the basis for controlling individuals in those institutions. For instance, scientific management rests upon detailed observations of the work of human individuals, and is used as a way of ordering and disciplining their lives in the factory. The *present* which Foucault desires to understand is one which is characterised by a "closely linked grid of disciplinary coercions" (1980, p.106). Disciplinary institutions (the school, factory, army, hospital, asylum, and so on) and technologies, dedicated to the detailed surveillance and control of the everyday life of those within them are a crucial part of modern society. Yet in studies of industrialisation and modernisation the importance of the invention and extension of these techniques and institutions has been neglected (Foucault, 1977a, pp.224-225). In *Discipline and Punish*, this question has been considered in detail; the focus of study being the prison, whilst other institutions (the factory, school, hospital and army) are considered more briefly.

In an interview in 1977 Foucault retrospectively summed up his essential concern in two words as having been "power and knowledge" (1980, p.109)[2]. Power and knowledge tend to reinforce one another, for as just discussed, the human sciences involve the creation of detailed knowledge about individuals which can be used to order and discipline them. Through the disciplinary technology itself more knowledge is created which adds to the power of the human sciences. In the case of scientific management, noted above, the results of the operation of the system itself, in terms of the performance of workers, can themselves be fed back into the system of knowledge in order to refine it. Foucault writes of discipline that:

> Instead of bending all its subjects into a single uniform mass, it separates, analyses, differentiates ... It 'trains' the moving, confused, useless multitudes of bodies ... Discipline 'makes' individuals; it is the specific technique of a power that regards individuals both as objects and as instruments of its exercise. It is not a triumphant power, which because of

> its own excess can pride itself on its omnipotence; it is a modest, suspicious power, which functions as a calculated, but permanent economy ... (1977a, p.170).

In a passage which implies disagreement with the Marxist critiques of industrial society he suggests that:

> We must cease once and for all to describe the effects of power in negative terms: it 'excludes', it 'represses', it 'censors', it 'abstracts', it 'masks', it 'conceals'. In fact, power produces; it produces reality; it produces domains of objects and rituals of truth (ibid., p.194)

Although 'knowledge' and 'truth' are part of the effects of power, they are not simply ideologies which legitimate it, for they help to create it in a positive way (Foucault, 1980, p.102). Thus the 'truth' accepted at a particular time and place in history is linked to the operation of power within that society.

Despite the tendency of power and knowledge to reinforce one another, change does occur. The presence of change reflects the ultimate inability of any system of power and its associated knowledge to totally dominate. The rich play of events in the world inevitably introduces instabilities and weaknesses. The task of the historian of the present is to explore the complex detail of the processes through which 'the truth' has changed.

Cost and management accounting is just one of the techniques through which the surveillance and detailed control of individuals in a business organisation is achieved. Its peculiar characteristic is that it replicates the production processes and makes it 'visible', in paper form and in monetary terms. The virtual 'encirclement' of the activity of work by financial measures is common in large companies. Considering an item being physically produced in an assembly line; the adding to it of brackets, the painting of it, and so on, are procedures which have already been planned in the office and their financial consequences assessed through the procedures of budgeting. After the physical processes are over, the record of the events is again translated into financial terms to be compared with the budget.

The paper replication in the office of events in the factory is an important part of the procedures through which the activity of work is controlled. In Foucault's terminology cost and management accounting is a *disciplinary technology* which has emerged within the institution of the factory. It is also a 'human science'; although scarcely comparable in elaboration with those such as medicine and psychology, the discourse which has developed around the technique- in textbooks, universities and so on- is indeed one which involves the creation and application of knowledge about man; albeit man reduced to the cipher of the number on the page. In the powerful management accounting systems presented to budding corporate managers throughout the world [through texts like Horngren (1984)], the whole hierarchy of the organisation becomes the object of management accounting systems. Workers most clearly so, for as far as the company who employ them are concerned they are simply a cost of production to be minimised. More senior employees, whilst being made responsible for controlling the costs of others' activity, are themselves made the subject of reports for the attention of individuals yet more senior. The theory surrounding and supporting the application of the techniques must be seen to be one intimately concerning man, for all its claims to be mere technique.

In *Discipline and Punish* (1977a), Foucault uses Jeremy Bentham's principle of 'panopticism' as a symbolic representation of the mode of control of disciplinary institutions (pp.195-230). Within Bentham's planned prisons, workhouses, schools and factories, a regime of incredibly intense and detailed control was laid out, based upon the idea of making activity visible, this was the principle of panopticism. It is a mode of control directed not against the physical body (in the old eye-for-an-eye, tooth-for-a-tooth way), but towards the improvement of, in some sense, the *soul* of the individual. The watching of the individual and the control and reform of that individual being intimately connected in this schema. The individual was to reform him or herself under the constant instructive, supervising and watchful eye of authority. The keeping of records of activity is a disciplinary technology discussed only briefly by Foucault. As it is the basis of the control exercised through systems of accounting it is appropriate to discuss it in depth here, and it is both interesting and fortunate that Bentham saw the potentiality for record-keeping to rationalise and intensify the control exercised in the panopticon. Bentham's writings are thus used here as an intellectual tool to explore the disciplinary nature of accounting systems.

Bentham's Panopticon: Visibility and Discipline

> I do really take it for an indisputable truth, and a truth that is one of the cornerstones of political science- the more strictly we are watched, the better we behave.
>
> Jeremy Bentham [quoted in Bahmueller (1981), Frontispiece]

In a letter to a friend in 1786, Jeremy Bentham wrote that his brother, Samuel, had hit upon "a very singular new and I think important, though simple, idea in Architecture ...." This idea was that of the Inspection House:

> ... a circular building so contrived that any number of persons may therein be kept in such a situation as either to be, or what comes to nearly the same thing to seem to themselves to be, constantly under the eye of the person or persons occupying a station in the centre which we call the Inspector's Lodge. You will be surprised when you come to see the efficacy which this simple and seemingly obvious contrivance promises to the business of schools, manufactories, and even Hospitals ... (Bentham, 1968-, Vol.3, pp.502-503).

Working first on the application of this principle of construction to prisons, Bentham designed a 'penitentiary panopticon'[3]. The key to the whole enterprise was to make every action of the prisoners visible to the guards, but without them knowing exactly when they were being watched. The prisoners were to occupy the cells around the circumference of a six storey building; the keepers to occupy the inspection lodge in the centre. Sitting, standing, or working, the actions of the prisoners were made visible by being silhouetted against the light from the windows for inspectors to observe. These inspectors were placed in such a way by "blinds and other contrivances" that they were concealed from the observation of the prisoners unless they saw fit to show themselves (Bentham, 1968-, Vol.4, pp.225-226).

Bentham wrote:

> Ideal perfection, if that were the object would require that each person should actually be in that predicament [being: "under the eyes of the persons who should inspect them"] during every instance of time. This being impossible, the next best thing to be wished for is, that, at every instance, seeing reason to believe as much, and not being able to satisfy himself to the contrary he should *conceive* himself to be so. (Bentham, 1843, Vol. IV, p.40)

The plan possessed the fundamental advantage of the:

> *apparent omnipresence* of the inspector (if divines will allow me the expression) combined with the extreme facility of his *real presence* (Bentham, 1843, Vol. IV, p.45).

The cell was to serve "for all purposes: *work*, *sleep*, *meals*, *punishment*, *devotion*: the unexampled airiness of construction conciliating this economy with the most scrupulous regard to health" (Bentham 1968-, Vol. 4, pp.225-226). The prisoners were not to be left idle, the powers of observation were to be put to good use. In the *Outline of a Plan of Management for a Panopticon Penitentiary House* Bentham noted how by a "mixture of laborious employment with sedentary" for the prisoners such a "distribution of time" would be maintained (allowing deduction of "what is necessary for meals and repose, and on Sundays for devotion") as "shall fill up the whole measure of it with either productive labour or profitable instruction". Prisoners were to be taught trades so that they could obtain employment when they left the prison and all inhabitants were to be taught "in the common and most useful branches of vulgar learning". The inmates were to be allowed a share in the produce of their productive labour to "attach them to industry" (Bentham, 1968-, Vol.4, pp.226-227).

Thus in this project observation and reformation were to be closely linked, individuals were to be transformed into law abiding citizens who would be useful to society. The process was to be open to society at large to observe- for the whole prison itself was to be open to the public gaze; the architecture which enabled "the whole establishment to be inspected almost at a view" would:

> ... render it a *spectacle*, such as persons of all classes would in the way of amusement be curious to partake of ... not only on Sundays at times of Divine Service but on ordinary days at meal times or times of work.

This would provide thereby:

> ... a system of inspection, universal, free and gratuitous, the most effectual and permanent of all securities against abuse. (ibid., pp.227-228)

The panopticon principle was one which Bentham saw as applicable to many different situations[4] where persons were to be kept under inspection, from schools and prisons to asylums and manufactories[5].

Bentham noted that the panopticon was so called "because of an eye stationed towards the centre" which exhibits everything that passes within it at a view (ibid., pp.289-290). He represented it graphically as an eye within a triangle surrounded with the words "mercy, justice, vigilance" (ibid., p.219). As Foucault points out, whilst the dungeon deprives of light and hides the inmates, the panopticon's full lighting enables better control of the prisoners- the visibility is a trap (1977a, p.200). Instead of a mass of prisoners kept in darkness, each prisoner becomes a subject who can be identified, known and reformed as an individual. They are caught up in an arrangement where power does not need to be actually exercised over them- things are arranged such that surveillance, and hence the operation of power is to a large extent automatic (ibid., p.201). The major effect of the panopticon is to "induce in the inmate a state of conscious and permanent visibility that assures the automatic functioning of power" (ibid., p.201). The fact that the inspector only looks occasionally is not important, for the inmate has no idea when the inspector *will* look but knows that he could look at any time. It is an "architectural apparatus", that is "a machine for creating and sustaining a power relation independent of the person who exercises it"; it is a mechanism which "automizes and disindividualises power". This power:

> ... has its principle not so much in a person as in a certain concerted distribution of bodies, surfaces, lights, gazes; in an arrangement whose internal mechanisms produce the relation in which individuals are caught up (ibid., p.201-202).

What is at issue here is not the actual impact of Bentham's plans[6], but the principle of making the activities of individuals in institutions visible in order to control them which Bentham took to its extreme. The panopticon is not only a "marvellous machine" for "producing homogeneous effects of power" (ibid., p.202) but is "the diagram of a mechanism of power reduced to its ideal form" (ibid., p.205). It is a symbol of the "disciplinary" forms of control of people which characterise our society today, and began to generally replace more traditional forms from the seventeenth and eighteenth centuries onwards (1980, p.119). The principle of controlling through making visible has become widely adopted in a great variety of institutional settings in the nineteenth and twentieth centuries; from schools (Jones & Williamson, 1979; Markus 1982) to asylums (Foucault, 1967) and factories.

The actual action of surveillance in factories tends to take the form of a pyramid structure of authority rather than a single gaze. A pyramid structure is suited to the factory for it has qualities helpful in the fulfilling of the dual requirements of production and discipline: it can be "complete enough to form an uninterrupted network ... and yet discreet enought not to weigh down with an inert mass on the activity to be disciplined". The "relays" of the disciplinary gaze in this pyramid structure are a specialised personnel- clerks, supervisors, foremen. Supervision becomes a very special function, one which forms an integral part of the production process (Foucault, 1977a, p.174). Foucault writes of the power in this hierarchised surveillance that it is:

> ... not possessed as a thing, or transformed as a property; it functions like a piece of machinery. And, although it is true that its pyramidal organisation gives it a 'head', it is the apparatus as a whole that produces 'power' and distributes individuals in this permanent and continuous field. This enables the disciplinary power to be both absolutely indiscreet, since it is everywhere and always alert, since by its very principle it leaves no zone of shade and constantly supervises the very individuals who are entrusted with the task of supervising: and absolutely 'discreet', for it functions permanently and largely in silence .... It is a power that seems all the less 'corporal' in that it is more subtly 'physical' (ibid., p.177).

Thus although it is individuals- clerks superintendents etcetera- who are doing the surveillance the supervisors themselves are watched in turn and thus everyone is in a sense 'caught' in a network of power relations.

In the 'relaying' of disciplinary power the making of *records* of activity becomes important for they can give surveillance a precise and accurate quality. This property will be explored in the following section, beginning again with the ideas of Jeremy Bentham.

Record-keeping and Discipline: Extending Visibility

Bentham's plans to build and run panopticon penitentiaries floundered, but the idea remained with him, to be used again when he developed his grand scheme to solve a problem of great public concern at the close of the eighteenth century, that of the paupers. In this scheme panopticon re-emerged but along with an additional aid to surveillance- that of book-keeping. He wrote to Arthur Young in 1797 that:

> Book-keeping *rationalized*- if thus I may have leave to translate your French- imported raisonne- Book-keeping extended in its limits as well as corrected in its language by human reason, is one of the main pillars of my system ... (Bentham, 1968-, Vol.5, pp.378-379).

Bentham's book-keeping system was to be an immensely thorough and detailed exercise involving the recording of many minute details of life in the organisation; as he writes:

> ... pecuniary economy, usually regarded as the sole object of book-keeping will here be but as one out of a number; for the system of book-keeping will be neither more or less than the history of the system of management in all its points (Bentham, 1843, Vol.VIII, p.392).

There were to be books for recording almost everything, entries were first to be made in a "chronological book" and from there copied into a "methodological book". Books were to be divided into the main categories: "1. Population Books, 2. Stock Books (including accounts of articles received, issued and consumed), 3. Health Books, 4. Behaviour Books and 5. Correspondence Books." The level of detail was great, for instance under the sub-heading of 'behaviour books' was a 'complaint book', whose twelve headings included 'time (day, hour, and minute); by whom; against whom, or what ... witness or witnesses examined; ... time employed in the examination ... (ibid., pp.393-394)[7].

The entire pauper population of half a million were to be kept, 2000 in each, in 250 of these Poor-Panopticons distributed evenly across the country. Management on this scale seemed to Bentham to "demand good book-keeping" as the "hinge" on which good management would turn (ibid., p.391). Bentham wrote: "book-keeping is one instrument in the hand of economy, architecture another" (ibid., p.392), these two systems of control were closely inter-linked with one another[8] and the architecture itself aided the keeping of the records:

> ... under the proposed system of management, as the *demand* for a copious system of book-keeping is in an unexampled degree urgent and extensive, so are the *facilities* afforded to the process of book-keeping, by the peculiar plan of architecture, equally unexampled. Compactness and simultaneous transparency- both of which properties it exhibits in perfection- are the principle points upon which the advantage turns. Elsewhere, the knowledge of the matter of fact requires to be communicated to the manager in chief, often through a variety of channels: *here*, it is present to all his senses, and requires only to be *preserved*- No false musters- no running to and fro- no mislayings and huntings- no crossings and justlings, for the purpose of survey and registration: every person, and every thing, within view and within reach at the same instant. A degree of minuteness which might elsewhere be impractical or unthrifty- would be without obstruction and without objection, *here* (ibid., p.393).

For Bentham this book-keeping was important because it could in a sense 'freeze' history. What happened last week, last year- at any time in the past- could be 'seen' by inspecting the books (see Bahmueller, 1981, p.193). These two objects, book-keeping perfected, inspection perfected coalesced in the rite of the "annual walk". This would take place in the Board Room of the Panopticon around a circular table sixty feet in diameter where the Directors of the Company could view the Books and "obtain a simultaneous view of the state of the establishment ... in the way of the ocular demonstration" (quoted in ibid., p.193). Thus the Directors could 'see' all that happened during the year without being permanently in the observation tower watching all that went on. As Bahmueller writes, book-keeping perfected was the ultimate Utilitarian victory over the messy disorderliness of social reality, and its ability to do so lay in its capacity to telescope all things and events into categories which, once condensed, could be displayed rigorously in written form and made literally visual at a glance (ibid., pp.193-194). However, control did not rest simply in making the past available to inspection but defined what should happen in the future; the analysis of the records was to be the basis for changes in the management policy:

> ... for the system of book-keeping will be neither more or less than the history of the system of management in all its points ... at each period it is necessary that it should be known what ... the state of management *is* and *has been*, in order that it may, in no *future* period be suffered to grow *worse*, but in every future period be made to grow *better and better* in as high a degree as may be (Bentham 1843, Vol. VIII, p.392).

The panopticons for the poor were thus to be used as an experimental laboratory for all sorts of medical and social research, from changes in diet to the best age for commencement of sexual intercourse. Any improvements found in one house were to be "taken in each instance for a pattern, and copied in every other" (ibid., p.397).

The relationship between the architecture, the keeping of records and the minute control to individual human beings can be seen with clarity in this scheme of Bentham's for solving the pauper problem. Control exercised through the process of making visible what is happening reaches a fetishistic level, a level which, from an intellectual point of view, is insightful because it illustrates how, and in what ways, systems of records can be powerful as a way of controlling. Just as the architecture of a factory- its light and space and division into pre-arranged workspaces- enables work to be observed so the recording systems present a 'frozen' record of productive activity. The paper replication of the activity of work in the form of records remains available for inspection after the events themselves have occurred.

Recording enables an 'objective' comparison of worker with worker, a worker's production yesterday with that he or she has achieved today. Foucault writes of the "whole meticulous archive constituted in terms of bodies and days" (1977a, p.190). Discipline refers the actions of each individual to the whole, each is measured and evaluated with respect to norms; the power of this 'normalisation' is that it at one and the same time imposes homogeneity and brings out the small individual differences which lurk beneath the sameness (ibid, pp.182-184). The nineteenth century industrialist William Brown of Dundee directed his under-manager thus:

> ... a desk to be placed in the reeling room and a new book begun for the keeping of accounts of the spinners and reelers work and waste, the weight of the yarn, the quantity spun etc. The overseer with your assistance will daily attend to it and it will be highly beneficial for you to spend a portion of time with it every day, examining and considering the state of the different hands' work and waste, comparing the one with the other, yesterday's with today's, and making yourself intimately acquainted with all their performances (quoted in Berg, 1980, p.194).

The individual workers were becoming describable and hence analysable objects of knowledge rather than being in a sense "below the threshold of description". To be written about in great detail would normally have been a mark of great distinction in pre-disciplinary times; it would have been the result of a judgement that you were a very special individual. Either very important in spiritual or secular life, or notorious- for example for committing murders. The disciplinary methods of watching and recording reversed this and made the record a document for possible use, a means of control and a method of domination (Foucault, 1977a, pp.190-191).

In the pyramid-like structure of authority which prevails in factories the creation of records is convenient for discipline- power is exercised on the basis of the 'truth' contained in the records. A worker whose record shows that he or she regularly trims 500 plates a day when other employees trim 800 can be disciplined on the basis of this record (bonus can be lost, ultimately the employment itself can be terminated). Through the records kept in an organisation each individual employee becomes identified and *known* to authority. Employees stop being an amorphous group of people, they become *individuals*, an individual will be assigned characteristics, for example: William Bede, born 7 June 1952, joined the company 9 December 1976, given clock number 2601552828; in files in the offices one will be able to find out all sorts of details about him: how many times he has been late this month, how long it took him to drill 578 widgets last week and so on.

Records are not just an enabling device for power to use, the creation of a record is an act of power in itself. Not only does it represent the result of a choice concerning what is important in the organisation but its creation can induce obedience. One feature of Bentham's panopticon is interestingly reflected in the control exercised through recording systems. The central tower enabled observation of the inmates of the Panopticon, yet without them being aware of it. Because they *know* that any offence against the rules of the establishment will result in punishment and that at any particular moment they *could* be being observed they will tend to obey the rules. As Bentham put it "in proportion as *punishment* is *certain*, *delinquency* will be *rare* (Bentham, 1843, Vol.VIII, p.394).

The individuals exercise control over their own behaviour because they know the potentialities of the system. In the *Dynamics of Bureaucracy* Blau describes how he found in his research that, what he refers to as 'statistical records', can act as a mechanism of control. A supervisor wanted to know the number of interviews completed by each of his subordinates in order only to take corrective action if any of them worked too slowly. In fact the very counting of interviews induced them to work faster and thus facilitated operations by making such corrective actions virtually superfluous. The use of 'statistical records' not only provided supervisors with information which enabled them to rectify poor performance, but often obviated the need for doing so (Blau, 1955, pp.34-35). The mere knowledge that what they had done had been made visible to management in the medium of a record had an important disciplinary effect. The creation of the knowledge about the work was both a result of power and a creation of it. As records are usually taken away from the place where they are produced to be summarised, stored and inspected, the exercise of discipline comes to have an automatic quality. Records are taken to offices where they can be inspected at will- by those with the authority to do so- the subject of the record normally has no control over it; in the case of factories (and indeed other institutions such as hospitals) not even the right to inspect it for him- or herself.

Records do not just define a 'truth' of greater status than memory but in a way they define what is important in the organisation and what is not. The record makes visible what those in authority deem to be important; there are many events happening in a factory in a day but only a small proportion of them will enter the official records. For instance, a worker's boredom and consequent depression will not be recorded[9], although it may be an important feature of work as that individual experiences it. It will not enter the records, and will not be summarised in the yearly annual report to be exposed to the public 'gaze', as records of production and sales will be. Without an event being turned into a record it only remains in existence in the minds of those who observed it. It remains 'visible' only in memory. The physical objects which have resulted from the production process may be available for inspection but the *detail* of their production so necessary to discipline is lost. In the factory memory has come to be regarded as unreliable and 'second-class' evidence; for instance the *record* of the number and type of widgets which a worker made on a particular day will have a more legitimate status as 'the truth' about what happened than the worker's own recollections based only upon memory. Every day the worker in a factory is reminded of the purpose of his or her presence by this continual recording.

In our society there is a fetishism for recording events, encouraged by the technology of a consumer society at a personal level, and endemic in bureaucratic institutions. Even our language reflects this, and seems to give a special authority to records for we talk of the 'record' a person has, as Wheeler (1969) notes. Institutions 'verify' characteristics of people by asking to see the official records which other institutions have made- birth certificates, marriage certificates, driving licences, examination certificates and so on. Once records are created they come to have a special status as evidence of the past through the very fact of being written, formalised, authorised, namely being given evidence in the world of documentation or computer files.

Weber writes how "the development of modern forms of organisation in all fields is nothing less than identical with the development and continual spread of bureaucratic administration" (1978, p.223); bureaucratic administration being "fundamentally domination through knowledge" (ibid., p.225). The *recording* of events in the organisation creates this knowledge which is at the root of bureaucratic administration. In business organisations it is the formal records and communications which ultimately dominate, despite the existence of less formal channels of communication, particularly at the higher levels of the organisational hierarchy. Even top management must face the yearly ritual of the presentation of the annual report, the record of the year's events summarised for the inspection of the owners of the company.

Through bureaucratisation all levels of authority are closely defined and jobs identified, analysed, and assigned their position in the organisational hierarchy. Individual employees become known subjects-with known positions, responsibilities and performances. Because of this the replacement of one individual by another becomes much easier.

Alfred Krupp, the German steel manufacturer, gave this notion is classic formulation:

> What I shall attempt to bring about (in the Krupp Works) is, that nothing shall be dependent on the life or existence of any particular person; that nothing of importance shall happen or be caused to happen without the foreknowledge and approval of the management; that the past and the determinable future of the establishment can be learnt in the files of the management without asking a question of any mortal (quoted in Baritz, 1974, p.6)

Records come to *define* the very existence which organisations have, they create an apparently perfectly objective representation, a 'regime' of truth within and about the institution. Yet records are things which are created, not a revelation of *what is*. They represent the result of a series of choices by management as to what records they want kept in order to try to control activity in the organisation. This is 'interested' knowledge in that it expresses the interests of management, it makes 'visible' a certain class of events in a certain format. It is a process of the creation of 'truth'.

Cost and Management Accounting as a Disciplinary Technique

The cost records which are a product of the work of those who operate cost and management accounting systems are records expressed in financial terms. The comments made in the previous section about records as a disciplinary technique apply to accounting records. However, because they involve the translation of records concerning diverse objects and events into a common terminology, that of money, they become a more powerful system of control. A strike by welders can be brought into direct comparison with the resources invested in supplying salesmen with cars, or a canteen for workers.

Different types of records about organisational activity are made comparable and capable of summarisation through this translation. It enables an aggregation of the 'facts' about past productive (or non-productive) activity in the organisation. It also enables disaggregation; a figure on a report which has resulted from a process of aggregation, say the cost of labour in X-plant for May 1985, can be examined more closely by tracing it back down into its component parts, in this case the individuals working in the different departments in the plant.

The making visible of productive activity through its paper duplication in the form of accounting records provides a representation of that activity which is very convenient to discipline. The particular power of the technique of cost accounting comes through the way in which it links (through translation into financial terms) the diverse events of the everyday process of production, to the goal of the enterprise of maximising profit. The small events of individuals going about their jobs in the organisation are recorded and processed through the accounting system, and identified as part of the greater whole which is the functioning of the entire organisation. The creation of accounting records enables control to be exercised far away in space and, to a certain extent, in time also (depending on how long the records are kept for). The decision to transfer a manager of a company from one plant to another may be made on the basis of a record of his contribution to company profit, at head office on a different continent, months or years after the events in question. Although, of course, events themselves cannot be altered by the later action of discipline, the knowledge of employees that accounts are being kept and will be open to examination can play an important part in inducing individuals to behave according to the instructions they have been given.

The potentialities for control in basic cost accounting systems can be illustrated in terms of a costing system described by Wheldon in his textbook published in 1932. Central to the system is a time recorder, which will punch the time onto a card, and four racks for cards. The first rack, labelled 'Out', contains the so-called 'gate cards' of employees not present. The second rack, labelled 'In', contains the cards of employees at work. The worker arriving in the morning finds his gate card in the 'Out' rack, records the time on it, and places it in the 'In' rack. The third rack is for 'Jobs Ahead'. Each job to be worked upon has a card made out for it and the foreman places these cards in this rack to be taken out and stamped by the worker when a job is begun. The stamped card is placed in the fourth rack, 'Jobs in Operation'. When the job is finished the worker 'clocks off' the job-card and places it in the 'Finished Jobs Box'.

The foreman files the finished job-cards consecutively according to each worker's clock number. Each morning a clerk from the Cost Department collects these cards. The recorded job times can be checked in the office against gate-times to ensure that all the time paid for is accounted for as time spent on jobs. Wheldon notes that:

> ... different-coloured cards may be used with advantage to denote the various departments, and different kinds of work, or to distinguish day-work from piece-work (ibid., pp.75-76).

The total cost for each job is collected in the 'Job Cost Ledger'. As an additional and overall control the profit shown by the cost books is reconciled with that shown by the financial accounts through the 'Profit and Loss Reconciliation Account'.

The racks adjacent to the clock provide a control which is at one and the same time general and particular. A glance at the first and second boards shows how many workers are present and how many are absent, whilst a glance at the third and fourth boards shows how many jobs are in operation and how many ahead. Closer inspection will identify the individuals involved and the work that they are doing. Information which can be verified at random by a manager walking around the relevant parts of the workshop or factory. The records produced by the system provide a powerful means for checking up on individuals; for note how it is suggested that the recorded job times can be checked in the office against gate-times, to ensure that there is not a minute of the worker's time which is not accounted for. Thus it is possible to know in minute detail what the worker has done during his time in the factory, not just simply that he or she has been present. Costs are aggregated, which means that broad general comparisons can be made between departments, and between different periods of time. Costs can also be disaggregated. It is possible to disaggregate the profit figure back through cost summaries to the work put in by, for instance, J. Kenton (No.26), on Friday, July 7th 1932. Someone examining the records can move from the general to the particular and back again.

Such systems of costing make visible the productive effort of the worker through a system of records which can be collated and compared in such a way that an individual worker's time at the factory can be divided into non-productive and productive. This productive time can be further traced into the commodities manufactured, even (if the production was in the form of discrete and identifiable jobs) into individual jobs. The principle of the disciplinary gaze being at its most effective when being complete enough to form an uninterrupted network, and discreet enough not to swamp the activity being disciplined, are clearly fulfilled in a most satisfactory way by cost accounting; it is so discreet that it does not even present itself to the worker as a watching 'supervisor' but as a collecton of pieces of card on which 'the facts' are recorded; it is so complete that it is linked into the very raison d'être of the whole institution, that of maximising the profit. Because the worker cannot watch the office staff going through the records, to him or her the accounts records are 'facts' about work which go into 'the system', the bureaucracy, to be examined. In this way the control becomes more anonymous; the person whose record is being examined does not experience this examination by another person- simply that they are subject to 'the system'.

The illustration was of a system modern in the 1930s in Great Britain. Systems of so called 'responsibility accounting' of more recent development, which involve planning and budgeting for the coming periods of time and allocating responsibility for the actual results through comparing the actual with the budget, link *the future* with *the past* in a powerful way. Events are surrounded by observations in time- for a budget lays down what should happen, the actual is recorded at the time, and after the event a comparison of actual and budget enables a very *precise* measure of the success or failure of the individual responsible. To each individual who is given a budget it acts as a framework for the future around which they must work. Such accounting systems enable the linking of the activities of individuals to the plans and purposes of the organisation as a whole, even in gigantic divisionalised corporations.

As I noted at the opening to this chapter modern society is characterised by a "closely linked grid of disciplinary coercions" (Foucault, 1980, p.106). It is these disciplinary coercions which make ours a "society of normalisation" (ibid., p.107). Individuals spend much of their lives in institutions- such as the school and the factory- where there is a very strict definition of what 'normal' behaviour is. People are coerced through the use of disciplinary techniques into acting according to these norms. Is it surprising, writes Foucault: "that prisons resemble factories, schools, barracks, hospitals, which all resemble prisons?" (1977a, p.228). In all of these institutions the individual inmates become the subject of a detailed knowledge about them; they and their activity are watched and measured. They are subject to disciplinary techniques and through these made the objects of the 'human sciences'- sophisticated knowledge systems which attempt to analyse, predict and control their behaviour. In a sense, as Foucault writes, discipline 'makes' individuals (ibid., p.170). In the factory the power of the disciplinary techniques is not just to be seen in the fact that they enable power to be exercised over employees. They actually produce a set of characteristics which 'is' the employee- a unit of production with a measured amount of training, skills and capacities. This power is exercised 'through' the employees, not simply over them.

Cost and management accounting is a sophisticated disciplinary technique which emerged in factories in the nineteenth century. Because of its use of money as a fundamental measurement standard it has the peculiar advantage of acting both as a 'rational'[10] means of making decisions regarding productive activity, and as a means of ordering and disciplining the employees of a business organisation. The characteristics of the individual created by the cost and management accounting systems are financial ones which locate that employee very directly as a factor of production. This happens all the way up the hierarchy of the large organisation in which a modern management accounting system is operating; the making of managers at each level responsible for certain costs and revenues allocates their contribution to ultimate profit in a way which 'creates' the supervisors themselves as subjects which are factors of production. It individualises people as part of productive activity, each individuals' work effort can be linked to the goals of the entire enterprise.

Cost and management accounting systems are apparatuses for producing knowledge in a very specific form. It is a knowledge of costs and profits, of waste and gain; a 'regime' of truth is created about the activity in the organisation. The cost records are an enabling device for power to act but at the same time the very fact of making the record, of producing knowledge, is an act of power.

Time, Accounting and Discipline

An important aspect of accounting not yet discussed here is its dependence upon, and furtherance of, a precise usage and measurement of time. Generally, within disciplinary institutions clock-time provides a rigid framework within which actions take place. The time-table imposed on school children is but one example of this. Within the factory the accurate measurement of time and intensive usage of it came to be seen as a crucial element in the organisation of production. The ancient belief that the longer the time a worker spends within the factory walls, the greater the amount of work he or she will perform, is brought into question. It becomes replaced with a new conviction: that it is the use made of the time which is more important than its length. Time becomes used "intensively" as opposed to "extensively" (Hobsbawm, 1968, p.356); every piece of time has to be used productively, activities are broken down into their constituent parts and each part given a time for its accomplishment. Acts become "temporally elaborated":

> ... the act is broken down into its elements; the position of the body, limbs, articulations is defined; to each movement are assigned a direction, an aptitude, a duration; their order of succession is prescribed. Time penetrates the body and with it all the meticulous controls of power" (Foucault, 1977a, pp.151-152).

To give an example, Frederick Taylor, one of the most ardent promulgators of the 'intensive' usage of time, wrote:

> The work of every workman is fully planned out by the management and least one day in advance, and each man receives in most cases complete written instructions describing in detail the task which he is to accomplish, as well as the means to be used in doing the work .... This task specifies not only what is to be done but how it is to be done and the *exact time allowed for doing it* (Taylor, 1911, p.39).

It is through procedures like these that a "positive economy" of time is arranged, it:

> ... poses the principle of a theoretically ever-growing use of time: exhaustion rather than use; it is a question of extracting, from time, ever more available moments, and from each moment, ever more useful forces (Foucault, 1977a, p.154).

The preparation of accounting statements depends upon a periodisation of time- for the preparation of daily balances, weekly summaries, monthly statements, yearly accounts and so on[11]. In cost accounting not only is a particular period of time taken as a reference period (e.g. the monthly report) into which events are categorised, but the precise time that they take provides the basis for allocating financial values to the events which make up the productive process (e.g. the drilling of a widget). The measurement of the times which the various activities in the enterprise take to perform play a fundamental role in the production of the 'facts' which are processed in the cost accounting system.

In the example taken from Wheldon's textbook (given earlier), of a fairly simple manual cost accounting system, the 'event' of a worker carrying out a job in a measured length of time, was recorded. This basic 'fact' of labour hours taken for a job was converted into a cost which became a basic unit in the costing system organised to control and co-ordinate activity. Cost and management accounting systems link the 'events' of production (in this case the individual jobs taking measured quantities of time) to the goal of profit maximisation. In standard costing systems which bring together costing and the scientific management techniques of simplifying, standardising and pre-planning work, the event of work and its concomitant cost are the subject of pre-set norms. Standard costing and scientific management together operate to predetermine the activity of work: the time to be taken, the materials to be used, the actions to be made in the performing of the task and the pay of the worker are laid out before the activity takes place. The 'exception reporting' system institutionalises the review of failures of the 'actual' to meet the 'planned'; only events which fail to occur as expected are reported.

Cost and management accounting thus relies upon a very precise usage of time. Such a usage of time was virtually unknown in the pre-industrial world, except in special institutions, in particular the monastery (perhaps the precursor of the acutely time-disciplined prisons, schools and factories which have come into existence during the last two hundred and fifty years). Cost and management accounting not only relies upon, but itself reflects a concept of time as something to be precisely measured and intensively used, a concept which pervades industrial society. Lukacs writes of how time has shed its "qualitative, variable, flowing nature" and has become frozen "into an exactly delineated, quantifiable continuum filled with quantifiable 'things'" (quoted in Gross, 1981-82, p.64). The 'quantifiable continuum' refers to the way in which time has been created as something existing independently of man with the property of stretching back to the past and forward to the future in absolutely regular portions. The quantifiable 'things' are the events occuring in the world fitted into this unilinear time. Time becomes like space that it is carefully measured and used.

Beyond relying upon and reflecting this concept of time accounting also plays a *constructive* role. Accounting, like other systems of control and co-ordination which measure and structure activity by reference to *the time*, continually reminds individuals how important time is. To Benjamin Franklin time was money; in the disciplined world of the modern organisation time is not *simply* money, but something which can be minutely sub-divided into units, each of which can be valued in money terms. Cost and management accounting aids, abetts and is an integral part of this process of the very precise valuation of life which characterises the modern age.

Disciplinary Power and the Question of Human Agency

So far, the discussion in this chapter has been based loosely around some of the ideas of Michel Foucault; rather more inspired by his work than being a direct application of it. One issue which Foucault touches upon in his earlier work, but has avoided more recently (this particularly applies to "Discipline and Punish"), is that of human agency. Who is it who does the disciplining, in whose interests do disciplinary institutions function? In the "Archaeology of Knowledge" (1972) under the heading of the "enunciation of discourse" these questions are raised using the example of doctors and medical discourse[12]; firstly, who is speaking?

> Who among the totality of speaking individuals is accorded the right to use this sort of language? Who is qualified to do so? Who derives from it his own special quality, his prestige, and from whom, in return, does he receive if not the assurance, at

> least the presumption that what he says is true? What is the status of the individuals who- alone- have the right, sanctioned by law or tradition, juridicially defined or spontaneously accepted, to proffer such a discourse?

In the case of, for example, medical statements they:

> ... cannot come from anybody; their value, efficacy, even their therapeutic powers, and, generally speaking, their existence as medical statements cannot be disassociated from the statutorily defined person who has the right to make them, and to claim for them the power to overcome suffering and death. (Foucault, 1972, pp.50-51).

Secondly: where are they speaking from?

> We must also describe the institutional *sites* from which the doctor makes his discourse, and from which this discourse derives its legitimate source and point of application (its specific objects and instruments of verification). In our societies, these sites are: the hospital ... , private practice ... , the laboratory... , lastly, what might be called the 'library' or documentary field, which includes not only the books and treatises traditionally recognised as valid, but also all the observations and case histories published and transmitted ... (ibid., pp.51-52).

In his inaugural lecture at the Collège de France, in 1970, he talks of the "appropriation of economic or political discourse", and of the 'social' appropriation of discourse on a broad scale; he asks what an education system is if not " ... a distribution and an appropriation of discourse with all its learning and its powers" (1971, pp.17-20).

These seem eminently important issues, but have not been followed up in later research in any depth. In the conclusion to the "Archaeology of Knowledge" the criticism is posed of his work that he has "tried to dispense with the speaking subject", that he believed that:

> ... one could cut off from discourse all its anthropological references, and treat it as if it had not come about in particular circumstances, as if it were not imbued with representations, as if it were addressed to no one (1972, p.200).

To this Foucault replied that the criticism was correct, but that if he:

> ... suspended all reference to the speaking subject, it was not to discover laws of construction or forms that could be applied in the same way by all speaking subjects, nor was it to give voice to the great universal discourse that is common to all men at a particular period ...

On the contrary it was to:

> ... show what the differences consisted of, how it was possible for men within the same discursive practice, to speak of different objects, to have contrary opinions, to make contradictory choices ... To show in what way discursive practices were distinguished from one another ... in short the aim was not to exclude the problem of the subject, but to define the positions and functions that the subject could occupy in the diversity of discourse (ibid., p.200).

It is these principles which lead to the 'subjectlessness' of such statements as:

> Power never ceases its interrogation, its inquisition, its registration of truth: it institutionalises, professionalises and rewards its pursuit (Foucault, 1980, p.93).

Power in Foucault's analysis is something that functions:

> ... power is not an institution, and not a structure: neither is it a certain strength we are endowed with; it is the name that one attributes to a complex strategic situation in a particular society (Foucault, 1978, p.93).

Power has no 'focus' in this analysis, even, apparently, in an institution such as the factory where authority takes a pyramidal form (as discussed earlier). There is an apex but:

> ... the summit doesn't form the 'source' or 'principle' from which all power derives as if from a luminous focus ... The summit and the lower elements of the hierarchy stand in a relationship of mutual support conditioning a mutual 'hold' (Foucault, 1980, p.159).

Hindess very appropriately describes Foucault as *gesturing* towards an alternative conception of power in terms of the organisation of strategic fields (1982, p.500): the gestures are rather ambiguous. If one considers the disciplinary mechanisms which operate in factories one surely must recognise that these operate in the interest of the owners who could be said to be at the focus of the hierarchy. With the separation of ownership and control in the large corporations, which have come to hold such a powerful position in the modern world, the focus may have become 'blurred' (there may be no directly identifiable mill owner living in a palatial residence just outside the town) but may still be there nonetheless. It is noticeable that Foucault has never devoted much effort to studying the disciplinary regimes of the factory, (there are some remarks in "Discipline and Punish") yet the social relationships of work affect most members of society on a daily basis[13]. Whilst not wishing to deny the importance of prisons, hospitals and asylums, it must be said that they are less important to the majority of members of society than the institutions of work. It is in this arena of work that the differences in the two perspectives are most clear: in Foucault's schema there can never be the all powerful and purposeful 'Capital' which in the Marxist schema directly controls events in the factory. Foucault is "notoriously cloudy" on questions of whose interests the disciplinary systems of the prison, asylum, and factory served (Ignatieff, 1981, p.176). Although at some points he refers in rather vague terms to the 'bourgeoisie' he often slips into "the use of the passive voice which makes it impossible to identify who, if anyone, was the historical agent of the tactics and strategies he describes" (ibid.).

This denial of focus, lack of consideration of the question of human agency and insistence on the study of power at the level of the disciplinary technologies themselves, rather than at the societal level, is part of Foucault's conscious rejection of the Marxist perspective of power. In trying to avoid the deterministic Marxist conception of agency, where the disciplining of work and other activities in capitalist society are apparently the result of the clearsighted actions of the bourgeoisie, Foucault has moved to what seems to be the opposite extreme. It is a critical perspective which begins from the small mechanisms of power rather than the global 'mode of production'. It causes him problems at times: in the discussion of the repercussions of the Council of Trent, Foucault analyses the situation as one in which power began from this single centre and filtered down to the minutest details of the forms of desire. When faced with this in an interview he confesses to have "inwardly blushed", admitting that he used the "metaphor of a point which progressively irradiates its surroundings"; but replying "that was a very particular case, that of the Church after the Council of Trent ..." (1980, p.199).

Within the institutions of the hospital, the asylum, the school and the factory which Foucault writes of, is there a smooth 'relay of power'? Power is surely mediated not smoothly, but 'lumpily' through professional groups, groups which have clearly socially appropriated discourse on a massive scale. Within the institutions of, for instance, hospitals and asylums, the human sciences of medicine and psychiatry are practiced by human agents, namely doctors and psychiatrists. These agents are members of the medical profession and the actions of this profession itself are important to the practice of the disciplinary controls of the human sciences of medicine and psychiatry. A profession does not simply apply pre-existing knowledge. As Freidson, who has studied the medical profession, writes, a profession is an:

> ... occupational organisation ...which, by virtue of its authoritarian position in society, comes to transform if not actually create the substance of its own work (1970, p.xix).

Underlying the critique of Foucault, and the introduction of the idea that the social organisation of practitioners can play a role in the creation and use of a particular disciplinary technique, is the oft debated problem of the extent to which human beings are able to create their own destiny. Abrams comments that the problem is one of:

> ... finding a way of accounting for human experience which recognises simultaneously... that history and society are made by constant, more or less purposeful individual action and that individual action, however purposeful, is made by history and society (1980, p.7).

I would add to Abrams' formulation, that despite the purposefulness of human action, the results of that action may be far different from those which were intended. These actions and effects help to 'make' the rich tapestry of history.

These points are all extremely relevant to the study of accounting. Thus whilst maintaining the Foucaultian position advanced earlier: that cost and management accounting is a disciplinary technique which is powerful because of the way in which it creates a 'knowledge' about the activity of work; this will be extended and developed from the viewpoint that the questions of who puts into practice disciplinary technologies, and from where in society they come, are important ones. Influencing not only the extent and intensity with which disciplinary techniques are used, but the very nature of those techniques themselves.

Professionalisation

The emergence in the factory, during the nineteenth century, of cost accounting as a disciplinary technique, and its elaboration into the management accounting of the twentieth, has not occured independently of the appearance of specialist practitioners, people who are members of a recognised occupation[14].

The relationship between these practitioners and the use of such disciplinary techniques is mediated through employers and managers, who apparently have the perfect freedom to decide who to employ, and how to run their businesses. Whilst, at first glance, it may seem that employees such as cost and management accountants merely enact the wishes of management, and are used or not used at their whim, the situation is really much more complex. The 'whim' of management may turn on whether or not they consider the techniques to be useful to them- and a belief in their effectivity may be greatly encouraged by the existence of respectable, specialist practitioners who write and talk convincingly of the *absolute necessity* of these techniques to the efficient running of a business. Not only this, the variety of cost and management accounting techniques actually available for management to consider using in their businesses, are shaped by the practitioners and the associations to which these practitioners belong. As the techniques become more elaborate, and thus more difficult for managers to understand, the power of the practitioners to define what *is* their work, grows. So, in trying to gain insight into how the figures, which are the products of cost and management accounting systems, came to be created (and to obtain a particular status as *truth*) it is important to consider the practitioners: to examine their role, and the way in which it is affected by the occupational or professional associations to which they belong.

In the United Kingdom the practitioners of cost and management accounting are usually members of a professional accounting body. The Institute of Cost and Management Accountants (ICMA) is directly involved, but also so are the other main professional associations, the chartered and certified bodies[15]. These professional bodies mediate between practitioners and the clients of their techniques in that they certify individuals as qualified to practice, and after qualification, their disciplinary procedures provide a continuing source of potential control over members' activities. Through the syllabi of their examinations they exercise a powerful control over what it is that is accepted to *be* cost and management accounting as distinct from some other technique. They may even have an affect on the body of accepted knowledge through their funding of academic research. Thus professional associations exercise influence over both practitioners and their knowledge.

The 'professional' position which accountants speak from is one of social privilege. Such people are not only privileged in the sense of being members of a privileged occupation, but also in the sense that the members of this elite are an integral part of the dominant elites of society (Portwood & Fielding, 1981, p.749). The words of those 'speaking from' this social position upon their areas of special expertise (and often also, through association, in areas they have not received special training) are normally understood to be especially valuable and 'true'. Doctors pronounce 'the truth' about illness; accountants operating as auditors are expected to state whether or not particular sets of accounts give a 'true and fair view' of the financial state of affairs of a business. Members of occupations understood to be professions obtain wealth, status and power in return for their apparently valuable work in society.

One of the most obvious characteristics of professions is that access to membership is restricted. Max Weber uses the concept of 'closure' to explain the way in which economic interests and social action are related to one another (1978, pp.339-343). When there is competition for a livelihood, offices, clients and other remunerative opportunities the participants become interested in curbing competition and some of them may get together and identify a characteristic of some of the other actual or potential competitors and use it as a basis for excluding them from these economic opportunities. If conditions are right the group will set up a regulated association, and later maybe obtain legal backing for their monopoly position. Weber writes that:

> This monopolisation is directed against competitors who share some positive or negative characteristics; its purpose is always the closure of social and economic opportunities to *outsiders* (ibid., p.342).

The economic interest of monopolisation of resources tends to lead to the social action of attempted exclusion and social closure. Parkin (1979) extends the notion of closure used by Weber to encompass *all* forms of collective social action designed to maximise claims to rewards and opportunities. Two main generic forms of social closure are identified: exclusion (Weber's concept of closure is of this type) and usurpation. The central feature of exclusionary closure is the attempt by one group to secure for itself a privileged position at the expense of some other group, through a process of subordination. A group of ineligible people is formed who are excluded from the benefits gained by the group who have defined themselves as 'eligible'. Usurpationary closure is the strategy used by less privileged groups, such as unions, when they go on strike. They attempt to 'usurp' the power of the dominant group (ibid., pp.44-47). Professionalism itself can be understood from this perspective as a particular form of exclusionary closure based on credentialism; i.e. the use of academic or professional qualifications and approval as a device for selecting the selected few from the general masses. It is characterised by strategies "designed to limit and control the supply of entrants to an occupation in order to safeguard or enhance its market value" (ibid., p.54).

Writing within this tradition, Larson describes professionalisation as "a collective project which aims at market control" (1977, p.50). Under the heading "Standardisation of Knowledge and Market Control" (ibid., p.40), she considers the relationship between some aspects of the knowledge base of a profession, and the success, or otherwise, of a project of professionalisation. She writes how such a project binds together two elements, "knowledge susceptible of practical application and a market- the structure of which is determined by economic and social development and also by the dominant ideological climate at a given time" (ibid., p.40). Through the social processes of professionalisation the tentative area of knowledge and practice which individuals are associating around, tends to begin to become standardised and codified. This has a number of advantages to the project, for, firstly, the professional 'commodity' is made more distinct and recognisable to its 'market'; secondly, it can form a clear focus to unify the group of practitioners attracted by the idea of creating a respectable professional body; and, thirdly, the knowledge can be taught effectively to a selected few, who can use it to justify the attempts to close off this set of social and economic opportunities.

Once a professional association is formed the process of expansion and growth will tend to bring a yet more close definition of the area of knowledge and competance in response to the need to provide a clear and unambiguous statement of the nature of the knowledge and techniques to the 'market' and to prospective members of the organisation. In this process of codification the knowledge becomes subject to analysis and to *abstraction*.[16]

In very practical terms the formation of a professional association itself creates a physical place for discourse about the role of practitioners and the nature of the knowledge and the practice. Discussions which help to define and codify this knowledge and practice. This relates to an issue which Freidson raises, which is that of "the role of the professional in creating and defining his own work" (1968, p.113). For through examinations and other means (such as the sponsoring of research) such a body comes to be involved with the creation of the knowledge which is at the root of the claim to the special status of the members themselves. Freidson writes that this role of professionals in producing their own work has been further confounded by the reification of knowledge. In the case which he studied, that of medicine, this is represented in the common view that disease exists independently of human action, and the physician is merely a diagnostician and therapist of what is objectively "there". In a similar way in the case of accountants, their role in creating and defining their own work has been confounded by the reification of the products of accounting systems: these figures are regarded as outside the realm of human value judgements. Esland suggests that it is through the wide acceptance, in society, of this claim to be providing *the truth*, that professionals have come to act as "reality definers" on important issues affecting society as a whole (1980, p.213).

This brings the discussion back to the issue of the relationship between knowledge and power; the power of professionals, and the truth which they claim to have a monopoly over, exist in a mutually supportative relationship with one another. Professionals have the power to play a role in creating their own work; work in itself which often appears to be playing an important role in maintaining the status quo in society; a status quo in which professionals are a privileged group. In the case of cost and management accounting such an analysis would lead to examining how such accountants play a part in creating a role for themselves in organisations. A role which involves creating knowledge through which employees in organisations can be disciplined and controlled; a situation in which they have a superior status to many of those whose efforts they create a measurement of.

However, this is very simplistic; the problem is that exaggerating the influence which professionals can have in defining their own work can lead to falling into a crude functionalistic analysis. An analysis which views a professions' knowledge and practice as something merely functionalist in maintaining its social position. Exaggerating the influence is as problematic as ignoring it altogether. Rueschemeyer sums up the problem succinctly:

> That the knowledge base and the conceptions about purpose, goals and propriety of expert intervention are subject to change and have important indeterminances, does not mean that expert groups can shape these changes and indeterminancies at will to their advantage . This view vastly underestimates the stability of major components of culture, in part due to their institutionalisation in differential institutional spheres, as well as the power of the major interests grounded in the basic structure of the division of labour and, finally, the difficulty of intentional intervention in long-term socio-cultural change (1983, p.53).

It is necessary to relate the knowledge and techniques of a profession to the cultural context as well as to the internal dynamics of the profession itself.

One important element in this context is that of the state, as will become apparent (see Chapter 4), it played a particularly important role in the developments in cost accounting in the period of the First World War. The involvement of the state with the furthering of disciplinary practices has not been considered in theoretical terms in this chapter. Even trying to define 'the state' inevitably involves one in implicit (if not explicit) theory of it, and that theory itself has been the subject of much intellectual debate (see Held & Krieger, 1984). It was not considered appropriate in the context of this thesis to use this theory, for the macro-perspective which it generally involves is precisely of that nature which this subtle detailed history is trying to avoid. Consequently 'the state' has been left undefined, but at the same time it being understood that 'the state' in 1918, was something very different to 'the state' in 1914. Not only this, but the very construction of the wartime state in Britain relied to some extent upon cost accounting. In the process of looking at the events concerning cost accounting in this period one is at the same time looking at the transfer of a disciplinary technique which emerged in the factory to to be part of the technology of the state. These are issues which will be returned later in the thesis.

Conclusion

The approach to research being suggested here is one which involves exploring in detail the relationship between the development of the disciplinary technique cost and management accounting, the social organisation of its practitioners, the content of the knowledge and practice, and the social and organisational context. The use of the word 'context' is not in any way to be taken as implying simple dependence- for accounting itself affects this cultural context; it provides a 'truth' about the world which influences the actions of those within it.

In the next chapters some of these issues are considered in the context of Britain in the period 1914 to 1925. For practical reasons certain aspects have been researched in more detail than others[17]. The work has focused upon the complex relationships between: firstly, the social context of the Great War and the years immediately following; secondly, the growth of interest in cost accounting; thirdly the 'coming into the light' of the practitioners, the growth of interest by chartered and incorporated accountants, and the formation of the ICWA; and fourthly, what it was that was regarded as the content and aims of the knowledge and practice themselves. The political and social turbulence, and the competition for this work, led to much discussion over the nature of that becoming known as cost accounting. It is in such periods of apparent *disorganisation* and turmoil that accounting 'reveals' itself more plainly. The debate forces basic considerations of the nature of the techniques, the knowledge, the role of the practitioners and so on, into the open. This makes it a very interesting period to begin the task of writing a 'history of the present'.

NOTES

(1) No distinction will be made here between 'genealogy' and 'archaeology', the generic term 'genealogy' being used to describe Foucault's method. Foucault used archaeology to describe his methodology up until finishing *The Archaeology of Knowledge* (1972). The two have similar principles underlying them but their focus is slightly different: archaeology concentrates on understanding the conditions for the emergence of a particular form of knowledge whilst genealogy is concerned with the descent of those knowledge to the present. Foucault's thought itself has shown shifts in focus, as opposed to the steady build-up and elaboration of *a* theory. Bearing in mind Foucault's own comment that "The only valid tribute to thought such as Nietzche's is precisely to deform it, to make it groan and protest" (1980, p.54); the principle applied to Foucault's thought here is that it should be *used*, rather than all its myriad nuances being analysed in detail. There are many books and articles discussing Foucault's work, Gordon (1980) and Weeks (1982) are perhaps two of the most relevant to the discussion here. Generally, in my opinion, most secondary literature on Foucault's work is disappointing.

(2) This was an issue which first caught his attention in the early 1950s, with the shock of the Lysenko affair and its suggestion of the association of science with ideology and politics. He decided that the issue of the relationship between a science such as theoretical physics and political and economic structures in society was exceedingly complex, asking:

> ... if one takes a form of knowledge like psychiatry, won't the question be much easier to resolve, since the epistemological profile of psychiatry is a low one and psychiatric practice is linked with a whole range of institutions, economic requirements and political issues of social regulation? Couldn't the interweaving of effects of power and knowledge be grasped with greater certainty in the case of a science as 'dubious' as psychiatry? (Foucault, 1980, p.109)

(3) So convinced was he of the practical utility of the idea that in 1791 he wrote to William Pitt, the Prime Minister, "give me the convicts", suggesting that he should himself act as contractor in the initial stages of the project and "take up my ordinary *residence* in the midst of them, and in the point of health to share whatever might be their fate." (Bentham, 1981, Vol.4, pp.228-229)

(4) Bentham even went so far as to suggest that young ladies should be confined in one designed as a boarding school, one of the great advantages of the design being the protection of their virginity, Bentham imagined the eagerness with which "gentlemen" would "crowd to such a school to choose themselves wives" (Bentham, 1843, Vol.IV, p.60).

(5) Manufacturies were considered very suitable targets for this form of organisation: "whatever be the manufacture, the utility of the principle is obvious and incontestible", particularly where workmen were "paid according to the time". Interestingly Bentham had a special place for the accounts office or 'compting house':

> Where a manufactury of any kind is to be established upon this principle, the *central lodge* would probably be made use of as a computing house: and if more branches than one were carried on under the same roof, the accounts belonging to each branch would be kept in the corresponding part of the lodge (1843, Vol.IV, p.60).

(6) The actual impact of Bentham's panopticon idea on the practice of institutional construction has been discussed by a number of authors (see for instance: Bahmueller, 1981, p.60; Steintrager, 1977, p.11; Burns 1978, p.23; Foucault, 1980, p.147).

(7) In more detail: The Behaviour Books were to be divided into: 1. Complaint Books, 2. Misbehaviour books, 3. Black, or Punishment Book, 4. Red or Merit Book. The heads of the Complaint Book were: 1. Time (day, hour, and minute), 2. By whom, 3. Against whom, or what, 4. Concerning what, 5. To whom, 6. By whom examined into, 7. Witness or witnesses examined, 8. By whom decided upon, 9. Time when decided upon, 10. Time employed in the examination, 11. Decision, 12. Decision by whom executed (if it be a case calling for execution), Time., &c., when executed. Interestingly the Red or Merit Book was to be kept by "the chaplain", the "recording angel" (ibid., pp.393-394).

(8) Interestingly, at the end of the year officers and governors of the panopticons for the poor were to be rewarded with "pieces of plate", the "act of remuneration to be grounded, in every instance, on *specific*, and specified, exemplifications of merit, with reference to the evidence presenting itself in each instance, on the face of the books" (Bentham, 1843, Vol.VIII, p.387).

(9) Except perhaps for the purposes of industrial psychology, a subject largely concerned with an attempt to understand worker behaviour in order to maximise the contribution of the workers to the business under consideration.

(10) Rational in the sense that the 'means' are related to the 'ends' through a consciously thought through series of logical (within that particular sphere of human understanding) steps.

(11) The preparation of basic accounting statements such as daily balances, weekly summaries, monthly statements and yearly accounts, depends upon a cutting up of time into equal parts. This idea is of comparatively recent origin. Chatfield writes:

> The striking difference between seventeenth century and modern book-keeping technique was the failure to balance and close the books regularly. The closing process was tied to random events; the end of a voyage, the filling of a ledger, the sale of a business, the dissolving of a partnership, a merchant's bankrupcy or death. *There was no concept of periodic reckoning* (italics mine) (Chatfield, 1977, p.59).

Not only are accounting statements now prepared periodically but they rely upon 'accruals' and 'matching' concepts. These determine that the receipt or payment of cash is no longer the basis for allocating events to different accounting periods, instead some notion of when the event occured, of which the cash is only a representation, is used.

(12) This was of course the subject matter of "The Birth of the Clinic"(1973). In this detailed study of the emergence of modern medicine, professional groupings and rivalries amongst the medical profession (those operating the disciplinary technology) are considered (see Chapter 5), in contrast to the approach in "Discipline and Punish" (1977a). Note that the original publication dates of these books in French was 1963 and 1975 respectively.

(13) At his death, in 1984, Foucault was beginning to become involved in this area through a project with students at Berkeley (Gandal & Kotkin, 1985).

(14) Indeed, I would suggest that the whole perception of a continuity between primitive costing techniques, the more elaborate cost accounting systems appearing in the late nineteenth and early twentieth centuries, and the sphere of knowledge and practice known today as 'management accounting', has been shaped by the practitioners through their professional associations. A similar point was made in a rather different way in note (2) of Chapter 1.

(15) Although many practitioners are not members of these bodies, most have had involvement with them through being students. The high

failure rate at the examinations provides a large number of trained, but 'unqualified' people.

(16) This paragraph represents my interpretation of some of the ideas in Chapter 4 of Larson's book (1977, pp.40-52) which seem relevant to the issue of the professionalisation of cost and management accounting. Theoretically the book seems to be rather confused, although it does contain some interesting ideas; for whilst Chapter 4 is clearly Weberian in inspiration, in the latter chapters of the book there seems to be a shift towards a Marxist position.

It is worth noting that in discussing the knowledge base at all, she moves beyond the analysis of most sociologists of the professions, who take it for granted. As Goldstein (1984, p.175) remarks, they usually take the intellectual core of a professions as a given factor around which the process of professionalisation takes place. Although I am in agreement with Goldstein on this point, I view the main theme of his paper, which centres around a simple identification of the 'disciplines' and the 'professions', as rather unsatisfactory.

(17) The study has only looked indirectly at what was happening in organisations themselves with regards to cost accounting. It is possible that records do exist which would enable further study of this aspect, but this must remain outstanding for further work.

CHAPTER 3

HISTORICAL INTRODUCTION

> ... it is more of a theoretical than a practical work. It does not purport to deal with the ordinary financial books. It is rather concerned with the wages and time books, stock books, and matter of a similar nature, which as a rule, do not come within the scope of the accountants' duties.
>
> *The Accountant*, reviewing the 1st edition of *Factory Accounts* by Emile Garcke & John Manger Fells (1887)

Introduction

In order to 'set the scene' for the events of 1914 to 1925 it is useful to review the development of cost accounting up to this date. The events of the First World War, in particular the transformation of the economy forced by the massive requirement for armaments, brought into far greater contact two previously relatively separate socio-historical developments: the emergence in factories of the disciplinary technique of cost accounting, and the appearance of an accountancy profession.

The importance of the prior existence of an accounting profession to the events concerning cost accounting in the period 1914 to 1925 must not be underestimated. The government gave established members of this profession great responsibilities during this time, in particular for cost accounting. As will be seen later, the existence of these professional bodies of chartered and incorporated accountants was a major factor in determining the actions of the individuals working with costing in industry who came together in 1919, to form the Institute of Cost and Works Accountants. Costing in Britain became the business of *accountants*, this was not a *necessary* development. In Sweden, for instance, it remained associated with the practitioners of scientific management, rather than professional accountants (Jönsson, 1984).

In Britain, in the nineteenth century, costing seems to have been associated with 'engineers', as opposed to 'accountants' (I use inverted commas here because it is not clear that either of these became distinctive occupations until the late nineteenth, or even the early twentieth, century). The research done on this involvement of engineers with costing in the nineteenth century by such writers as Wells (1978) and Urwick & Brech (1949), must, I feel, be interpreted with caution. This is because my research on accountants leads me to consider the way in which such earlier researchers assume that the occupation 'accountant' was a clearly defined one at this time (see, for instance Wells, 1978, pp.121-122), extremely misleading. It seems quite likely that the same applies to the simple and straightforward occupation 'engineer' which they assume- a description I consider to be likely to have covered a range of occupations from skilled workmen, to the owners of large factories. This involvement of engineers with cost accounting is not considered in this chapter, mainly because the focus of this thesis is upon the period after 1914. By this time, I would agree with Wells (1978, p.vii), that engineers had largely left the field to accountants[1] (both groups now having more clearly defined professional roles).

As regards the study of the appearance of costing systems in factories, it is as well to point out here that there are a number of awkward problems in trying to unravel when, where and how costing systems came into being in factories in this early period. Part of the problem is caused by the fact that many manufacturers regarded their costing systems as a trade secret (Garner, 1976, p.30; Wells, 1978, p.62). The lengths to which this secrecy went is illustrated by Webster Jenkinson's comment in 1907 that:

> ... it is the custom to add a further percentage to the actual oncost, which amount is known only to the management, so that the office staff may not see the profit made on each job (quoted in Wells, 1978, p.62).

In his detailed survey of the literature of cost accounting up to 1914, Wells found only four examples of costing systems described as in use in Britain, where the firm in question was identified (ibid., p.63). More fundamentally though, the question arises as to the point when a systematic set of costing records amounts to 'cost accounting'. This is nicely illustrated by the reply I received from a veteran member of the ICMA, to my request to discuss his experiences of cost accounting in the inter-war period. He wrote:

> I do not consider myself a suitable candidate for interviewing, the reason being that up until I joined Smiths Industries in 1941 my whole working time had been taken up with costing as distinct from Cost Accounting. The firms where I worked up to then had no integrated accounting systems, the financial

accounts being entirely separate, and the costing side being used simply to arrive at the material and labour costs of the product, with an addition for overheads, for pricing purposes (private correspondance).

This is a comment certainly relevant to the earlier periods[2].

Both the emergence of cost accounting and of professional accountants must be understood in their social context, if the history is to follow the principles outlined in chapter 2. As previous work on the history of accounting has not tended to follow these principles[3], it has been necessary to construct this chapter as best as is possible from a wide variety of secondary sources. The chapter is divided chronologically into four parts. In each section costing and professional accounting will be considered in relation to their social context, with a view to providing a background to the later events examined in more detail.

1. The Industrial Revolution in Britain: 1750-1840

Cost accounting is a sophisticated means of disciplining and ordering work which emerged in factories, largely not until the nineteenth century[4]. The basic and fundamental step in the historical movement towards the detailed control by 'employers' of the work[5] of individual 'workers', came with this late eighteenth century movement of work into factories.

It was in Britain that what has become known as the 'Industrial Revolution'[6] first occurred. In the early eighteenth century a good deal, maybe most, of the industries and manufactures of Britain were rural; the typical 'worker' was a village artisan or smallholder who made cloth, hosiery or some kind of metal goods at home. Often this was done under a 'putting-out' scheme, whereby a merchant would regularly visit homes, taking raw materials and collecting finished goods (Pollard, 1968, p.20). By the mid-eighteenth century this system had begun to break down and work, particularly in the cotton industry, was increasingly performed in factories. Hobsbawm describes cotton as the "pacemaker" of industrial change, stimulating trade and industry in general as well as being important in itself [in the post-Napoleonic decades something like one half of the value of all British exports consisted of cotton products (Hobsbawm, 1969, p.69)]. The reasons for the disintegration of the putting-out system around the middle of the eighteenth century appear to be rather complex, but centre around a growth in demand for the products (see Landes, 1969, pp.56-60). Merchants could not force workers to produce more to meet the demand, raising the wages paid often led workers to work less hard, not more, for beyond a certain point they preferred leisure to income. Additionally embezzlement of the raw material by the workers was a problem- despite it being made a criminal offence for which the corporal punishment could be imposed (Landes, 1969, pp.56-60; Marglin, 1976, p.35). The movement of work into factories also enabled the use of new industrial technology, such as the spinning frame and the steam engine. Whether the motivating force behind the building of factories was the use of this new technology (as traditionally believed by historians), or whether it was the need to discipline and control work, are matters for dispute (Evans, 1976, p.6; Marglin, 1976). Which came first is not important here, what is relevant is the nature of the social organisation of the factory. Its essential characteristic was the way in which the activity 'work', could be watched, and hence ordered and controlled, in a way which it could never have been when performed by workers in their own homes. Andrew Ure wrote that:

> In my recent tour ... through the manufacturing districts, I have seen tens of thousands of old, young, and middle aged ... earning abundant food ... in apartments more airy and celubrious than those of the metropolis ... In those spacious halls ... (1835, pp.17-18).

Such spaciousness enabled the inspection of those at work to ensure that they were both at their work and producing good work. Also, in some factories (although certainly not all), the work pace was governed by machines:

> ... the benignant power of steam summons around him his myriads of willing menials, and assigns to each the regulated task, substituting for painful muscular effort on their part, the energies of his own gigantic arm, and demanding in return only attention and dexterity to correct such little aberrations as casually occur in his workmanship (ibid., pp.17-18).

The adjustment of workers to the regularity and discipline of factory work was difficult (Pollard, 1963, p.254). They found it hard to accept the time-discipline which the factory imposed, for they had a conception of time related to the carrying out of tasks rather than to the regularity of the clock (Thompson, 1967, p.60). This adjustment was not helped by the modelling of many works, either deliberately or by accident, on workhouses or prisons (Pollard, 1963, p.254). Since men did not take spontaneously to these new ways, they had to be forced- by fines and by Master and Servant laws such as that of 1823 which threatened them with jail for breach of contract. Fines were the most usual reaction to minor transgressions of rules and regulations in the early years of industrialisation, particularly bad time-keeping (Pollard, 1963, p.261). The general level of fines was high and meant to hurt, the fines for miners at Merthyr were alleged to average as much as 1s. or 2s. out of a wage of 13s. (Pollard, 1965, p.220).

Some of the earliest employee records probably owe their origins to the practice of fining: McKendrick writes that at Wedgwood's factory the wage sheets were marked with the time of arrival, the time of departure and the time they had off for meals (1961, p.42). The keeping of records, as discussed in the previous chapter, is a disciplinary technique which extends the control which can be exercised over workers. For it enables the 'seeing' of events at a distance both in time and in space from their place of occurence. Once records begin to be kept the *office* takes on a far greater significance, for no longer is the 'observation' of work limited to the moment and place when it occured. It is relevant to note, however, that there was not simply an abrupt change, from the undisciplined cottage industry to disciplined work in factories. The organisation of work in the early nineteenth century was to a certain extent anarchic, for there was widespread use by employers of contractors. For example, an engineering employer might sub-contract the building of a locomotive to a 'piece-master' who would employ and pay his own craftsmen out of the price; and these in turn would employ and pay their own labourers (Littler, 1982, pp. 65, 68; Hobsbawm, 1964, pp.297-298). Hobsbawm refers to this as the "sub-contracting" of exploitation and management" (ibid.). Interestingly, Littler advances the hypothesis that one of the advantages of such internal-contract systems is that they act as a substitute for accounting in that the employer is saved from numerous complex cost calculations. The 'cost' of work being simply the price agreed in advance with the subcontractor (1982, p.67)[7].

It is in two of the seemingly most organisationally and technically advanced companies in Britain, in the period of the late eighteenth and early nineteenth century, that quite well developed forms of what later became known as 'cost accounting' have been identified. One of these, Boulton and Watt, will be discussed here, the other, Josiah Wedgwood & Co., is discussed by Hopwood (1986).

In Boulton and Watts' Soho foundry, opened in 1796, technical and economic innovations went hand in hand- particularly in the years 1800 and 1801 when the major changes were made (Roll, 1930, p.194). This was probably connected with the expiration of Watt's patent in 1800 and the subsequent transformation of a monopoly situation to one where there was keen competition (ibid., p.237). However it is notable that standardisation of production had begun much earlier, in the old works. This development towards standardising, or as it was called 'methodising', the production was apparently originally caused by the necessity of producing duplicate parts for Cornish engines. This increased in scope after 1782, when rising demand resulted in a desire to restrict production to a certain number of standardised sizes of engines (ibid., p.267).

The layout and plans for the operation of the Soho Engine Manufactory reflected what appears to have been a definite systematic and preconceived plan. For instance, the machinery was laid out in contemplation of a certain sequence of production processes (ibid., pp.171, 174). Similarly the operations to be performed in making the parts and for assembling the steam engines were laid out in great detail. Roll writes that such fixing of a "definite standard regulation on the part of the management" relieved the workmen "of the larger part of their independence and individual responsibility" (ibid., pp. 177-179). Whereas up to 1795, in the previous works, there was little pressure on workmen and they could only be paid on the piece-rate system for the articles which were standardised, in the Soho Works the advent of more machinery, greater division of labour and standardisation meant the piece-rate system could be extended (ibid., p.194). All the workers were employed by the firm, rather than by internal-contractors- although some vestiges of the old system survived in that, for instance, the foremen on a nozzles job got a profit based on the difference between the mens' piecework earnings and time wages (ibid., p.200).

At this same period the engines themselves were becoming more standardised and the prices at which they were to be sold were calculated on the basis of the total estimated cost of the engine plus (by 1801) a standard 25%. The cost of production was estimated on the basis of material cost, direct wages, indirect wages and general charges. Elaborate records were maintained for the purpose of calculating the actual profit realised on each engine (ibid., pp.238-243). Roll writes that overall the new methods of paying employees and of pricing engines were accompanied by "a great number of new books of a statistical character ... the method of price fixing naturally reacted on the costing and book-keeping system; and in this respect ... Soho seems to have been far in advance of the time ..." (ibid., p.244). The time-sheets of the workmen, for instance, fulfilled four objects: they were the basis for ascertaining the workers' wages, the basis for calculating the labour costs of engines, the starting point for making changes in the methods of production (eg. speeding-up or the introduction of more machinery) and the computation of new wage rates. In a similar way, most of the departmental records of indirect charges, wage-bills, etcetera were used in maintaining a standard of efficiency (ibid., p.250). In 1800 and 1801 analyses of profit according to departments are appended to the trading accounts (p.256). Roll describes the amount of work which the small number of office staff must have performed as "amazing" (ibid., p.251).

Soho appears to have been exceptional as regards the extent and nature of the organisation of business and record keeping which the systems involved (ibid., pp.171, 244). It does not seem that it had any great influence on contemporary practice. What is so interesting about it is the close relationship between three things: firstly, the physical standardisation of types of engine produced, of the parts for them, and of the methods used in construction; secondly, the extension of the piece-work system; and, thirdly, the requirement perceived by the owners for knowledge of costs in order to price the product and run the factory efficiently at a time when they faced competition from other manufacturers. Sophisticated cost accounting systems go hand in hand with the standardisation of products and production methods. The 'facts' which cost accounting systems demand can only be created with enormous difficulty where work is carried on in a disordered, anarchic way. The opposite also applies, for the operation of a complex and detailed system of organisation may be virtually impossible without records. Roll points this out, noting that many aspects of the reorganised Soho Works were such as to make any check except that through written records impossible (ibid., p.252). Cost accounting records are particularly convenient to an organisation because they can easily be aggregated and disaggregated, and they enable comparisons to be made between quite diverse events and activities.

Beyond the realm of very exceptional businesses, such as those of Boulton and Watt, and Wedgwood, there were, perhaps, other firms with systems for finding 'costs' on a systematic basis. William Stone describes the cost accounting systems in operation in a Manchester cotton mill, the earliest account still in existence beginning on September 1, 1810. The mill itself came into being sometime in the period 1764 to 1785, by 1810 it was a large and well established business (Stone, 1973, p.71). The accounting system contained cost accounts which followed the cost flow of the mill's manufacturing process. Stone writes that the mill ledger shows that the cost accounting system was amazingly complete:

> The cost records were integrated with a double-entry system which produced a balanced trial balance on a bi-monthly basis ... Prime costs for labour and materials were collected for each of fourteen cost centers and general expenses were allocated to these centers using pre-determined rates. Transfers of materials-in-process between cost centers made use of intracompany pricing. A manufacturing gain of loss for each of thirteen of these cost centers and the selling profit or loss from the warehouse room were included in the bi-monthly trial balance (ibid., p.71).

Stone made no comment on whether or not he believed the system in operation at Charlton to be very exceptional, or perhaps just one of many which existed, unbeknown to historians now. He simply points out, as Johnson (1972) does, that the existence of this system suggests that the traditional view that "modern cost accounting methods were not in use before the late nineteenth century", is challenged by this finding.

The question of where such methods originated is a difficult one. Of the many British (and indeed, European) accounting textbooks produced between the sixteenth and early eighteenth centuries, few even considered production costs, let alone considered in detail the accounting needs of industrialists. Pollard attributes this to the dominance of accountancy in Britain by the requirements of the merchant- from whom all the formal training and prestige were derived (1968, p.250). He suggests that the mercantile system of double-entry bookkeeping, arising out of the practices of merchants and bankers, was the most influential of the three main systems of accounting available to the industrialists in the second half of the eighteenth century[8]. The reason for this probably being that many, perhaps most, of the accountants to be found in works offices, and much of the accountancy they learnt, had been derived from the counting houses of merchants (ibid., p.245). There certainly do not appear to have been any detailed texts in existence laying out how such systems as that at the Soho Works could be constructed. It seems unlikely that these exceptional systems had a direct impact on later developments. Perhaps this is precisely because there were virtually no texts, journals, or professional bodies, through which the discussion and transmission of ideas could occur. In Foucaultian terms, one could say that there was no *discursive domain* beyond the realm of the discussion occuring within the enterprise itself.

2. The Age of Capital: 1840 to 1872

In this period there was an extraordinary economic transformation and expansion: Hobsbawm describes the years 1840 to 1875 as the "age of capital" (1977). I should like to put forward the suggestion that this transformation opened the way to a growth in bureaucratic record-keeping systems in organisations, or perhaps more accurately, a growth in record-keeping systems was part and parcel of this transformation. As discussed in Chapter 2, the keeping of records about productive activity is, in a theoretical sense, the precursor of cost accounting systems, for they involve the systematic translation of records into the terminology of money. Generally, historically, it would be expected that moves towards the disciplining of work through the systemisation of production and the regular keeping of records would precede cost accounting. In practice, however, the course of events may not be so simple. In the development of a cost accounting system in a particular enterprise the order of such events may indeed even be the reverse- the introduction of a cost accounting system may itself prompt the creation of record-keeping systems to create basic facts, such as the time required by a skilled worker to make a certain item.

This discussion is inevitably speculative, for as Johnson points out, very little is known about the accounting records of firms in the period from 1840 to 1890 (1972, p.466); however, his own research on American companies did suggest that some firms, even by mid-century, had sophisticated cost accounting systems (ibid.). Similarly little is known about the position in Britain during these years. Edwards notes the correspondence in 1870 concerning one "Montague Whitmore of 41 Clerkenwell Green, London", who advertised in *The Engineer* and who apparently installed a satisfactory job costing system for £10-10s (1937, pp.283-284). Perhaps the interest caused in the columns of the journal is indicative of the rarity of the occurrence, or perhaps there were a number of people involved in this way with costing- only a great deal more research in the area would reveal which was the case.

On the following pages some aspects of the changes in the way in which businesses were organised in this period are discussed which would appear to be associated with the growth in record-keeping systems, and thus probably with cost accounting.

One of the most important features of the economic transformation which occured in these years was the growth of the railways; their construction used up huge amounts of capital and brought into being large companies with many employees (Hobsbawm, 1969, p.110-115; Pollins, 1956, pp.332-333). The rapid investment brought, in the 1840s, the problem of fraud. Railway Acts were introduced which imposed specific rules of accounting[9]. At the same time it is probable that companies developed an internal bureaucracy to attempt to control and co-ordinate their affairs[10]. In 1850 Dionysius Lardner published a book entitled *Railway Economy* which was perhaps the first attempt to lay down principles for railway administration and accounting (ibid., p.339). It is interesting to note that John Manger Fells, one of the joint authors of the pioneering work *Factory Accounts* (1887), started his commercial career in the accounts office of a railway company around the early 1870s (Kitchen and Parker, 1980, p.36). In other industries firms were growing larger, particularly in the engineering, ship-building and machinery fields (Hobsbawm, 1969, It was in these larger companies in particular, that a more intensive management of labour began to develop. Employers became concerned with the quantity and quality of work performed during the hours of a workers' employment, rather than just simply with obtaining the greatest possible number of hours per week[11]. This was encouraged by new laws: Factory Acts were passed, the first in 1833, which began to curb the exploitation of employees (Stacey, 1954, p.16). In 1847 the Ten Hours Act, limiting hours of work, forced employers to look to 'intensive' rather than 'extensive' methods of exploitation in the cotton industry. It is notable, however, that without any such legislative pressure the same tendency was to be seen in the industrial north (Pollard, 1963, p.264). The 'stick' disciplines grew less important. In the 1860's non-economic compulsion of labour, such as the Master and Servant Acts were abandoned. Long term hiring contracts, for instance the 'annual bond' of the northern coal miners, disappeared as did the practice of truck payments. Labour was hired on a weekly, or even daily, basis and thus the 'market' in labour could operate more freely (Hobsbawm, 1977, p.257). Positive incentives to persuade employees to work were introduced; in a great many enterprises the 'discovery' of payment by results was greeted as an innovation of major significance (Pollard, 1963, p.264). More intensive methods of labour exploitation usually meant an increase in record keeping. The keeping of records facilitates the co-ordinating and the disciplining of work, it enables workers' performances to be compared with each other more easily, payment by results introduced, and so on. I do not want to suggest, in a functionalist way, that records are a *necessary* element in the intensive disciplining of work, merely that they can play an important role in facilitating it.

At the same time as the organisation of work inside the factory was changing, ownership and control of business were beginning to become more separate, for through the Companies Acts of 1855 and 1862 limited liability Joint Stock companies were given a legal basis (Edey & Panitpakdi, 1956, p.356; Stacey, 1954, p.7)[12]. The 1862 Act released "the flood-gates of company promotion" and the number of companies registered grew at a great rate: in the period from 1862 to 1873 inclusive, 8,627 companies were registered, with a total of £1162 million nominal share capital (Stacey 1954, p.8). The growth of large businesses was facilitated- particularly in the rail and heavy industry sectors of the economy. In addition to creating a situation where capital could more easily be acquired, the companies legislation of 1855 to 1862 brought a legal compulsion to companies to keep certain accounting records. Each company had to appoint a person legally responsible for the keeping of these records, known as 'the company secretary'. Urwick and Brech suggest that this company secretary would often also play the role of company accountant, as the two tasks were closely related (1949, Vol.II, p.132). However, despite these developments, the majority of companies remained fairly small in size. In the 1850s a factory employing 300 workers could still be considered exceptional, and as late as 1871, the average works manufacturing machinery had only 85 employees (Hobsbawm, 1977, p.250). Traditional management practices, such as internal contract, probably remained common throughout the nineteenth century (Littler, 1982, pp.64-69). Hannah remarks that the family company continued to dominate the industrial scene until well into the twentieth century (1983, p.23). Thus British industry in this period presents a very varied picture, the old and the new existing side by side. It was in the new and larger firms, often limited companies, that the bureaucratic record keeping which would appear to both precede and accompany cost accounting, seems to have been developing.

One of the ways in which this growth in bureaucracy can be identified is through the growth of a clerical workforce. In 1851, there were 43,741 commercial clerks working in Britain, by 1881 this number had increased by more than fourfold (Lockwood, 1958, p.19; Census 1911, Summary Tables, p.274). However, in 1871 Orchard concluded that the average number of clerks in commercial offices in Liverpool was four (Lockwood, 1958, p.19). The division of labour in the offices was often along the lines of: the employers or partners who made the important business decisions, the book-keeper/cashier who wrote up the financial records, and the ordinary clerk, who was responsible for correspondence, filing, and other routine matters (ibid., p.20). The education suitable to such employment was described in *The Clerk: a sketch in outline of his duties and discipline*, published in 1878 as:

> A little instruction in Latin, and probably a very little in Greek, a little in Geography, a little in Science, a little in arithmetic and book-keeping, a little in French, with such a sprinkling of English reading as may enable a lad to distinguish Milton from Shakespeare are considered enough preparation for aught that may turn up in the way of employment.

The book went on to note that book-keeping was:

> ... justly considered the essential accomplishment of all clerks, speaking of them as a class: and excepting those who are attached to a particular profession, such as to the law or to offices under government, it is the ordinary business of their lives (quoted in Lockwood, 1958, pp.20-21).

The clerk was one of a new middle-class emerging out of the division of labour; the manufacturer, Mr Thornton, in Mrs Gaskell's novel *North and South*, published in 1854-5, comments:

> It is one of the great beauties of our system, that a working-man may raise himself into the power and position of a master by his own exertions and behaviour; that, in fact, everyone who rules himself to decency and sobriety of conduct, and attention to his duties, comes over to our ranks; it may not always be as a master, but as an overlooker, a cashier, a book-keeper, a clerk, one on the side of authority and order (1970 edition, p.125).

The Development of an Accounting Profession: 1840-1872

Whilst the changes discussed in the previous section were going on within business organisations, the extraordinary economic transformation and expansion, of which Hobsbawm writes (1977), encouraged the growth of an occupational group becoming known as 'accountants'. The early developments are briefly described in a note to this chapter[13]. There were quite marked differences between the developments in Scotland and those in the rest of the country, but here the discussion will focus on England and Wales for reasons of brevity.

In England and Wales the profession is described by H.W. Robinson as having been:

> born through bankruptcies, fed on failures and frauds, grew on liquidations and graduated through audits (quoted in Chatfield, 1977, p.147).

In 1835 a Municipal Corporation Act gave the legal right to all persons to set up shop, many set up small businesses as contractors, coal merchants etcetera (Stacey, 1954, p.17). In the 'hungry forties' many went out of business and 'accountants' became involved with this bankruptcy work. According to Mr Robert Bell's book *Ladder of Gold*, published in 1850, the problems of the age of 'railway mania' (the loss by individual investors of huge sums of money, due in part to inadequate legal protection) brought "a colony of solicitors, engineers and seedy accountants" to settle "in the purlieus of

Threadneedle Street" (quoted in Jeal, 1937, p.525). Ernest Cooper, recalling the 1860s, wrote that accountants:

> ... were regarded as associated with and dependent upon insolvency, and I well remember that to be seen talking to or having your offices entered by an accountant was to be avoided, particularly in the stressful times of 1866 (1921, p.554).

There were gibes that:

> ... if an accountant were required, he would be found at the bar of the nearest tavern to the Bankruptcy Court in Basinghall Street (ibid.).

The Companies Act of 1862 became known as "the accountants' friend", for it created the position of official liquidator for the purpose of winding-up insolvent companies and this job was usually given to a professional accountant. In addition , by requiring that dividends could be paid only from income, it made the services of skilled accountants more necessary (Chatfield, 1977, p.147).

Whereas in London in 1850 there were 264 accountants, by 1883 their numbers had risen to 840 (Stacey, 1954, p.18). Already, by the 1860s, there was an elite of accountants appearing who were involved with the better paid and more 'respectable' work[14] (Cooper, 1921). Whilst at the other end of the scale 'accountants' undertook book-keeping work for small businesses; Sidney Webb's father worked in this period as one[15], he apparently earned "small and irregular fees from doing the books of local shop-keepers" (Mackenzie & Mackenzie, 1977, pp.56-57). The business of auditing was only just beginning for accountants. The

Railway Acts, which were described earlier, actually provided for the appointment of shareholder-auditors by railways and specified that they could hire professional accountants to assist them (Chatfield, 1977, p.147). As representatives of the stockholders these auditors assumed a quasi-judicial position (ibid.), theoretically independent of management- a role which has been developing ever since. However, in the 1860s professional auditors were the exception and "comparatively few large concerns, railways or banks, were audited by accountants" (Cooper, 1921, p.554).

Thus in this period accounting was an expanding occupation, this growth being associated with the increase in bankruptcy and the legislation passed to deal with it. There seems to have been an increasing division of labour within the occupation, the elite aspiring to the social acceptability and monetary remuneration of professional status. However, to write of a 'division of labour', as I have just done is perhaps a little misleading, for there is also another process at work here, and that is the gradual identification of a variety of people involved with financial work of themselves as *being* 'accountants'. This is an aspect of the formation of occupations and professions which will be discussed further later.

It seems very unlikely that these people calling themselves 'accountants', and operating from professional offices, or from their homes, were involved with the early development of costing in industry. Although it is possible that the chief clerks in larger companies who were dealing with accounts were beginning to *call* themselves 'accountants' [16], it also seems unlikely that they were involved with anything other than what were known as the mercantile books (see the next section in this chapter).

3. The Great Depression: 1873-1896

Traditionally, in established accounting wisdom, this is regarded as the era when cost accounting emerged in Britain. Not only a period when it emerged, but also one when English cost accountants led the world, Garner writing that it was they who contributed a large proportion of the original ideas and procedures under discussion by 1900 (1954, p.342). Americans are generally regarded to have quickly taken over the lead after this date. In writing about this period Solomons remarks that:

> ... the last three decades of the nineteenth century were marked by what can only be described as a costing renaissance in the English speaking world (1952, p.17).

Whilst on the same page that:

> ... there is plenty of evidence that even at the turn of the century anything that could be called a costing system was still to be found only exceptionally both in British and American industry (ibid., p.17).

These statements seem, on the face of it, more than a little contradictory. Behind them there looms what I regard as the major fault of the histories of cost accounting written concerning this period. The 'renaissance' identified is in the appearance of articles in journals and textbooks, but little is known about the extent to which these systems were installed in practice. To deal with this difficulty here the discussion will take the form: firstly, looking at the social context of the Great Depression, a context which would appear to have encouraged the appearance of cost accounting systems; secondly, at the discourse which would appear to have developed around the emergent cost accounting in the form of articles and texts; and, thirdly, at the growth of an occupational group engaged in the everyday creation of accounting 'facts', that of clerks.

The Great Depression has been described as "what happened when the Railways were built" (quoted in Hobsbawm, 1969, p.130). At a time when there was a sharp reduction in the costs of the primary products used in industrial processes (one major factor leading to this being the transport revolution), and an expansion of capacity for output of manufactured goods, there was a less than proportionate increase in demand. The world market became more competitive, for other countries had become industrialised and were producing the goods which hitherto only Britain could supply. There was a twenty year deflation which reduced the general price level by about a third (ibid., pp.127-132). The drastic slackening of demand for engineering products and machinery led to intense competition and price-cutting (Wells, 1978, pp.63-64). As the:

> ... titanic profits of the industrial pioneers declined, squeezed between the upper millstone of price-reducing competition and the lower of increasingly expensive and mechanised plant with increasingly large and inelastic overheads, businessmen searched anxiously for a way out (ibid., p.129).

The pressure from competition occured at a time when the *real* cost of labour was increasing (with deflation), and the labour movement was becoming more powerful[17]. Labour efficiency, as well as the efficient use of raw material and equipment became of concern to manufacturers (Hobsbawm, 1968, p.358). In the attempt to intensify control over the activities of the factory there was an increasing disciplining of work. It began (probably only in the larger engineering works) to include "a careful analysis of the production process, its break-up into simple segments and the establishment of labour norms for each"; and "the elaboration of systems of incentives or supervision capable of making workers labour at maximum intensity" (ibid.). The development of record keeping systems such as to enable the above practices, would, it seems likely, have facilitated the emergence of systems actually orientated towards discovering the labour costs of each operation.

As well as aiding the disciplining of labour there was another aspect to costing. It could be seen to be very useful in the decision concerning the price to charge (or accept) for finished engineering goods (Solomons, 1952, p.19; Wells, 1968, p.70). The accountant John

Mann, writing in 1904, suggested that the keeping of records of cost originated in this way:

> ... in the need of data required in estimating, especially in engineering and kindred trades where the work is specially contracted for, and where there is no scale of market prices (quoted in Solomons, 1952, p.20).

The editor of *Engineering*, wrote, in 1891, on the subject of "practical prime costs", that he was of no doubt as to the origins of the development of costing:

> ... the present-day conditions of the engineering and manufacturing trades, as regards keenness of competition and consequent narrowness of profit, render this subject of an increased importance.

Up to twenty years earlier conditions had been different:

> Selling prices could generally be fixed at figures leaving good margins, and a 'rough and ready' cost of a certain article or piece of work, upon which could generally be fixed a fancy profit, with a liberal contingency allowance, was as a rule found all that was required .... It is during the past 15 or 20 years that prime costing has been developed to the elaborate systems in operation in many of our large and well-managed firms (quoted in Solomons, 1952, p.19).

In addition to the above factors, the growth in size and complexity of businesses created a situation where written records were perceived as being more necessary. It is likely that many of these were records of costs. This growth was associated with a movement towards a separation of ownership and control, for there was a huge increase in the numbers of limited companies (although, as noted earlier, the family company dominated the industrial scene until well into the twentieth century). At the opening of the year 1864, 891 companies had been registered under the 1862 Act (Cooper, 1921, p.554). By 1880 there were around 6,300 limited companies, with a total capital of £380 million; by 1900 the comparable figures were 29,730 companies, with an aggregate capital of £1,622 million (ICAEW, 1966, p.42).

It is interesting to note that the 'technology' through which cost accounting systems could be operated more easily was also developing. Prior to the 1870s the usual means of keeping records was through their writing up into books. The source documents for such records being collected on spikes, eventually to be bundled up and transferred to drawers. Delgado places the origin of the modern sophisticated systems of recording and reference at 1876 when "a new principle of loose filed vertical cards was introduced" (1979, p.68). Such a system enabled records to be more easily accessed and this increased the possibilities for their use. At the same period the box-file also appeared, in it papers were filed flat between sheets of card on which were printed the letters from A to Z. This enabled the source documents previously kept on spikes and in bundles to be retained in a much more accessible form. The concertina file had similar advantages, and was probably the forerunner of the vertical file, which was introduced in 1892 (ibid.). Thus whilst production itself was being ordered in a more systematic manner, these new developments in office technology rendered this paper replication in the office also more systematic. It seems likely that such innovations have played an important role in the history of cost accounting, although this has not yet been studied.

Cost accounting was emerging as a matter for discussion and debate and there was a body of knowledge developing concerning its practice. This can be seen most clearly in the discussion in the newly appearing textbooks and in the engineering journals. In March 1899, it was noted that there was an:

> ... awakening in everything relating to workshop administration, including organisation, cost-keeping, provision of depreciation of plant, ... these subjects appearing in prominent journals on both sides of the Atlantic ... (quoted in Jenks, 1960/61, p.428).

The most important of the early texts on cost accounting had already been published, this was *Factory Accounts* (1887), by Emile Garcke and John Manger Fells[18]. By the end of 1922 seven editions had been brought out. Garner comments that it "probably had more to do with the advancement of cost accounting practices than any single book ever published" (1968, p.217). Kitchen and Parker in turn have stated that it was "*the* work of the costing renaissance" (1980, p.38). In the "Introductory" to the first edition the authors wrote that:

> Although the term Factory Accounts may be familiar, and its meaning sufficiently evident of persons acquainted with manufacturing business, or experienced in any operations requiring records to be kept of materials, plant, and stock, yet it is not infrequently assumed, even by accountants, that the ordinary commercial method of book-keeping by double entry, supplemented by the special subsidiary books which every trade demands, suffices for every kind of business (1887, p.4).

Describing these methods as inadequate they go on to recommend their special methods of book-keeping which integrated the cost accounts into the double entry system and enabled the employer to determine:

> ... accurately and scientifically, not merely approximately and by haphazard, the actual profit they make or sustain, not only on the aggregate transactions during a given period, but also upon each individual transaction. In a business the operations of which vary widely in character, this special knowledge as to the profitableness or otherwise of a particular piece of work is of paramount importance, for it is not only conceivable but very probable that the presence or absence of this information may have the most vital bearing on the policy to be pursued in in accepting or rejecting large contracts (ibid., pp.5-6).

Fascinatingly, despite its designation as the first cost accounting text it is interesting to note that the early editions contained much information that we today would consider outside the scope of cost accounting: such as the details of the Factory Acts and the laws relating to fire and boiler insurance. Details of various schemes of organising, for example, co-partnership were given, along with the opinions of the authors thereon. Cost accounting, it seems, was not at this time a clearly defined set of ideas and techniques with definite 'boundaries' distinguishing it as an activity distinct from factory administration more generally. In the revised 1922 edition the subjects included in the text are much nearer to the matters today considered within the ambit of cost accountancy.

During this period number of clerks employed grew rapidly. The censuses reveal the following figures:

Year	1886	1891	1901
Total engaged in occupations:	11,161,716	12,751,995	14,328,727
Commercial and Business clerks:	181,475	247,229	363,673

Thus over a twenty year period, when the total employed increased by less that 30%, the number of clerks increased by over 100%.

There was thus a process of social differentiation occuring during this period amongst clerks. The beginning, it seems apparent, of a division of labour in the office which would eventually lead to the emergence of a spectrum of occupations ranging from aspirant professionals such as office managers and cost accountants, to poorly paid office drudges like filing clerks. Already, by 1871, Orchard, in his study of Liverpool clerks, could see two distinct sets. Distinct in their income, their opportunities, and their social behaviour. At the upper end were those earning perhaps £150 per annum, rising in later life to as much as £350; they mixed in respectable society, went to the opera and kept servants. In the lower and more numerous class were those earning around £80 per annum; often the wife of such a clerk worked at home to supplement the family income- such work being appropriate to those who desired extra money but wished to appear respectable (Lockwood, 1958, p.28). Clerks, however, low their income, still saw themselves as socially above those who worked with their hands, rather than their brains. Charles Booth reported in his *Life and Labour of People in London*, published in 1896 that, despite the fact that the lower paid class of clerks earned amounts similar to skilled artisans:

> From top to bottom clerks associate with clerks and artisans with artisans- but comparatively seldom with each other. A clerk lives an entirely different life from an artisan- marries a different kind of wife- has different ideas, different possibilities, and different limitations ... differences ... invade every department of life (quoted in ibid., pp.28-29).

One disillusioned clerk noted that "foolish parents wish to see their sons in broadcloth instead of fustian; they think that a clerk is a gentleman and an artisan not" (*The Clerk's Journal*, 1890, quoted in ibid., p.29).

As the basic skills of reading and writing became more widespread amongst the population[19], competition arose for the job of clerk. Orchard observed that apprentice clerks were willing to work without salary to learn the job, he described them as "lads of good family, well supplied with pocket money" (quoted in ibid., p.26). Later the employment situation appeared to be aggrevated by cheap clerical labour from Germany and Scotland [whether or not this was really the case is a matter of dispute, see Anderson (1976)]. Continuous employment could not be guaranteed as far as a clerk was concerned. Garcke and Fells, writing in 1887, discussed how unfortunate it was that the retrenchment in times of depression often led employers to dismiss one or more of their clerks, considering this appropriate as they were "unproductive workers" (1887, p.10). They emphasised the importance of systematic record keeping by a permanent office staff[20], writing that:

> ... one of the disadvantages of insufficient records being kept is that book-keepers and clerks have often to spend much time obtaining from foremen and workmen, after the event, information which should reach the counting-house in a regular and systematic manner. This not only savours somewhat of espionage and is likely to create animus but is also contrary to the principle that true economy is to be found in the specialisation of labour, and in clerks devoting themselves to clerical and foremen to mechanical work (ibid.).

Unfortunately little seems to have been written about the early cost clerks. The following piece about them, written by an incorporated accountant from Rugby, suggests that they were of low status in clerkdom:

> The subject of Cost Accounts has, in late years, received very careful attention, which cannot fail to grow as manufacturers improve their methods and organisation. Until very recently, in almost all establishments, the clerks engaged on Time and Cost Accounts were amongst the most poorly paid, and this condition of things exists very largely at the present time. No doubt, in many cases the men receive what they are worth, but the salaries offered for the work cannot be expected to attract men of high intellectual capacity (Rider, 1904, p.178).

In 1896, J.Slater Lewis, head of the electrical engineering department of the Salford Rolling Mills, published *The Commercial Organisation of Factories*, described as the "first modern book on factory organisation"

(Jenks, 1960/61 p.428). Although almost certainly in some senses ahead of its time, it is interesting to consider the position of clerks within the 'ideal' organisation described in the book. Lewis writes in the introductory chapter that:

> Engineering, save in the matter of factory accounts, is endowed with acknowledged formulae, rules, tables and data of every description, the acquisition of which is deemed to be of national importance ...

However:

> Notwithstanding the progress of the age, every manufacturer still devises his own system of accounts has his own books and forms specially drafted and printed and his clerks educated in methods which may be of little or no value to them in other factories (1896, p.v).

Through following his "practical handbook" (ibid., p.xxv), the manufacturer could obtain a "complete and intelligent office organisation" which was generally based on the principle of division of labour in the office; the idea being that reducing the clerical work to pure routine would make it economical in the same way as division of labour in the works had done.

A Staff Organisation Diagram was provided, of which part is reproduced here (ibid., p.544):

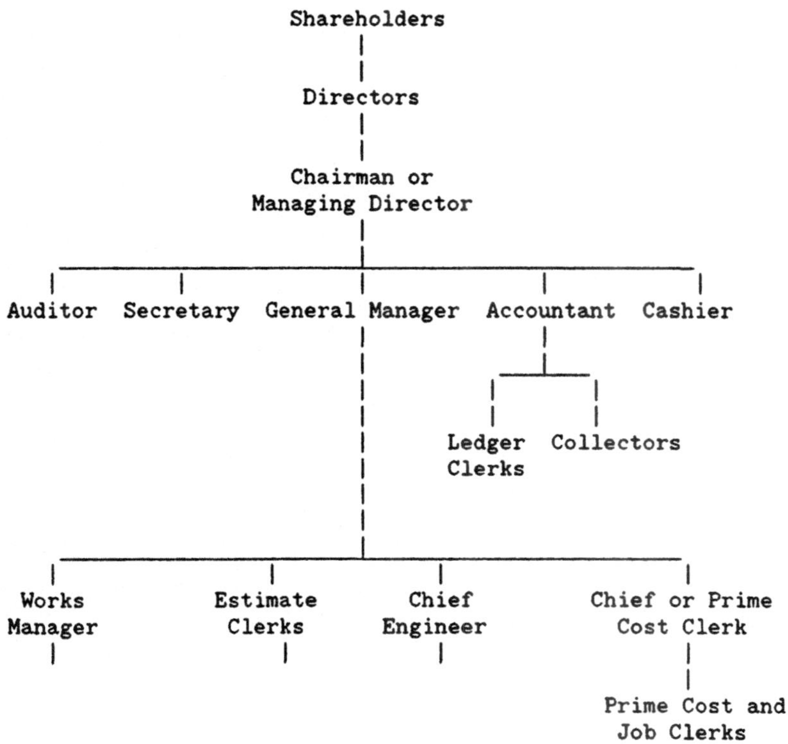

Little significance can be attached to the 'levels' in the chart-ledger clerks are obviously not above the chief engineer in the organisational hierarchy. Placed as it is amongst the 'miscellaneous' items in the last chapter. the chart seems rather 'incidental' to the work. As Urwick and Brech remark (1949, Vol. II, p.81), this perhaps indicates that the need for definitions of formalised relationships in industrial enterprises was not perceived as being so important, in the late nineteenth century, as it is today.

In Lewis's work there is nothing in the description of the role of the accountant which suggests any involvement with costing records, the attributes of the good accountant being that he should be an "enthusiastic book-keeper, thoroughly versed in the system of double-entry", balance the books promptly, keep intelligent control over the accounts of the concern and collect together "various items in such a form as they may be required by the Directors or the Auditor" (ibid., pp. 16-18). The costing records are kept by the cost clerks, responsible, as it can be seen from the diagram, directly to the general manager, not to the accountant. These records themselves are not kept in the 'counting house' but in the job clerk's office which Lewis writes should be as "near to the Shops as possible"[21] (ibid., pp.168-169).

It is in the estimating department[22] that the information from the costing records and the counting house are brought together, the labour and the material from the job clerk's records, the establishment (or indirect) charges from the accounting records through the medium of the general manager:

> Generally speaking the Estimate Clerk will receive instructions from the Manager as to the rate of Establishment charge which he has to include in the estimates (ibid., p.106).

Although it is impossible to assess the impact of *The Commercial Organisation of Factories* on the practice of organising, the very fact of it having been written and published is important. The ordering and disciplining of work had become a subject which could be discussed in a systematic manner, and in a way which embraced the whole of the activities of the organisation. The office work itself was becoming subject to the division of labour, the tasks of individual clerical employees specified. The procedures for *knowing* the organisation were rationalised in the sense that means and ends were laid out in detail.

The Professionalisation of Accounting: 1873-1896

In England and Wales this was a period when accountancy began to establish itself as a profession, if not yet a quite reputable one. In Edinburgh and Glasgow professional associations of accountants had obtained Royal Charters in the 1850s[23]. Whilst in England and Wales, although local societies were formed in the 1870s, it was not until 1880 that such a Royal Charter was granted (Macdonald, 1984, pp.187-188).

Bankruptcy work had remained the staple of accountants' work. The Bankruptcy Act of 1869 had brought "a large accession of business to accountants" (Cooper, 1921, p.559). Whinney wrote that there had been a great influx of persons:

> ... who thought they had nothing whatever to do to become accountants but to put up a plate and designate themselves as such, in order to become rich men (quoted in ICAEW, 1966, p.4).

In 1875 Justice Quain commented on the operation of the Bankruptcy Act to the effect that:

> ... the whole affairs in bankruptcy had been handed over to an ignorant set of men called accountants, which was one of the greatest abuses introduced into law (quoted in Stacey, 1954, p.24).

The first local societies were formed from members of the elite of this occupation, they appear to have been anxious to distinguish themselves as being professional people. The draft rules and regulations circulated prior to the formation of the London Institute, in 1870, defined the objects of the Institute as being:

> To elevate the attainments and status of *professional* accountants in London, to promote their efficiency and usefulness, and to give expression to their opinions upon all questions incident to their *profession* (italics mine) (quoted in ICAEW, 1966, p.6).

One of the main ways in which they made themselves exclusive was through setting very high entrance fees and subscriptions. The entrance fee for a Fellow was 50 guineas[24] (ibid., pp.6-7), at a time when most clerks only earned around £80 per annum. They applied for a Royal Charter, but were refused.

Whilst bankruptcy work remained the staple of accountants' business, other work gained in importance. Kitchen and Parker comment that:

> From the 1870s there was, for large organisations, a steady movement away from audits carried out by lay auditors (amateurs elected at general meetings by shareholders from among their own number) and towards the employment in their stead of professional accountants to undertake the audits and to report to shareholders on the annual accounts (1980, pp.2-3).

This is clearly associated with the huge growth in the number of limited companies, and the increasing complexity of business. In other spheres, such as public utilities, banks and industrial, provident and friendly societies, Acts were also passed requiring audits to be carried out, often by professional auditors (Jeal, 1937, p.526).

Cost accounting, though, was considered by chartered accountants to be outside their sphere of work: *The Accountant* (which described itself on the front cover as "The recognised weekly organ of chartered accountants and accountancy throughout the world") reviewed the first edition of *Factory Accounts* by Emile Garcke and John Manger Fells, first published in 1887, in the following terms:

> ... it is more of a theoretical than a practical work. It does not purport to deal with the ordinary financial books. It is rather concerned with the wages and time books, stock books, and matter of a similar nature, which as a rule, do not come within the scope of the accountants' duties (*The Accountant*, 5 May 1888, p.278).

The reviewer took exception to Garcke & Fells' statement that "for a manufacturing or trading concern to be well organised":

> ... the storekeeper or warehouseman should be able to state, by referring to his stores or stock ledgers, the actual quantities of any kind of material, or stock, on hand with the same facility and precision as the accountant can ascertain from the Commercial ledger the balances of cash at the bankers or the amount of securities in the safe (1887, pp.6-7).

The reviewer asked what accountant would agree to these remarks for "the ideal sought after is simply unattainable in most cases" (*The Accountant*, 5 May 1888, p.278). Recalling the attitudes of accountants in 1891, John Mann remarked on how "he was laughed at as a faddist in proposing to record at all the intricacies of costing, especially in an engineering works", when he brought up the question at his own professional Institute in Glasgow (*The Accountant*, 26 January 1901, pp.114-115).

To return to the late 1870s, it seems that accountants were gradually gaining in status, perhaps due to their involvement with the more prestigious audit work. Eventually (after much dispute between the local societies who came together to make the charter application), in 1880 a Royal Charter was granted to the new 'Institute of Chartered Accountants in England and Wales' (ICAEW, 1966, pp.12-13). By 1882 there were 1,193 members (ibid., pp.22-24)[25]. It seems, however, that despite the grant of a Royal Charter they were still not *quite* socially *au fait*, for Ernest Cooper recalled how:

> There was an expectation that the Queen's Jubilee of 1887 would bring a flood of titles, and it was hoped that the President of our Institute would receive a knighthood. Some of us anticipated the honour by jocularly calling Mr Whinney Sir Frederick, but our hope was disappointed ... (1921, p.555).

It was not until the during the First World War that accountants seem to have finally consolidated their position as professionals. After the war they did indeed receive a flood of titles (see Chapter 4).

The professionalisation process brought three related forms of standardisation to accounting. Firstly, the beginning of the 'standardisation' of practitioners; secondly, the standardisation of a field of knowledge and practice called 'accounting'; thirdly, a movement towards the standardisation of accounting practices. Practitioners began to become 'standardised' in the sense that rigid conditions were set for entry to the Institute; conditions which included five years of articled clerkship and the passing of examinations. In addition, they forbade the combination of the accountancy with other classes of business, such as auctioneering and estate agency (Garrett, 1961, pp.3-5). Those organising the Institute perceived that if the title 'chartered accountant' was to become one indicating a competant professional man (women were excluded) and one which would bring status and high remuneration to its holder, then they must ensure that their members had the appropriate characteristics.

This 'standardisation' of practitioners was accompanied by a process of definition of accounting, of what it was that distinguished accounting from other related knowledge and practice. This had begun with the publication of a journal for accountants in 1874. Jones, analysing the contents of the first issue of *The Accountant*, reports that 94% of the space was taken up with articles on bankruptcy law and practice, reports of law cases on bankruptcy, and "summaries of the figures in bankrupt estates in the principal towns". Interestingly, some of the small remaining space was devoted to the relations of accountants with solicitors and the evils of touting. Income tax was not mentioned once (the rate was 2d in the £) (1937, p.181). The subjects covered by the journal reflected the concerns of accountants in practice, at the same time they represented a definition of what accounting was and what an accountant did. They quoted one gentleman who wrote round to prospective clients:

> I take the liberty of enclosing my card. I have recently commenced business as a Law Stationer, Law Bill Clerk, Public and Private Auditor and Accountant, House, Land and Estate Agent, Rent and Debt Collector, and Trustee in Bankruptcy (quoted in ICAEW, 1966, p.12).

He had obviously *not* understood the nature of the accountants' role as perceived by its more 'professional' practitioners. This process of definition became much more pronounced once the ICAEW was formed. Through their examinations they defined what practitioners should know, and hence, to a large extent, what their role was. In the first final examination of the ICAEW, held in 1882, questions covering the rights and duties of liquidators, trustees and receivers; bankruptcy and company law; mercantile law with the law of arbitration and awards; book-keeping, auditing and the adjustment of partnership and executorship accounts, were asked (ICAEW, 1966, p.27). The inclusion of auditing reflects the growing involvement of accountants with that business. In addition to examinations, meetings also facilitate the closer definition of the accountants' role, albeit unintentionally. In 1887 at the first autumnal meetings of the ICAEW, the addresses and speeches reflected the predominant concern with liquidations, receiverships, bankruptcies, deeds of arrangement and absconding debtors; although some time was devoted to auditors' certificates (Jones, 1937, p.182).

The standardisation of practice itself is enhanced by examinations, through discussions at meetings, and through the professional journal; an article by Edwin Guthrie written in 1882 and entitled: *The want of uniformity in the modes of stating accounts; the frequency of inconsistency between the title and subject-matter of published accounts, and the employment of non-correlative terms in accounts*, seemingly arousing considerable interest in the columns of *The Accountant* (Kitchen and Parker, 1980, p.11).

4. The Pre-war Period: 1897-1914

Writing in 1937, Edwards was of the opinion that cost accountants had added little to the *theory* of the subject since the early years of the twentieth century and that by 1906 it was clear that cost accounting had come to stay (1937, p.344). The putting into *practice* of this theory in business organisations in Britain was a different matter however. The exigencies of the First World War had led, in 1916, to the setting up of a Board of Trade investigation into costing in the engineering trades. In the final report the authors commented that:

> Of course all efficient firms in this country have proper systems of costing. We think, however, that the essential value of a careful system of costing to ensure the maximum economy has not yet received from many houses the attention it deserves. Certain large works are known to have no systems of costing at all. Other works are known to have a system of costing based upon conventional rates of wages in those works some years before. It may be assumed that most small works have only a costing system more or less reduced to a rule of thumb (Cmnd. 9073, 1918, p.11).

The huge variation in the quality of costing systems noted here reflects the more general situation of British industry, the old and the new existing side by side.

Britain left the problems of the Great Depression behind, not through having modernised the economy to any large extent, but by exploiting the last remaining possibilities of the traditional hegemony [26]. More was exported to countries with poorly developed economies (as in the case of cotton) and much was made of the last great technical innovations (as in the case of the iron steamship) (Hobsbawn, 1969, p.151). There was a lack of extensive industrial rationalisation, but change was coming slowly to British industry. Between 1888 and 1914 an average of 67 firms disappeared in mergers each year, a number far greater than that of the previous period; these may well have been encouraged by the desire of firms to become large enough to raise capital on one of the stock exchanges (Hannah, 1983, pp. 20-21).

A growth in the size of a firm tends to encourage the use of bureaucratic record-keeping systems, such as cost accounting, in order to facilitate control and co-ordination. Rationalisation, in the form of workshop reorganisations, did occur in several industries, especially engineering (Littler, 1982, p.84). Associated with these reorganisations was a far more detailed management of the *cost* of labour. It became a factor to be carefully measured, watched and controlled. Workers were directly paid and controlled by the firm rather than through internal-contractors or piecemasters (ibid., p.90) and complex payment and incentive schemes were introduced, such as the premium-bonus system[27]. Under this latter scheme workers were given a time allowance for work to be performed plus a bonus for any time saved- often calculated in a complex manner (ibid., pp.84-85). Work was generally more disciplined- by the early 1900s feed and speed inspectors, quality-control inspectors and rate-fixers had all started to appear on the shop-floor (ibid., p. 89). This concern with the cost of labour and the disciplining of work may well have been encouraged by the atmosphere of confrontation, for the last years before the First World War saw acute and widespread labour unrest. This was caused by, amongst other factors, an end to the rapid improvement in the real incomes of workers- which had characterised the period of the Great Depression (Hobsbawm, 1969, p.159). Associated with this was more widespread trade union membership: whilst in 1889-90 there were two million members, by 1911-13 there were four million (ibid., p.165).

It would appear to be no coincidence that in the United States, where scientific management and similar practices were introduced on a far wider scale than in Britain, cost accounting was in greater use[28]. The Americans were more advanced both in the intensive application of cost accounting techniques within the firm and the extent to which they had spread throughout industry, before the First World War (1984, p.127). As Jenks comments:

> ... the development of cost accounting practices as distinct from doctrine, depended upon the rise of standardised shop conditions (1960/1961, p.434).

It seems likely that the lack of consistency in the development of costing in Britain found by the Board of Trade investigation remarked upon earlier, reflected the varied degrees of rationalisation which had occured. Even as early as the first decade of the century there was an awareness that America was more advanced in this field, Rider writing in 1904 that it was "well known" that the subject had received "much greater attention" and its application brought to "greater perfection" than in Britain (1904, p.178). The comments made in his article about the role of cost accounting in estimating are interesting, the British usage being explicitly compared to that of "foreign competition"[29]. A need was perceived for Britain to copy the American developments[30], Webster Jenkinson commenting that:

> Uncle Sam, at home, always counts the cost; and if we do not admire all his business methods, yet this one is well worthy of imitation (*The Accountant*, 9 March 1907, p.316).

William Plender made a similar remark in his Presidential speech to the Tenth Provincial Autumnal Meeting of the ICAEW in 1910 (reported in *The Accountant*, 8 October 1910, p.479). The belief that American methods and American consultants were superior to their British counterparts is one which forms an undercurrent to all the later developments in Britain.

There is little direct evidence concerning the emergence of specialised clerks dealing with costs. It would not seem unreasonable, however, to assume that in the larger and more organised businesses division of labour amongst clerks would bring such specialists. In 1911 Rawlinson commented that:

> ... there are many great works in England which have their separate cost staffs, with a separate set of offices, whose duty it is to lay before the head manager periodically statements of the whole output of the works, divided in its departments, and showing the result of the week's or month's transactions ... (*The Incorporated Accountants' Journal*, p.265).

Clerks were generally more numerous and better educated. There were two and a half times as many "commercial and business clerks" in 1911 as as in 1881, a period in which the total engaged in occupations increased by less than 50% (1911 Census, Summary Tables, p.274). In a book published in 1915 Arthur Williams recorded the workings of a Swindon locomotive factory where he had been employed for 23 years. He wrote of the clerks as being "the most numerous of all the trained classes at the factory": of the 12,000 employees, over 1,000 were clerks (Williams, 1915, pp.133, ix, 135). The expansion of the state education system had led to a higher level of literacy, and thus a greater availability of the 'raw-material' of clerkdom. Individuals were entering the occupation with vocational training in commerce[31]. As will be discussed in detail later, it was from the amongst the elite of these clerks that the majority of the early members of the ICWA seem to have come.

There was no subdivision of the census classification of "commercial and business clerk" until the 1921 census, when "a more scientific classification of both occupations and industries" (Census 1921, Industry Tables, p.3) was adopted. It is worth noting at this point that it revealed that out of nearly a million "clerks and draughtsmen (not civil service or local authority) and typists", nearly 20,000 were "costing and estimating clerks" (Census, 1921, Occupational Tables, p.21). An analysis by industry revealed most of these to be working in engineering and basic manufacturing (*The Cost Accountant*, September 1925, p.94); this analysis is reproduced in the Appendix to this thesis. Although there would appear to have been an increase in the membership of this occupation during the war (see chapter 4), it seems probable that there were a fair number employed in such a specialist post in the prewar years.

To move to the issue of the installation of cost systems, there is evidence that consultants were installing systems for manufacturers at this period, some with an engineering background, others with an accounting one. Competition for the work appears to have existed[32]. Wells comments that there was some acrimonious criticism of accountants by engineers, for example, Holden A. Evans, a naval engineer, writes in 1910:

> The employment of an expert accountant to devise and install a cost system in a manufacturing and repairing plant is an absurdity. Yet this mistake has been made by many and the results are almost invariably unsatisfactory (quoted in Wells, 1978, p.123).

Who were these 'expert accountants' being criticised by the engineers? It is possible that they were chartered accountants. The contents of an editorial in *The Accountant* (which described itself as a magazine for chartered accountants the world over) in 1909, suggests their involvement:

> ... of the numerous inefficient so-called systems of Cost Accounts in existence, by far the larger number have been evolved by practical manufacturers without the aid of professional accountants ... (*The Accountant*, 27 April 1909, p.549).

Webster Jenkinson writes of them being: "called upon to advise in the construction of a costing system" and it being "desirable" that they be "fully acquainted with the principles underlying such accounts" (*The Accountant*, 13 February 1909, p.238). However, as discussed later, Webster Jenkinson's enthusiasm for cost accounting was not shared by a goodly proportion of his colleagues, who continued to consider such activities as too closely connected with the activities of 'traders', to warrant be the proper concern of professional men.

A second alternative is the incorporated accountants, the next tier down in the status hierarchy of the occupation; or, more accurately, the accountants doing this work may have been joining this body. It is worth noting here that Fells (who held the post of 'accountant and secretary' in 1887), described himself as a 'business organiser' on his marriage certificate dated 1897, and it was not until 1902 that he joined an accounting body, and then he became an incorporated accountant (Kitchen and Parker, 1980, p.36).

It is interesting to raise a number of interconnected issues concerning cost accounting in this period. Firstly, the question of responsibility for cost records and accounts. Were they under the supervision of a general, or works, manager (as Slater Lewis suggests in his book *The Commercial Organisation of Factories*, published in 1896), or did they come under the supervision of the financial accountant? Secondly, *where* in the enterprise were cost records kept? Were they kept in the offices connected to the works (again, as Slater Lewis suggests), or were they kept in the 'counting house' (traditionally the home of the financial accounts)? Thirdly, and perhaps the key to the other questions is, to what extent were cost records integrated into the financial accounting systems? The evidence which Wells presents indicates that the integration of costing records into the financial accounting system was associated with the increasing dominance of accountants (as against engineers) in the matter of installing them (1978, pp. 128). According to Wells engineers had largely left this field to accountants by 1914 (ibid., p.125). Such a dominance by accountants would be expected to be associated with the keeping of costing records in the 'counting house', rather than the works-office, and their supervision by an accountant, rather than a general manager. Perhaps it is in this change that costing records became cost *accounts* (see the introduction to this Chapter). To raise yet another related issue: the whole history of estimating, and the appearance of 'estimators', would appear to be linked to the history of costing in Britain. As I have discussed, it has been suggested that the difficulties in estimating for engineering work during the Great Depression, was an important factor in the development of costing in Britain during this period. Writing in 1904, Rider comments on how "highly technical" estimating staff apparently considered "information compiled by clerks" as not worth taking into account when they prepared estimates[33]. This suggests that they were a specialist occupational group, perhaps separate from cost clerks in some works. The use in the 1921 census of the category "costing and estimating clerks" suggests their association, however. All these questions would make interesting subjects for further research.

Professional Accountants and Cost Accounting: 1897-1914

In the 1911 census the number of "accountants" was given as nearly nine and a half thousand but the census compilers complained that these included "some accountants' clerks and commercial clerks notwithstanding efforts made to exclude them" (Vol. X, p.xxxiii). Between, on the one hand, professional accountants (members of the

Chartered or Incorporated bodies) and, on the other, clerks, were a growing number of individuals calling themselves 'accountants'. Some of these were joining associations such as the Central Association of Accountants and the London Association of Accountants, formed after the Chartered and Incorporated accounting bodies made long periods of training and the passing of examinations a requirement for membership[34].

There was a gradual warming of interest in costing by chartered accountants. In 1901, the editor of *The Accountant* reported that a chartered accountant acting as an auditor had applauded his clients action in abandoning a system of preparing cost sheets which were "not accurate" and cost £1,200 per annum and had stated that in his, the auditor's experience "extending over fifty years" he had "never found a Cost Book to bring out a correct result" and that "the adoption of such a system would cost more than could be gained by it". The editor commented that he was surprised, as he viewed a knowledge of costs as "vital" (*The Accountant*, 1 June 1901, p.638). In 1897 O. Holt Caldicott FCA bravely urged the:

> ... necessity for our acquainting ourselves with many of the technicalities of manufacturing and commercial concerns in order that we may be qualified to speak as experts, not merely in figures and intricate calculations, but also in regard to the cost of production and distribution of various commodities, and in regard to the soundness or unsoundness of our clients' trading having regard to the special conditions affecting the particular business of each one (*The Accountant*, 22 May 1897, p.524).

He goes on to admit, however, that, "I believe that my professional bretheren are not all of my opinion on this point ... " (ibid.). He discusses the difficulties of a student acquiring such technical knowledge during his term of articles and lamely concludes that "if he is observant and thoughtful, the special knowledge of which I speak must come ... " (ibid.). This latter comment reflects the ambiguity with which professional accountants regarded cost accounting, some regarding it as beneath their professional integrity to get involved with cost accounts, others, like Webster Jenkinson, giving it their full support, he noted that:

> Although not part of the regular duty of the auditor to check the Cost Accounts, yet, ... it is very desirable that he be fully acquainted with the principles underlying such accounts. .... It must always be remembered that although legally we are not, as auditors, called upon to advise our clients in the conduct of their business, yet as Chartered Accountants we are expected by them to be competent and ready to give an expert opinion when they themselves are baffled (*The Accountant*, 13 February 1909, p.238).

The possible involvement of chartered accountants in installing cost accounting systems has already been discussed. Some may have been actually *employed* by companies, rather than simply being used as consultants: in the official history of the ICAEW it is suggested that chartered accountants were being appointed in growing numbers, to the post of secretary or accountant to a company, at this time (ICAEW, 1966, p.43).

In 1888 the reviewer of the first edition of Garcke and Fells' book *Factory Accounts* had written, as I discussed earlier, that it was considered to deal with matters which "as a rule do not come within the scope of the accountants' duties" (*The Accountant*, 5 May 1888, p.278). When they reviewed the sixth edition in 1911, however, they wrote "a reliable guide to all matters pertaining to factory accounts (*The Accountant*, 22 July 1911, p.123).

Questions had begun to appear on the examination papers of the largest body, the Institute of Chartered Accountants in England and Wales (ICAEW). For example at the November 1911 Intermediate examination candidates were asked:

> What are Cost Accounts? State shortly how they are prepared and give an example.

In the Final at the same sitting a question was asked on the charging of standing and establishment expenses in a system of costing. However, such questions were generally descriptive and fairly simple. Moreover, whole examinations, for example that of November 1914, passed without any question being asked on the subject (ICAEW Archives). Articled clerks scarcely came into contact with cost accounting during their training. They were expected to learn accounting 'on the job' (which meant preparing simple sets of accounts and, in the sphere of auditing, ticking off ledgers to one another and to summaries). They were tutored for their examinations by correspondance courses sold by privately run colleges. Such colleges would not have any interest in teaching their students anything about cost accounting beyond the minimal level seemingly demanded by the examiners.

In concluding this section it is interesting to note that when Miles Taylor returned from the United States in 1914 and, as he writes, "with more enthusiasm than commonsense" put up a plate describing himself as a "Chartered Accountant and Efficiency Engineer" the Institute accused him of using a term which was "discreditable to a Chartered Accountant" (*The Accountant*, 28 June 1919, p.552). So although interest was generally growing, it is more accurate to say that some Chartered Accountants took a great deal of interest in it and tried to persuade others to do so, but the majority were only beginning to see it as something which could be relevant to them, and then only in the form of information to help in the process of auditing.

Conclusion

By the eve of the First World War cost accounting systems had apparently been introduced into many of the larger, and more well organised works in Britain. It has been suggested that this was associated with the workshop reorganisation which occured in several industries, especially engineering. However, if we accept the findings of the Board of Trade investigation begun just two years after the end of this period, namely in 1916, then it seems that some large works had no system of costing, and others, a totally inadequate one. They suggest that small works had "only a costing system more or less reduced to a rule of thumb" (Cmnd. 9073, 1918, p.11).

This is about as far as a traditional history would go in describing the situation on the eve of the war, but there are other aspects which are important to a 'genealogical' history. The techniques were not only being practised in factories, a discourse had developed about them. A discourse which is evidenced by the articles in trade journals and in the textbooks which had appeared. This emergence of a field of *knowledge*, cost accounting, and a discussion about what the role of such techniques in controlling and co-ordinating work in the factory, was associated with the rise of specialist practitioners of the craft who were involved with installing these systems. What their background was is difficult to say, but there is some evidence that by the eve of the war, either those of an accounting background had come to predominate, or the practitioners were *calling* themselves 'accountants' in greater numbers.

By 1914 the elite of professional accountants, the members of the ICAEW, were coming to see costing as something associated with the accountancy which they practiced. Whether their arena of professional knowledge and practice should include cost accounting, was a question seeming to have been answered in the positive when questions, albeit of an elementary nature, began to appear on their examination papers in the years prior to the war. However, whether their involvement with cost accounting was to be central to their future position as prestigious professionals, was a matter for dispute. Many regarded it with distaste as a business too closely connected with the world of grimy industry to bring them the greater status they desired as gentlemanly professionals.

Within factories the division of labour in the office brought specialist clerks dealing with costing. It seems likely that the old system of a separate 'counting house' (where financial books were kept), and a 'works office' (where records concerning production were written up), was being replaced in the most 'advanced' (in organisational terms) works, by an 'accounts office'; where production records became the raw material for a complex integrated cost accounting system. However, such developments were seemingly not common, and many manufacturers ignorant of costing matters; cost accounting had come into being, but not yet 'into the light'.

NOTES

(1) It is interesting that there does seem to have been some residual competition in the war, this can be seen in the apparently rather strained relations between the Technical Costing (engineering based) and Accountancy Costing branches at the Ministry of Munitions.

(2) It is interesting to note that Wells claims that it is the failure to recognise the distinction between cost records and cost accounts, which has led to the confusion surrounding the origins of particular costing techniques (1978, p.67).

(3) With the possible exceptions of: firstly, Hoskin and Macve (1986), who discuss the early history of accounting in terms of Foucault's power/knowledge analysis; and secondly, Burchell et al (1985), who discuss the recent rise and fall of interest in value added statements. Neither of these works is directly relevant to the emergence of costing in the nineteenth century.

(4) Garner, however, claims that many cost accounting practices and theories pre-date the British Industrial Revolution. He writes that:

> In fact, they date back to about the fourteenth century when, as a result of the growth of Italian, English, Flemish and German commerce small industrial enterprises began to be established by various individuals and partnerships to engage in the production of the few staples of that era, such as woollens, books, coins and wine (1968, p.211).

He describes cost accounting in Britain as having begun in the reign of Henry VII (1485 to 1509), when workshop owners who were resentful of the many guild restrictions established their own industrial communities with the aim of producing goods to be sold through channels other than the organised guilds. As the owners of workshops found themselves competing against the guilds, as well as amongst themselves, "more accurate records of costs became imperative and almost a prerequisite for success" (1968, p.212). Although it is interesting to note these developments it seems improbable that these developments had any direct influence on those in Britain in the nineteenth century. The last comment: that cost accounts became 'imperative' betrays a rather functionalistic attitude. It is not clear to me that cost accounts ever become absolutely 'imperative'.

(5) To put these comments in context it is worth briefly considering the concept of 'work' which underlies activity in business organisations as we recognise it. 'Work' is a culturally specific concept, and the very words 'work', 'to work', and 'worker', took on

their meanings in our language in a certain period (Godelier, 1980, m.164). As Lukes writes, the "meanings of words generally incapsulate ideas, even theories" (1977, p.1). Looking mainly at French economic vocabulary (but similar comments would probably apply to English vocabulary), Godelier notes how it was not until the eighteenth century that the words for wage earner, worker, and capital acquired their modern meanings. The modern French verb 'to work', *travailler*, for instance, came from the Latin *tripaliare* which meant torturing with a *tripalium*, an instrument made of three stakes (1980, p.165).

The coming into being of the modern meanings of 'worker', 'work', etcetera, was associated with, amongst other things, the rise of 'political economy', one of whose key concepts was the idea of work (ibid., p.166). Hannah Arendt points out that to ancient thought the very term 'political economy' itself would have been a contradiction in terms, for whatever was 'economic', related to the life of the individual, and 'political', to the public life (1958, pp.28-29). To the Greeks the sphere of the household was the sphere of the maintenance of life, a sphere which involved the 'economic', a sphere in which man existed not truely as a human being but only as a specimen of the animal species man-kind (ibid., p.46). This household sphere was considered one form of life, the other, the political life (*bios politikos*), a totally separate one where men were free. Necessity was a 'pre-political' phenomenon to be satisfied in the private household organisation (ibid., pp.22-23). Arendt writes of the 'rise of the social', as one of the most important events in the coming of the modern age; the economic affairs of the household realm have been brought into the public realm, "in the modern world, the two realms constantly flow into each other like waves in the never resting stream of the life process itself" (ibid., p.33). The rise of the social has been accompanied by a huge expansion of economic activity. Activity which no longer takes place in the household, but in specially constituted organisations as 'work'. Politics in itself has come, in large measure, to serve these economic interests which in Greek society were in an independent and inferior arena of life. This glimpse of Greek attitudes brings to light how our idea of 'work' is not a universal given, but culturally and historically specific.

(6) The question of why it was Britain that became the first 'workshop of the world' and why this breakthrough occured towards the end of the eighteenth century, and not before or after, remains a subject for debate by academics (see, for instance Hobsbawm, 1969).

(7) Littler seems to imply that this advantage was one of the main reasons for the use of the system. Clawson, who studied the internal contract system operating in America in the period 1860-1920, argues rather differently however. He stresses the way in which this system enabled factory owners and managers to minimise costs. Contractors

"had huge incentives to maximise output and keep costs to a minimum; thus ensuring capital an agent in the work group (1980, p.110).

(8) The other two being: the master and steward system, developed largely in the administration of large landed estates; and the accounting developed by manufacturers operating the putting-out system (Pollard, 1968, p.245).

(9) It is interesting to note that Stacey argues that:

> It was in the first Railway Acts that accountancy made its debut in the modern sense. The accounts of railways and public utility undertakings were regulated by special Acts of Parliament which imposed specific rules of accounting which later became known as the "double account" system (1954, p.13).

(10) Pollins hints at this, commenting that although he had not had the opportunity himself , he felt that "the development of the organisation and methods of the accounting departments of railway companies would repay study" (1956, p.353).

(11) Hobsbawm writes how economic behaviour by employers and workers in the early years of the industrial revolution tended to be based on custom, empiricism, and short-term calculation, rather than on any long-term rational analysis of the market (1968, pp.344-345). By the period under discussion here, 1840-1873, there had been a "partial learning of the 'rules of the game'" by both sides (ibid.). A new generation grew up who knew no other life than factory work, they began to understand that 'labour' was a commodity to be sold, whilst employers began to learn the value of intensive, rather than extensive labour utilisation. This was a slow change however, when they had any choice in the matter workers still tended to fix the basic asking price and the quantity and quality of work done, by non-economic criteria. Likewise, employers still tended to measure the degree of labour utiisation by custom rather than empirically (ibid.).

(12) To summarize this development briefly:- The Bubble Act of 1719 had denied limited liability status to all bodies not incorporated by the Crown or by parliament. Despite this a large number of joint stock companies and partnerships were formed founded on the principle of limited liability, but without legal acknowledgement. Unfortunately the liability of the shareholders in such companies was not limited to the value of their shares and they could be held responsible for the whole of a company's debt. Fraud became a great problem (Stacey, 1954, p.6; Edey and Panitpakdi, 1956, p.357). Incorporation by registration, but with unlimited liability, was first made possible by the Joint Stock Companies Act of 1844, but through

the Companies Acts of 1855 and 1862 limited liability was introduced (Edey and Panitpakdi, 1956, p.356; Stacey, 1954, p.7).

(13) There were professional bodies of accountants in Italy existing from the sixteenth century onwards, perhaps earlier (Brown, 1968, p.175), however, this is not likely to have affected the later British developments, which began in Scotland. There the occupation of 'accomptant' emerged in Glasgow and Edinburgh from rather different roots (Macdonald, 1984, pp.180-181). In Edinburgh it was closely associated with the legal profession and there were, apparently, several instances of the members of the leading Solicitors' society in Scotland practising as accountants. Brown, writing in 1905, comments that "moreover, until comparatively recent times much accountants' work was done in solicitors' offices" (1968., p.182). Both the esteem with which such individuals were held, and the association with the legal profession, are demonstrated in a letter written by Sir Walter Scott in 1820, where he gives advice as regards possible professions for his nephew to follow:

> If my nephew is steady, cautious, fond of a sedentary life and quiet pursuits, and at the same time a proficient in arithmetic, and with a disposition towards the prosecution of its highest branches, he cannot follow a better line than that of an accountant. It is highly respectable- and is one in which, with attention and skill, aided by such opportunities as I may be able to procure for him, he must ultimately succeed. I say ultimately- because the harvest is small and the labourers numerous in this as in other branches of our legal practice .... (quoted in ibid., p.197).

A little later it was said that the profession of accountant was "certainly more varied than that of a lawyer, and I believe is certainly not less dignified" (quoted in Jeal, 1937, p.522). Towards the middle of the nineteenth century there seems also to have been a strong connection with banking and insurance, for many accountants were directors. managers and agents for these institutions (Macdonald, 1984, p.182).

In Glasgow, on the other hand, "it had its origin as a distinct calling in commercial circles and it was not an uncommon thing for an individual to be designated 'Merchant and Accomptant'". In the commercial crises of 1777 and 1793 accountants were employed to wind up bankrupt companies (Brown, 1968, pp.198-199). By the third quarter of the nineteenth century stockbroking was also important there and over 40% of the profession were engaged with it (Macdonald, 1984, pp.182-183).

Less is known of the early development of the accountancy profession in England and Wales (ibid., p.188). Stacey writes that by the end of the eighteenth century there were around 600 accountants and "most of them were carrying on the practice of accountancy as a sideline to other more important and lucrative business, such as auctioneering, rent-collection and stockbroking" (1954, p.17).

(14) For instance, in 1864 the head of the firm of Harding Whinney and Co. was appointed to be a Commissioner to inquire into the working of the Bankruptcy Acts (ICAEW, 1966, p.4). Others, apparently, became wealthy: Ernest Cooper recalls that the name which most impressed his youthful imagination was that of E.J. Coleman, head of the firm of Coleman, Turquand, Youngs & Co: he was reputed to be living as a Buckinghamshire Squire (Cooper, 1921, p.555). William Quilter, to become the first president of the London Institute of Accountants in 1870, was described as an "accountant, art collector and somewhat of a financier" (ibid.).

(15) Sidney Webb's family were described as coming "from the genteel fringe of the lower middle class". His mother's hairdressing business provided most of the family income, whilst his father was described as an 'accountant' he "spent more than half of his time on politics, avidly reading newspapers, following parliamentary debates and serving unpaid on the local vestry and as a Poor Law guardian" (Mackensie & Mackensie, 1977, pp.56-57).

(16) Urwick and Brech suggest the 'company secretary' would also play the *role* of company accountant, although they do not indicate whether the person would *call* themself 'an accountant' (1949, Vol.II, p.132).

(17) By the early 1870s trade unionism was officially accepted and recognised where it had succeeded in establishing itself, mainly amongst the skilled craftsmen of the manual trades, but also in the core of the basic industries, such as coal mines and the cotton mills and in the machine building and ship building trades. The great expansion of 1871-3 raised the number of organised workers to something like half a million; by 1889-90, this had grown to one and a half million (Hobsbawm, 1969, pp.155, 165).

(18) At the time of its writing Emile Garcke was an electrical engineer and John Manger Fells "the Accountant and Assistant Secretary of the Anglo-American Brush Electrical Light Corporation" (having begun his career in the accounts office of a railway company) (Kitchen and Parker, 1980, p.36). It is interesting to note that both were members of the Fabian Society (Hobsbawm, 1968, p.257).

(19) Elementary education up to the age of twelve became compulsary for all children in 1870, and in the twenty years following the

average school attendance rose from one and a half to four and a half million, whilst the money spent on each child doubled (Trevelyan, 1964, p.219). This basic education was sparsely supplemented by the addition of some of a technical and commercial nature by independent schools, mechanics institutes, the YMCA and other similar bodies. Reports on technical and commercial education showed, as early as 1867, that Germany, Belgium, France and the USA were ahead of Britain in this field. It was gradually realised that the basic education provided in England and Wales was not providing adequate numbers of technically and commercially trained men. This realisation led to a general movement in support of technical and commercial education which reached a peak in the 1880s (Andersen, 1976, pp.89-93).

(20) It is interesting to note the link here between the division of labour to be seen in the specialisation and clear separation of roles between the office staff and the workers; and the attempt, in a sense, to 'purify' the abstraction of information.

(21) This is in accordance with Garcke and Fells' scheme in *Factory Accounts* (1887), where they describe the "counting house", in the glossary to the book, as "the place in which *mercantile* book-keeping is conducted" (italics mine).

(22) It is worth noting that Lewis writes that the estimating section is a:

> ... strictly confidential section ... indiscriminant admission of pupils and outsiders would be improper and inimical to the interests of the firm ... The 'pupil' ... pays his premium and is put through the shops and the drawing office and thus acquires a practical knowledge of the manufacturing operations, but in so far as commercial duties are concerned, particularly that of estimating he is ignorant ... (1896, p.106).

(23) Macdonald suggests that it was the connection with the legal profession and the existence within the membership of the established middle-class, that led to this early professional development in Scotland (1984, pp.187-188).

(24) A guinea was £1-10s; in present terminology, £1.05.

(25) By 1885 a new professional body had been formed, namely 'The Society of Incorporated Accountants and Auditors'(SIAA), as it became known in 1908. The competition between professional bodies of accountants, which had died down with the formation of the ICAEW, began again. According to Garrett:

> Those who might claim to be members of what was then almost a nascent profession were not wholly covered by the membership or facilities provided by existing bodies of accountants.

Thus the SIAA came into being (1961, p.3). Amongst the first members of the new association were practising accountants who apparently could not fulfil the ICAEW's rather rigid conditions for membership; these included municipal and county treasurers and accountants, and "in smaller numbers, accountants occupying responsible positions in business and the Government" (ibid., pp.3-5). The launch was not looked upon favourably by the ICAEW:

> From references to various published directories and other sources and an inspection of the Society's list, we find represented among its members, a formidable array of clerks of all kinds- rent collectors, corn merchants, shop-keepers, valuers, collectors of taxes, bailiffs, secretaries of various concerns, civil engineers, school board clerks, overseers, timber agents, pawnbrokers and manure merchants" (from *The Accountant*, 1886, quoted in Stacey, 1954, p.28).

In 1887 the Society instituted examinations, although members continued to be admitted on the basis of apparent competance, backed up by testimonies (Garrett, 1961, p.6) . It was possibly in response to that body's growth in size that the ICAEW changed its bye-laws in 1891 and 1893, allowing the admittance of accountants of ten years practice. Some of the members of the Society took advantage of this offer (ibid., pp.6-7). Competition between the two gradually waned, although disgreements arose every time a Bill was promoted for the registration of accountants (ie. to legally restrict the practice of accountancy in the way in which the practice of medicine is restricted).

(26) Whilst manufacturing industry was in decline (compared to other industrial nations such as America) London prospered as a financial centre. Much 'invisible' income came from Britain's position as intermediary in the world's system of payments, through the provision of trading services and through shipping. By 1900 British ships carried 55% of the cargoes entering through US ports (Hobsbawm, 1969, pp.151-152). Foreign investment increased greatly and by 1913 Britain owned perhaps £4,000 million abroad, compared to less than £5,500 million by France, Germany, Belgium, Holland and the USA put together (ibid., p.152).

(27) For instance in 1886 only 6-7% of turners were paid through piece rate and bonus systems, but by 1914 this figure had risen to 46% (Hobsbawm, 1968, p.360).

(28) To briefly summarise these developments. In the latter part of the nineteenth century cost accounting in the United States was given impetus by the rationalisation of production methods and organisation of business associated with the rise of the professional mechanical engineer (Nelson, 1974, pp.480-81; 1980, p.13). These engineers believed that if shop management were undertaken with the same knowledge and forethought as the building of a complicated machine, the plant would run with similar efficiency (Nelson, 1980, p.12). Cost accounting systems were one of the tools to be used in the realisation of this plan (ibid., p.13). Efficiency became "a craze" by the early twentieth century (Haber, 1964); In the factory this 'efficiency' manifested itself in the implementation of 'systematic' and later 'scientific' management systems, the more advanced schemes involved introducing cost accounting. The standardardisation which went with 'efficiency' in itself laid the way open to systematic cost accounting (Epstein, 1978). Harrington Emerson, one of the pioneers of standard costing (Sowell, 1973, p.1), was an 'efficiency engineer' making his living selling efficiency to businessmen, he claimed a hundred employees and offices in six cities (Haber, 1964, p.56). F.W.Taylor himself, known as the 'father' of scientific management devised a costing system to be implemented alongside his other managerial innovations (Nelson, 1980, p.54); amongst the reasons he needed to install improved accounting systems was to measure the precise benefits of his reorganisation work (Merkle, 1980, p.13).

At the same time as work was becoming rationalised through Taylorite and other similar systems, firms were growing very much larger. The rise of the integrated industrial enterprise, which , by 1917, had become the most powerful institution in American business, brought with it a "visible hand of managerial direction" to replace the "invisible hand of market forces" (Chandler, 1977, p.286). The 'visible hand' brought with it sophisticated accounting systems for co-ordinating, administering and allocating resources (Chandler & Daems, 1979). Management quickly became professionalised in the twentieth century, Chandler writes that the "appurtances of professionalisation- societies, journals, university training, and specialised consultants- hardly existed in the United States in 1900, By the 1920s they were all flourishing" (Chandler, 1977, p.468). Cost accounting was included in this process. In 1915 the newly formed American Association of University Instructors in Accounting included cost accountants. By 1916, 116 colleges and universities offered accounting courses which covered, amongst other things, auditing public accounting and cost accounting. In 1919 a National Association of Cost Accountants was formed (ibid., p.465).

It is interesting that Littler writes of the bureaucratisation of the labour process as taking place in the period from 1900 to the 1920s in the USA, a process which did not occur until the 1920s to the 1930s in Britain (1982, p.,184).

(29) James Rider (an incorporated accountant) wrote:

> I have been recently reading, with great interest, a series of articles in the *Engineer* on the subject of Estimating. The author, who evidently has obtained his knowledge from the inside, institutes comparisons between estimates for large contracts for constructional work, the figures of which have been published; and the information at his disposal has enabled him to dissect the various tenders, and show the bases for the respective portions of the work tendered for. The result is rather humiliating reading for commercial men, particularly when we remember how English manufacturers have recently been thrust to one side again and again on this particular class of work by foreign competition. They prove one thing most conclusively, namely, that in most, if not all, of the establishments, submitting the tenders reviewed in the articles, there can either have been no intelligent consecutive system of Cost Accounts, or the estimating staff, being (as is usually the case) highly technical, had considered any information compiled by clerks as not worth taking into account (Rider, 1904, p.178).

These clerks were apparently working from an 'accountant's' department' (the old 'counting house'). For in discussing the checking of "cost accounts with specifications", he writes:

> If the drawing office, works department, and storekeepers have properly fulfilled their part of the work, the checking by the cost clerks will be very simple. But it is necessary that there should be a consecutive plan, intelligent connection, and smooth working between all departments concerned. Too frequently the investigations and questions of the accountant's department are resented by the works staff, who, being practical men are somewhat disposed to look with something akin to contempt upon clerks (ibid., p.181).

For an understanding of the organisational context in which these developments were taking place, Arthur Williams' (1915) first hand account of life in a railway factory is invaluable. Although how representative it is of large works at this time is impossible to say.

(30) It is notable that whilst *Factory Accounts* (1887), by the British authors Garcke and Fells, remained a classic text in the field, when reviewing works on cost accounting Rawlinson comments on the "many interesting articles" in "business magazines ... principally based on American methods, and usually dealing with card systems of record" (1911, p.267). Even the initiative in creating cost accounting knowledge was moving to America.

(31) Under the Technical Instruction Acts of 1889 and 1891 Committees of the County Councils and County Boroughs were empowered to grant rate aid in support of secondary technical and manual instruction in their districts. During the twenty-five years from 1889 to 1914 there was a slow but steady growth in technical education, including commercial education, from a variety of different institutions such as the London Chamber of Commerce, the Royal Society of Arts (RS A) and the National Union of Teachers (Urwick and Brech, 1949, Vol.II, p.138). Andersen looked specifically at commercial education in the North-West of England. There the growth in commercial education can be seen in the increasing numbers of candidates sitting the Union of Lancashire and Cheshire Institute's commercial examinations: in 1882, 599; in 1889, 1393; and in 1891, 3068; practical subjects such as shorthand and book-keeping attracted over half the students (1976, pp.92-93). Thus by the early 1900s it can be assumed that many more clerks had received some vocational training, than twenty years earlier. After the turn of the century Balfour's Education Act of 1902 brought in state aided secondary schools and, in the field of further education, in the same year commerce faculties were set up at Birmingham and Manchester Universities (Urwick and Brech, 1949, p.136). In the latter part of 1902 The London School of Economics (LSE) issued a sessional programme which included an optional course of sixty lectures over two years in 'Accountancy and Business Methods' for the London BSc. (Econ.). However these university courses catered for very small numbers in comparison with the technical colleges and other similar institutions which were being set up, or expanded. It is interesting to note that there were 96 graduates from a newly introduced London Chamber of Commerce commercial teachers certificate in 1905 (ibid., p.138).

(32) Although I feel that this was largely the case, as I noted in the introduction to this chapter, I consider Wells' work must be regarded with caution. This is because of the assumption which runs through his book that there were simply two sorts of people involved with this work, on the one hand professional engineers, and on the other, professional accountants. In my opinion this is a very misleading assumption. The book is also problematic in that it jumps from the American to the British developments as if they were just part of one unending stream. Concomitantly, there is little attempt to relate these to their social context. The whole book is overlain with Wells' smug desire to explain 'where we went wrong' in accounting for common costs. The origin of these problems is to be found in his use of Kuhn's (1970) notion of changing paradigms in science, to understand (and further) the development of accounting. A usage which I consider to be entirely inappropriate.

(33) See note (29).

(34) Sidney and Beatrice Webb made an analysis of the accounting profession as part of a study for the Fabian Society published in 1917; it is interesting to briefly summarise this. They pointed out that the profession of 'Public Accountant' was "ill-defined" and it was hard to "make any general statements as to the characteristics and results of its professional organisation" (p.30). They analysed accountants into three groups as follows (in descending order of status):

Name	Date Formed	Number of Members
Group 1		
Institute of Chartered Accountants in England and Wales (ICAEW)	1880	
Scottish Societies of Chartered Accountants (Edinburgh, Glasgow, Aberdeen).	1853-1867	
Institute of Chartered Accountants in Ireland	1888	
Total		6,000
Group 2		
Society of Incorporated Accountants and Auditors (SIAA)	1888	3,000
Group 3		
Corporation of Accountants	1891	
Institute of Certified Public Accountants	1903	
Central Association of Accountants	1905	
London Association of Accountants	1905	
Total		4,000
Grand Total		13,000

Figures to the nearest 1,000.

Source: Webb & Webb, 1917, p.30

Thus there were around 13,000 members of one or other of the associations of accountants at this time. Webb and Webb suggest that there were possibly half as many more persons again professionally engaged in some sort of accountancy who were eligible to join one or other of these associations (ibid., p.30). This last figure is, of course, a matter for conjecture, for matters had probably altered little since 1911, when, as I noted earlier, the census compilers complained about the difficulties of excluding accountants' clerks and commercial clerks from the census category 'accountant'. The organisations classified in group 3 were of varying degrees of laxity in their admission of members, from whom, often, neither apprenticeship nor examination were required. The Webbs commented that the new societies for accountants had in total:

> ... over four thousand members, among whom there are a certain number of quite successful Public Accountants having extensive general practices but the membership shades off indefinitely through Accountants, Treasurers, or Controllers of Municipal Corporations and other Public bodies, salaried chief accountants or book-keepers of large commercial and industrial enterprises, and the teachers of accountancy of various grades, down to the mere debt or rate collector or auctioneer who, on the strength of occasional jobs at accounts or in keeping books, chooses to dub himself a Public Accountant (Webb & Webb, 1917, p.30).

CHAPTER 4

THE FIRST WORLD WAR

... the most microscopic investigation into
the cost of production ...

Dr Addison discussing the procedures used
by the Ministry of Munitions, June 1917.

Introduction

The First World War was a war fought on an unprecedented scale. Five million men entered the armed forces and over both individual citizens and business the power of the state increased tremendously. As A.J.P. Taylor remarks, until August 1914 a sensible law-abiding Englishman could pass through life and hardly notice the existence of the state beyond the post office and the policeman, but this was all changed by the impact of the Great War when the mass of people became, for the first time, active citizens whose lives were shaped by orders from above. Their food was limited and its quality changed by Government order, their freedom of movement was restricted and their conditions of work prescribed (1970, pp.25-26). The relationship between the state and its citizens "altered profoundly" (Middlemas, 1979, p.14). Much of the legislative power of Parliament was sidestepped as "departments, bureaux, committees, controllers were created and piled on top of each other" (Mowat, 1955, p.13). The business world and the government were brought into intimate contact as, on the one hand, business leaders were brought into government and, on the other, business life was transformed as some industries were reduced or closed and others artificially fostered in the attempt to provide the men and the capital for the making of munitions on a vast scale (Taylor, 1970, p.26, p.99). To give just one example of the results of this transformation, before the war the output of shells was just 55,000 rounds per annum but in the period from the outbreak of war to the armistice 200 million rounds were produced (117 HC.deb.5s, col.50).

The scale upon which production was organised was enormous and unprecedented. Whilst in 1913 total government expenditure for all purposes was £184 million, by the year ending 31 March 1918 the turnover of the Ministry of Munitions was £2,000 million and its net cost to the taxpayer £620 million (Marriner, 1980, p.130). It was claimed to be "the biggest buying, importing, selling manufacturing and distributing business in the world" dwarfing its nearest rival the United Steel Trust (The Financial Secretary to the Ministry of Munitions, speaking in April 1918, quoted in ibid., p.130). By the end of the war the Ministry employed a staff of sixty-five thousand men and women, controlled over three and a half million workers, ran directly two hundred and fifty factories, quarries and mines, and supervised twenty thousand controlled establishments (Stevenson, 1984, p.70). The War Office, who supplied commodities for the Army other than munitions, and the Admiralty, which controlled shipbuilding, naval accessories and munitions (Pigou, 1947, pp. 108-109), are not included in these figures. They were also mammoth spenders. In June

1917 the annual value of War Office purchases was estimated to be £350 million and amongst its purchases up to that date were included 35 million knives, forks and spoons, and 400 million pounds of bacon (*The Times*, 29 June 1917, p.3).

As Churchill said, "an extraordinary improvisation without parallel in any country in the world took place in our industrial system" (Ministry of Munitions, unpublished, Vol.3, Pt.1, Ch.1, p.11). It was under these exceptional conditions of war that cost accounting 'came into the light', largely as an unanticipated result of the way in which the government mobilised the industrial resources of the country.

The Control of Industry

Prior to the First World War it is likely that it was only in the area of armaments production, that the government, in purchasing its requirements, was regularly involved in anything other than market transactions with industry. From 1880, when the Director of Army Contracts at the War Office and Admiralty, had begun to deal directly with the trade in purchasing items (and civil agents eliminated), the principle *theoretically* in operation was that of competitive tendering. Whilst nominally the departments were committed to the principle of free competition their practice was often very different; particularly in the case of specialised armaments for which they were the only customers. There the contracting departments became involved in a 'special relationship' (Trebilcock, 1966, p.367) with contractors, where a small number of approved firms obtained the benefit of getting the work. The government attempted to prevent monopolistic and unreasonable prices by carefully allocating orders between firms, and between these firms and the Ordnance factories owned by the government (ibid., p.365)[1].

Once the war had begun, the huge increase in demand put pressure on both the normal system of competitive tender used for ordinary commercial articles, and the 'special relationship' with armament contractors. In July 1914 the Army Contracts Department of the War Office had a staff of only 56 officials and clerks, it was totally inadequate (Lloyd, 1924, pp.13-15). Lloyd reports that for "every item of Army clothing feverish buying and selling went on" and "army socks became a favourite gambling counter in the city" (ibid., pp. 26-27) as profiteers attempted to (and succeeded in) exploiting the slow and bureaucratic purchasing system. It had become a 'sellers market', the buying departments were faced with a serious shortage of supplies and prices were rising steeply. Competitive tendering did not only mean that there was delay in the allocation of contracts, but also it lead, in an indirect way, to rises in the price of materials by encouraging forward-buying on the part of all firms submitting tenders. In turn, it became difficult for manufacturers to price contracts because they did not know what price raw materials would be (Pigou, 1947, p.111). Additionally, it was charged that industrial resources were not being adequately used, for in respect of armaments such as shells[2], the War Office refused to extend its list of authorised contractors, and deluged those firms with orders which they could not possibly fulfil (Taylor, 1970, p.50).

The government were generally reluctant to interfere with business. Most of the cabinet ministers in the Liberal government were Free Traders, hostile to the interference of government in the supply, by free enterprise, of the necessary items for fighting the war. The President of the Board of Trade told the House of Commons that:

> No government action could overcome economic laws and any interference with those laws must end in disaster (quoted in Taylor, 1970, p.41).

This was despite the fact that government policy had been less explicitly free market when it had come to matters concerning what appeared to be the 'national interest'. As I have already noted the War Office had been developing a 'special relationship' with some munitions manufacturers, and it was a considerable employer in the form of the Royal Ordnance Factories and the dockyards.

Some explicit controls over business had been introduced early in the war[3], but to Ministers who had spent the greater part of their political careers in exploding the fallacies of protectionism on the one hand, and socialism on the other, the idea that industry would have to be deliberately organised for war production on a large scale, encountered resistence (Lloyd, 1924, quoted in Stevenson, 1984, p.69).

Gradually the problems, both at home and at the front, were building up which would lead to the introduction of a coalition government in May 1915, the setting up of the Ministry of Munitions in the following month, and the extension of Government control over industry. Amongst the pressures which finally led to this were the interlinked problems of simmering industrial unrest, growing concern by many sections of the community over the extent of war profiteering and the so-called 'shells scandal'.

In 1915 the war was escalating; it no longer appeared, as it had done at the start of the war, that it would be over quickly. The production of munitions with which to fight it needed to be increased, but there were problems. Almost a fifth of engineering workers had joined the armed forces, and the strength of trade unionism in the industries relevant to munitions production was great. It appeared that these trade unionists had, somehow, to be cajoled into easing their restrictive working practices and accepting 'dilution', the use of unskilled and semi-skilled workers to do work traditionally reserved for skilled craftsmen. There was a strong tradition of militancy in the engineering trades central to munitions production and unless compromises were made on issues which the unions were concerned about, then further industrial conflict looked likely[4] (Stevenson, 1984, pp.67-68). In mid-March the principal union leaders met and formulated the 'Treasury Agreement', in which the unions accepted dilution and the lifting of restrictive practices. In return Lloyd George agreed that some limitations would be placed on profits, as well as traditional craft privileges restored at the end of the war. Unions would be given some share in the direction of industry through being given positions on specially set up local committees (Stevenson, 1984, p.68).

The issue of profiteering was one of great concern to many workers. They were afraid that if dilution occured, and restrictive practices lifted, their employers would make even greater profits, at their expense. At a Labour conference held in the same month, a suggestion that all profits in excess of 10% should go to the state, was given "hearty approval"; they took the attitude that "the settlement of this question on these lines is a necessary corollary to the problems which the trade unions have been called upon to face" (*The Times*, 20 March 1915, p.12). Ben Tillett, General Secretary of the Dock, Wharf, Riverside and General Workers' Union issued a news bulletin in which he declared:

> In too many cases the employers are taking malicious advantage of the war and the necessities to reap huge profits, and refuse to even meet the growing obligations caused by the increased cost of living (ibid.).

It was not only the Unions who were concerned with profiteering, for by 1915 it had reached a level which could simply be no longer tolerated, even by the Free Traders in the government. In March 1915 contractors trying to sell urgently needed sandbags to the Government at 100% profit became the victims of an old regulation which allowed the army to requisition items and pay 'a fair market price in the opinion of the purchasing officer' (Lloyd, 1924, p.37). In the 'City Notes' in *The Times*, the complications of limiting profits were commented upon, and the questions raised:

> What are profits? and at what point do they become unreasonable? If a Government Department is to decide these questions it will have a great deal of difficult accounting to do and some very subtle problems of equity to solve ... (23 March 1915, p.16).

However, an article in the same edition, entitled "Patriotism and Profits: a cause of unrest: how to remove it", struck a more positive note, it was suggested that:

> The problem of how to supervise and control profit on work for the State in time of war is by no means insoluble. It means a full and fair disclosure of the prime cost of all Government Contract work, an audit by well-qualified supervisors, standardised scales of profit for each class of work, and a simple and ready method for referring disputes to arbitration (23 March 1915, p.5).

The 'shells scandal' of the late spring of 1915 brought further calls for government action in the area of munitions production. It originated in the problems at the front in France. The British had begun a major offensive in France in early 1915, although unfortunately they were not very successful. This appeared to be at least partially due to a great shortage of shells, only a certain number being allowed to be used each day. Lord Northcliffe, proprietor of *The Daily Mail*, the daily newspaper with the largest circulation, and of the *The Times*, launched a campaign against the government's failure to ensure a sufficient supply of shells (Taylor, 1970, pp.55-56). The lack of adequate munitions for the men, who had so bravely volunteered to fight, became a major issue.

In May 1915 a Coalition government was created. Although Northcliffe's campaign against the shortage of shells had begun too late to affect the Liberal Government, which was already weakened beyond repair, it did give the final push to Lloyd George's demand for an independent ministry controlling the provision of munitions (Taylor, 1970, p. 60). In June 1915 the Ministry of Munitions was created to take over from the War Office the duty of supplying munitions to the army, and Lloyd George took command of it. Control over the munitions industry was extended by the Munitions of War Act of July 1915, which incorporated the concessions negotiated in the Treasury Agreement some months earlier. Amongst the additional regulations was one creating a category of 'controlled establishments', covering any plant regarded as essential to the manufacture of munitions. In these establishments wages and conditions came under the direct control of the Ministry; and manning levels, choice of operatives and even the organisation of work were now under the control of the state (Stevenson, 1984, p.69). Profits of employers were also to be limited in those establishments, by a so-called 'munitions levy', which attempted to prevent them from rising above a standard based on pre-war levels (*The Accountant*, 30 June 1917, p.597)[5]. At the same time the Ministry initiated the construction of a number of national factories to meet the excess demand for shells (Pigou, 1947, p.111).

The cost of producing armaments became an issue of concern. In his diary of 12 August 1915 Addison, at this point in time an Undersecretary at the Ministry of Munitions, wrote:

> For some time I have been getting very anxious about the Financial Arrangements; about the nature of some of the contracts and so on. The astounding thing is that nobody seems to be able to tell us what things cost to make (Addison, 1934, p.116).

The pressure of demand for production brought a greater involvement by government in business in many different spheres. Statistical information began to be collected about businesses and their activities. In the early days of the Ministry of Munitions whilst, on the one hand a statistics department was set up to assemble a detailed account of the armaments needs of the army, on the other, an analysis of the industrial capacity of Great Britain was begun. To formulate the best possible programme for producing armaments, James Stevenson, head of the Department of Area Organisation, initiated a survey of the factory districts. In the latter part of June 1915, questionnaires were sent to 65,000 different manufacturing workshops throughout the United Kingdom requesting details as to the machinery the shops possessed, how many hours a day it was working, what types of contracts the firm was fulfilling etcetera. By mid-July 45,000 replies had been received (Adams, 1978, p.64). By September 1915, over 700 of the main engineering plants were classified as 'controlled establishments' (ibid., p.70). However, overall control was only at an "elementary stage". It represented "little more than the substitution of collective agreements between the Government and business associations for competitive tendering and individual contracting", and it soon proved insufficient (Pigou, 1947, p.112). An example of the problems can be seen in the negotiations which were entered into with the Brass-Makers' Association, in the latter part of 1915, to obtain a reduction in the apparent excessive price of certain items supplied to the ordnance factories. The Association was able to resist the Government proposal for a price reduction because the armament firms, whom they also supplied, were willing to pay the higher prices (ibid.).

Further control was inevitable. Gradually dealings in more and more commodities were restricted through the issue of licences, and associated with this was control of prices (see below). Each control imposed seemed to lead to more controls, as Sidney Pollard has written:

> Some relatively minor control, to deal with an immediate issue, often had repercussions which required Government intervention forther and further back, until the State found itself directing a major part of the country's industries, and controlling or licensing most of the remainder (quoted in Stevenson, 1984, p.70).

For example, the consequence of the fixing of metal prices by the Ministry of Munitions at the end of 1915, was that it had to allocate supplies between competing users by means of a priority system (Pigou, 1947, p.113).

It was through the problems of pricing items where there was no clear market price and where the government required most of the country's production, that cost accounting became an issue of concern.

The Pricing of Munitions Contracts and the Question of Cost Accounting

Because there was no way of establishing a 'fair market price' for many of the items required for the war, in early 1916 a new clause was embodied in the Defence of the Realm Act concerning the price to be paid:

> In determining such price regard need not be had to the market price, but shall be had to the cost of production of the output so requisitioned and to the rate of profit usually earned in respect to the output of such factory or workshop before the war.

The power to examine manufacturers' figures was bestowed through the general clause:

> ... and may require such particulars to be verified in such a manner as they may direct ... (quoted in Lloyd, 1924, pp.58-60).

Taylor suggests that the House of Commons "did not realize what it was doing" when it passed this legislation, which was so absolutely the antipathy of the old notions of free trade (1970, p.66).

Samuel Lever[6], a chartered accountant who had spent much of his working life in the United States, was brought in to be in charge of, as Addison writes:

> ... arrangements for cost accounting, for the control of the cost of new munitions factories, for revising our present tenders and so forth (1934, p.119).

Three basic ways of ascertaining costs were used by the Ministry of Munitions:[7]

(i) Technical costing: "the estimate of costs by engineering experts resulting from an analysis of the process of manufacture into its elements, and the calculation of what the costs of each of these ought to be in the light of all known conditions".

(ii) Accountancy costing: "the ascertainment of any given contractor's actual costs of production by examination of his books".

(iii) Using the cost returns from National Factories where similar articles were being produced. (Ministry of Munitions, unpublished, Vol.3, Pt.2, Ch.1, pp. 10-11).

The last of these methods was very successful in reducing prices paid for shells and it is interesting to note the sophistication of the systems which were set up in many of the national factories (which were publically owned). In the case of the National Shell Factories:

> A system of cost accounts was devised which should yield for each process of shell manufacture a statement of the output, its cost in material, wages and establishment charges, and the extent to which each of these items was affected by faulty materials or defective workmanship. The average cost of each process through which the shell past was ascertained, and the addition of these costs gave the total cost of the shell. The costs so obtained are known as 'Process costs'.... This method permitted the closest comparison of the costs of each operation, not only at each factory week by week, but also as between one Factory and another. The results thus indicated the relative efficiency of the management, and within each factory provided managers with a clue to any leakage or extravagance (ibid., pp.12-13).

There was difficulty in obtaining staff with any knowledge of costing and representatives of the Government visited the factories and gave instructions as to the books to be kept and the method of preparing cost returns. When private shell manufacturers were offered the use of these special costing forms a "large number" apparently took advantage of them (ibid.).

In a letter to *The Accountant* it was suggested that the methods of costing introduced by Sir Samuel Lever into the munitions works controlled by the government were "far superior" to any thing known in this country previously (19 May 1917, p.482). As in the case of the national shell factories, given above, great emphasis was placed on the use of costing to make production more efficient. This principle was even followed in the canteens. Webster Jenkinson (Controller of Factory Audit and Costs, Ministry of Munitions) wrote how:

> In the early days heavy losses were made, which continued until the introduction of a proper accounting system, which showed monthly the costs of the various types of provisions, consumption percentages,and running expenses. As a result of

> the information thus afforded and the comparisons which could be effected, various economies were made possible, the reduction in the losses indicating the value of these cost statistics. The percentages of these losses were as follows:-
>
> For the period ending 31st March 1917, 20.23%.
> For the half-year ending 30th September 1917, 13.78%.
> For the half-year ending 31st March 1918, 6.43%.
>
> But for these reductions through proper economic management the probable result would have been an increase in the cost of the meals to the workers (*The Accountant*, 8 March 1919, p.187).

It is interesting to note the accuracy of measurement implicit in the presentation of these statistics to two decimal places.

The Ministry of Munitions evolved a number of different types of contract based on estimated or ascertained costs of production. Basically there were two types, the first where the price was fixed in advance, the second where actual costs were paid with the addition of an allowance for profit. Some contracts were even entered into on the basis that the price would be settled later. The problems which were encountered by the government and contractors using these systems can be imagined (some of these are outlined in ibid., Ch.1, pp.16-35; Ch.2, p.59). After the war stories were told about the failures and inconsistencies, such as the "big government department" who told a manufacturer that:

> ... we cannot possibly grant you an on-cost (overhead) of over a certain amount, but what we can do is, you take your foremen from the expenses side of your account and put them on to what is termed the productive side of the accounts (reported in *The Cost Accountant*, March 1922, pp.184-185).

Another was told of the managing director who obstinately refused to set up a systematic cost accounting system. On investigation it turned out that he was charging all of his overheads to each of the contracts he was working on for five different government departments (reported in *The Accountant*, 19 June 1920, p.723).

The scheme seems to have been effective in reducing prices as far as the few large armaments firms were concerned, S.H.Lever (Assistant Financial Secretary to the Ministry of Munitions), explained to Parliament in the following terms how the Ministry had compelled the big armament firms to reduce their prices for shells:

> ... the Ministry consulted accountants and engineers, and having arrived at what they considered the actual cost, set out to cut the prices of shell bodies. The big armament firms said the work could not be done for the prices named by the Ministry. The firms were then asked to produce their costs, and, as the Ministry had power under the Munitions Act to see the firms' books, they immediately brought the prices down. The price of shell bodies had now been cut between 25 and 30 per cent (quoted in *The Times*, 11 October 1916, p.5).

He gave many examples, such as the price of 18-pounders, formerly 20s to 23s, cut to 12s 6d. The Chairman of one of the large armament companies, Cammell Laird & Co. (Limited), protested at the charge (*The Times*, 17 October 1916, p.5). However, Dr Addison, Minister of Munitions, supported Lever strongly and noted how:

> ... careful and scientific examination of costs, applied, as they have sought always to apply them, with scrupulous consideration and fairness, have tended to promote efficiency and economy in works management, to the undoubted benefit in many cases of the contractors themselves, and have certainly

saved the State very many millions of pounds (reported in *The Times*, 23 October 1916, p.10).

In the ensuing debate in the House of Commons the members seem to have been generally on the side of Addison and Lever. Addison receiving "cheers" and "hear hear" for his description of the work done in reducing prices for munitions (reported in *The Times*, 25 October 1916, p.10)[8].

Beyond the realm of the large factories making standard products there were more problems however; 20,000 small factories were hurriedly built, or converted, to catch the £2,000 million the Ministry of Munitions was dispersing. Often costs had to be set at the level of the least efficient firm. The result was "a crop of profiteers, men who shot up from nothing to great fortunes (and often later down again)" (Taylor, 1970, p.66). Hobsbawm described the war as "a paradise for profiteers" (1969, p.275). In a report on National Expenditure published in 1918, the Select Committee investigating the financial methods of the Ministry of Munitions complained of the large scale of the profits earned by munitions firms. Examining the profits earned by 26 firms who had been subject to excess profits duty or munitions levy (selected at random), they found that on average the firms had earned nearly five times the amount of their standard profit (a measure of the profit earned before the war). Of this they retained as special depreciation on new capital expenditure more than half of their standard profit and a slightly larger amount for additional cutput. After deduction of munitions levy the firms in the aggregate retained nearly twice their standard profits over and above the special depreciation. (reported in *The Times*, 12 March 1918, p.3). Amongst the examples given was one of a company making a chemical product:

> The company asked £17 per ton, stating that the cost of manufacture was £22 10s, but that they could afford the apparent loss as they were selling to the public at a very high price. An agreement was reached that the firm should be allowed 10 per cent. profit on the cost ascertained by an independent arbitrator, which was about £13. Another Department of the Ministry had, at the same time, a contract with the same firm for the same commodity at £19 and £20 (quoted in ibid.)

The cost investigations required were carried out through cost investigation departments. Qualified (chartered or incorporated) accountants were employed to lead teams on the accounting side; on the technical side engineers were employed. There was apparently "great difficulty" in "finding competent persons" to do this work but the staff was gradually increased. It was estimated that in 1917 alone about 2,500 technical estimates and about 1,000 accountancy investigations had been made (Ministry of Munitions, unpublished, Vol.3, Pt.2, Ch.2, p. 58). The cost investigations were unpopular with some manufacturers (ibid., pp.52-53). In the summer of 1918, in response to a protest by the Federation of British Industries at the methods of costing and price-fixing, the matter was referred to a government committee. The committee found that enormous savings to the nation had resulted from the inspection of books, and that the right should not be abandoned (ibid., pp.60-61).

Despite this unpopularity, after the war many were of the opinion that these investigations had encouraged manufactures to take a greater interest in cost accounting. E.T. Elbourne's book, *Factory Administration and Accounts* (1914), which synthesised administrative methods, including cost accounting, with the planning of production and control of stock, sold some 10,000 copies during the course of the war-apparently principally among the executive staffs of the government contracting firms (Urwick and Brech, 1949, Vol.1., p.149). The re-issue of the book in 1918 was greeted in the *Ministry of Munitions Journal* with a strong recommendation, the editor remarking that it must already be known to many of the readers (January 1918, p.40). Speaking in the House of Commons in March 1919 the Deputy Minister of Munitions said:

> The contractors at first were very suspicious of this system for although it had been a common industrial practice in America for some years, it was foreign to the practice of this country. I believe today we can say that it has become an integral part of the method of most up-to-date industrial firms ... (113 HC. Deb.5s, col.485).

In a leading article published just after the war *The Accountant* summed up the situation:

> Many manufacturers are today keeping Cost Accounts who hardly knew that there were such things five years ago. Many others are thinking of installing a costing system who, five years ago would have discounted the idea as ridiculous, or at least not applying to the condition obtaining in their work. Now there is abroad a healthy spirit of inquiry into the matter, and a disposition to give costing methods a fair trial (1 March 1919, p.150).

It is notable that during the war lectures in cost accounting were introduced into the curriculum at the London School of Economics (LSE), one of the foremost institutions for the study of commerce (Dev, 1980, p.4). Although one student of the ICAEW frustratedly wrote:

> ... where can I obtain *practical* instruction in subjects which will be of the utmost importance to accountants in the near future? Neither factory costing or scientific management are taught anywhere in London. Professor Dicksee conducts some classes at the London School of Economics, but these are intended for students working for a university degree, and are purely theoretical (*The Accountant*, 19 May 1917, p.482).

This new interest in cost accounting went hand in hand with a general transformation of industry as businesses strove to meet war-time requirements. Hannah notes how Churchill's hope of 'business as usual' during the war was to prove profoundly wrong; the war brought mergers, large scale enterprises, new industries and standardisation (1983, p.28). As industrialists had been impelled to bring in unskilled labour to work in the factories (including many women), there was an increasing division of labour and erosion of skill differentials (Littler, 1982, p.99). Among major industries, engineering changed the most (Pollard, 1962, p.55). In the "storm centre, the engineering industry", wrote Cole, "the specialised shop or works, concentrating upon a single type of product, has long been established in America, and is making great headway here" (1917, p.16). The general engineering shops which had previously made mainly specialised orders began to make standardised items for stock as the war brought an unlimited demand for many items (ibid.). At the same time interchangeable standardised parts were increasingly used (Hannah, 1983, p.28).

The Effect of the War on Chartered and Incorporated Accountants

The war brought accountants into the public eye. As Urwick and Brech wrote, "a profound metamorphosis seems to have overtaken the accountants in the five years of hostilities" (1949, Vol II, p.138). In this section this will be discussed in some detail as it is relevant to the 'coming into the light' of cost accounting and cost accountants in a number of different ways, some direct, others more subtle. As accounting was brought to the awareness of the public through the increasing interference of the government with business, so chartered and incorporated accountants gained in professional status. Cost accounting was the most important area of war work for them, an area which, as already discussed, was previously regarded by many of them as somewhat beneath their dignity. From the May 1918 sitting of the ICAEW examinations onwards there was a dramatic increase in the number of examination questions asked on the subject of cost accounting; at the same time they became far more sophisticated and were not just of a descriptive nature, as they had generally been previously. In the auditing paper questions appeared on the auditing of costs (ICAEW Archives). After the war this had implications both for their professional development and for the attitudes and actions of those who worked in the field of costing in industry.

The involvement of accountants, working on the governments' behalf, began early in the war. Ernest Cooper wrote of how:

> Immediately on the outbreak of war, the Government called for the assistance of a Chartered Accountant to take control of the whole of the enemy banks established in this country. Our colleague engaged the services of several other members of whom I was one ... (1921, p.555).

The employment of accountants by, and on behalf of, the government, went hand in hand with increases in the control by the state of business activities. Thus, despite the early involvement noted above, it was not until the latter part of 1915, with the creation of the Ministry of Munitions, that their employment really began to rise. Eminent accountants were appointed to senior positions in Government service, notably at the Ministry of Munitions, the Ministry of Food and the Office of the Coal Controller (*The Accountant*, 10 May 1919, p.396). Among the most prominent was Samuel Hardman Lever, who became Assistant Financial Secretary to the Ministry of Munitions and later Financial Secretary to the Treasury[9]. Gilbert Garnsey became Controller of Munitions Accounts; W.H. Peat was Financial Secretary at the Ministry of Food; William Plender was placed in charge of the affairs of banks owned by the enemy and served on many government committees; M. Webster Jenkinson, Controller of Factory Audit and Costs at the Ministry of Munitions (*The Accountant*, 10 May 1919, p.396); Arthur Whinney became an advisor on costs of production at the Admiralty, and was later made Assistant Accountant-General of the Royal Navy; Arthur Roberts was Assistant Director-General of the Royal Army Clothing Department and later Chairman of the Financial Board of

Control at the Air Ministry, and Albert Wyon, Government Auditor of Railways (ICAEW, 1966, pp.59-60). All of these, and others, were knighted for their services during the war. Much of their work came to involve questions of cost. The reason for this being, as noted in the previous section, that as fair market-prices became harder and harder to identify under war conditions, the acceptable compromise between 'business as usual', and simple appropriation by the government, became the notion of recompensing manufacturers on a 'cost plus' basis.

Many accountants were employed directly by the Government. In mid-1918 it was reported that there were about 340 chartered and incorporated accountants, many of them members of the best known firms, on the staff of the Ministry of Munitions (*The Incorporated Accountants' Journal*, July 1918, p.187). Webster Jenkinson talked of how:

> ... quite 200 of the men on his staff at the Ministry had learned a good deal about costs during the last two years. There was a reserve of accountants who had some practical training, and who would, when they left, be able to spread their knowledge up and down the country (*The Accountant*, 18 January 1919, p.46).

Similarly the Admiralty and the War Office employed accountants to carry out cost investigations and in other financial work. The Admiralty Costs Investigation Department, for instance, employed 69 qualified accountants at the height of its activity (117 HC. Deb.5s, cols. 937-38). Others worked for the Inland Revenue (*The Accountant*, 25 May 1918, p.392)[10]. In national and other government factories, accountants were apparently to be found "acting not only in their usual capacity but as managers, commercial superintendents, cost accountants, and stores accountants" (*The Accountant*, 5 January 1918, p.1). The chief sources of supply for such accountants included those over military age, those unfit for military service, accountants in the army detailed for home service because of wounds or illness, those given exemption from service as they possessed "special experience" and, interestingly, accountants brought over from the United States (ibid., p.3).

Many others were employed indirectly. For instance in the bulletin prepared by Turquand, Youngs and Co., to be sent to their staff at the front, it was noted that:

> ... nine members of our staff have, on the application of the firm, been exempted from service in the army till January next year. They are, every one of them, engaged from time to time upon government work, directly occasioned by the war and their services are on that account rightly regarded as indispensible ... (quoted in Jones, 1981, p.126).

At the first Annual General Meeting held after the end of the war, the ICAEW President wrote of this government work:

> Many of our members, while not giving their whole time, have rendered valuable assistance to the Government in various ways, such as supervising, controlling and winding-up enemy banks and other enemy-owned businesses; investigating and reporting to the Food Controller as to the cost of various classes of food; serving on Advisory Committees in connection with the Tribunals under the Military Service Acts, and otherwise advising in connection with the supply of accountants for military and other Government services ... (*The Accountant*, 10 May 1919, p.396).

Others were employed by the forces themselves, for example in the pay and canteen departments of the Expeditionary Forces (*The Accountant*, 22 January 1916, pp.114-115).

Jones reports that government work generated 6% of Whinney Smith and Whinney's fees in 1915 (1981, p.132). Despite not being directly employed by the government some of these accountants became involved with costing through this indirect work. Lloyd writes how, throughout the country, "prominent" firms of chartered accountants were selected by the Ministry of Food to be District Supervising Accountants and investigate the books of any manufacturer or trader on the instruction of the Ministry 1924, p.318). One of the chartered accountants involved with this work, Mr. Clare-Smith, reported how it had been "quite an eye-opener to him to see, particularly when acting for the Ministry of Food, how very little traders knew about their costings, and how impossible it was to get at true figures" (reported in *The Accountant*, 18 January 1919, p.44). Other accountants, not employed on any government work, may well have come into contact with cost accounting through having to deal with their clients' problems in this area. The imposition of the Munitions Levy and Excess Profits Duty on companies made the calculation of 'profit' an important issue. This brought yet more concern with the calculation of costs.

There was a shortage of accountants, which became more acute as the war went on. There was apparently some understanding on the part of the government of the necessity for accountants as early as 1916, when conscription was first introduced. Chartered and incorporated accountants were declared to be engaged in work "of national importance" and included on the "list of certified occupations". In their submission to the committee dealing with this matter the ICAEW had emphasised the "vital importance" of the work of professional accountants and their staff to the finance and commerce of this country. There were, by 11th December 1915, said to be 4,489 of them already in the forces; of the 11,070 remaining engaged in the profession (excluding 1,370 women, the large majority of whom were typists), 5,550 would have been taken for service if the occupation had not been certified (reported in *The Accountant*, 22 January 1916, pp.114-115). Thus married men of over 31, and single men of 41 and over, were excused military service, unless a tribunal could prove that their work was not required in the national interest. Due to public criticism they were excluded from the second revised list, however government pressure brought them exemption again in 1917, although the conditions for obtaining it were more onerous (Garrett, 1961, pp.106-107). Accountants were obviously in some demand by this time, for in an appeal for volunteers published in *The Times* of 25th May 1917, it was declared that if potential recruits were not medically of category "A" (ie. completely fit) they could still be taken for other forms of service:

> Men with a good knowledge of horses, motor drivers, men with clerical and accountancy experience, with police experience, and domestic experience are required ... (p.7).

The general shortage of accountants was recognised more clearly after enquiries by the Public Accounts Committee of the House of Commons, and a Select Committee on National Expenditure. These enquiries revealed huge financial losses, seemingly caused by the inadequate accounting systems of the Ministry of Munitions. Marriner wrote how the "dismal history of failure" of the Ministries' accountants until 1918 "sparked off public scandals", for many millions of pounds of taxpayers' money could never be accounted for and had to be written off (1980, p.130). One of the recommendations of the Select Committee was that:

> ... the War Office should order the release of qualified accountants for National Service in the Ministry ... (reported in *The Times*, 12 March 1918, p.3).

They commented that:

> Immersed in their work and exercising the whole of their energies in extending the manufactures which they were organising, the supply officers seem to have underestimated the importance of the financial aspect. We do not observe sufficient recognition on their part that they stand towards the notion somewhat in the position of trustees who have money entrusted to their charge" (ibid.).

The issue was debated in the House of Commons. However whilst Sir Gilbert Garnsey, the Controller of Munitions Accounts, issued a letter asking the practising members of the profession to send him full particulars of those on their staffs serving in the Army, in order that further action should be taken, there seems to have been a reluctance on the part of the War Office to facilitate the return to Britain of members of the profession serving in the forces overseas (*The Incorporated Accountants' Journal*, July 1918, p.188).

At the same time there were problems in preventing accountants from being called-up, and on June 20th the subject was discussed in Parliament (reported in *The Accountant*, 29 June 1918, pp.460-461). The Deputy Chairman of the Appeal Tribunal of the House of Commons, G. Bettesworth-Piggott, anxious about the shortage of accountants, wrote to the *The Daily Telegraph* to complain that the "trade unions" in the accounting profession were insisting on far more years of training and experience than were necessary. He asked why, if gunners and airmen could be trained in a few months, accountants could not (reported in *The Certified Accountants' Journal*, 1918, p.66).

Ernest Cooper wrote how "the war brought our profession prominently forward" (1921, p.554). During the war, and directly after, they were showered with public honours for their work. Cooper recalled that five members of his firm were knighted for their work (ibid.). The war seems to have accelerated a process of upward social mobility remarked upon by F.W. Pixley in 1897 in *The Profession of Chartered Accountant*:

> ... those who have been articled to our members since the date of the charter come from the same class as do those who are now at Woolwich, Sandhurst and the Inns of Court. They have been educated at the same class of schools... (quoted in Jones, 1981, p.137).

Arthur Whinney was knighted for his work as Advisor to the Board of the Admiralty on the costs of production and as Assistant Accountant General of the Navy (*The Accountant*, 18 January 1919, p.39). His father, Frederick, president of the ICAEW from 1884 to 1888, died plain 'Mr.', despite the hopes raised in the Jubilee year of 1887, that he would receive one (Cooper, 1921, p.555). It is interesting, however, that his death in 1916, at the age of 87, did warrant a mention in *The Times* (19 May 1916, p.15).

Curiously it was upon the question of accountants' liability to taxation that formalised in law the social acceptance of accountancy as a profession. Excess profits duty was defined as not applying to the professions[11], and the government was thus inadvertently faced with the problem of what constituted 'a profession'. Speaking at the Annual General Meeting of The Society of Incorporated Accountants and Auditors[12], the president, C. Hewetson Nelson commented upon the progress towards "ultimate consolidation of the profession" made in 1915:

> ... the position of accountants has been more clearly defined, in that oft-debated question whether accountancy was or was not a profession had been authoritatively answered in the affirmative by the Chancellor of the Exchequer, when he stated that members of the institute and the society were excluded from liability to excess profits duty on the ground that they were included in the professions (reported in *The Times*, 19 May 1916, p.15).

Clerks and Accountants Working in Industry

Contemporaneous with this were effects on the clerks and accountants working with costing in industry. The importance of the role of the cost accountant and clerk were brought to the attention of the public at large, and in particular to manufacturers. One cost accountant, reflecting back on the pre-war period, remarked that:

> Cost and Works Accountants had for many years exercised their mysterious functions in obscure corners of great industrial concerns, but their aims, their aspirations, and their achievements were rarely understood or appreciated by the busy world around them (*The Cost Accountant*, March 1922, p.178).

During the war this disinterest was rapidly changed, particularly where pricing was done on a 'cost plus' basis. Not only did manufacturers become more aware of cost accounting, but many more people (mostly women and those unfit for military service), were trained in the skills as fit male cost clerks were sent to fight.

A difficulty which manufacturers had to face in the war, which worsened as more and more eligible young men were called up to join the forces, was a shortage of clerks. The size of clerical staffs required by companies was large, for although the amount of clerical work undertaken by companies had been increasing over the preceding decades (see Chapter 3), the use of office machinery (other than the typewriter) was in its infancy. The possibility of a shortage of clerical labour was recognised in a government report issued in 1915. It was estimated that the number of men of military age in clerical and commercial employment was over three hundred thousand, of which perhaps half would be available for military service (Cd. 8110, 1915, p.3). The report suggested that women without clerical experience would have to be employed. In this connection it is interesting to note that the emergency course through which they were to be trained (full-time for 3 to 4 weeks), included the elementary principles of double-entry book-keeping and the calculation of the cost of goods (ibid., p.4). By October 1915 there were already "considerable numbers of young women, mainly the friends and relatives of existing staffs" working in "large banking, insurance and other offices, as well as Government departments" (*The Times*, 30 October 1915, p.5). Under the conditions of war clerks' work became womens' work; for example, a manufacturer complaining about a clerk who had left his employment to take a more lucrative job making out pay and time-sheets at Woolwich Arsenal, wrote that such work was "surely womens' work" (*The Times*, 22 September 1915, p.9). Such a comment would have been unthinkable before the war.

Government departments had to recruit (and often train) new workforces from scratch. At the Ministry of Munitions it was reported in July 1918 that:

> In the finance , contracts, accounts and audit departments of the Ministry there are unfortunately less than 1% of permanent civil servants, but we have secured the services of many business men, and about 340 Chartered and Incorporated Accountants ... The direction and control of the work is thus provided for, but the clerical work had necessarily to be done by those of less experience; the accountant clerks and the book-keepers of peace time are in the trenches, but their

> substitutes are training on, and are becoming more efficient every day (reported in *The Incorporated Accountants' Journal*, July 1918, p.187).

Given the nature of the work of the Ministry of Munitions it is likely that a goodly number of these clerks came into contact with the problems of pricing items being purchased, and hence costing. In addition, others were employed as assistants on teams investigating the costs of manufacturers. Similar work was carried out at the War Office and the Admiralty. A breakdown of the staff of the Admiralty Costs Investigation Department was given in the House of Commons as:

Qualified Accountants	69
Assistant Accountants	78
Clerical Staff	47
Recorders	103
Total	297

(117, HC. Deb5s, Cols.937-938)

In retrospect, after the war, it was felt that costing investigations were not so effective as they could have been, one of the problems being the lack of training of those carrying them out (*The Accountant*, 19 July 1919, p.60). It was probably men such as J.J. Wood whom a manufacturer was complaining about when he commented that the Government "sent us men from heaven knows where to investigate the cost" (*The Cost Accountant*, March 1922, p.186). Wood went into the army on leaving school and in 1918, apparently having not been to college or sat any examinations went into a job as a "travelling factory auditor, in the Department of Factory Audit and Costs, Ministry of Munitions". In this position, he writes: "I assisted in auditing the books- both costs and financial- at many of the Government National Factories in England" (ICMA Archives, Wood personal file)[13]. They must have learnt gradually however, for the manufacturer whose complaint I noted above, went on to grudgingly admit that "of course as time went on they got more experience. They were bound to get it going one place to another" (*The Cost Accountant*, March 1922, p.186).

The national factories had large clerical staffs. After the war the advertisments for the sale of the factories revealed that, for example, the National Ordnance Factory at Nottingham had office accomodation for 145 clerks and mess room accomodation for 1000 persons. Even if it is assumed that meals were taken in two or three sittings, the proportion of clerks in the workforce nevertheless appears large (*Engineering*, 21 March 1919). The National Projectile Factory at Sheffield apparently had office accomodation for 209 clerks and mess accomodation for 1500 persons (*Engineering*, 25 April 1919). As was noted earlier in this chapter, there had been difficulty in recruiting staff for these factories with a knowledge of costing and representatives of the government visited the factories and gave instructions as to the books to be kept and the method of preparing cost returns (Ministry of Munitions, unpublished, Vol.3., Pt.2, Ch.1, p.13).

The awareness of manufacturers of the importance of the role of the cost accountant may well have been enhanced by the popularity of Elbourne's[14] book *Factory Administration and Accounts* (1914). The representative staff arrangement diagram showed clearly the role of the works accountant:

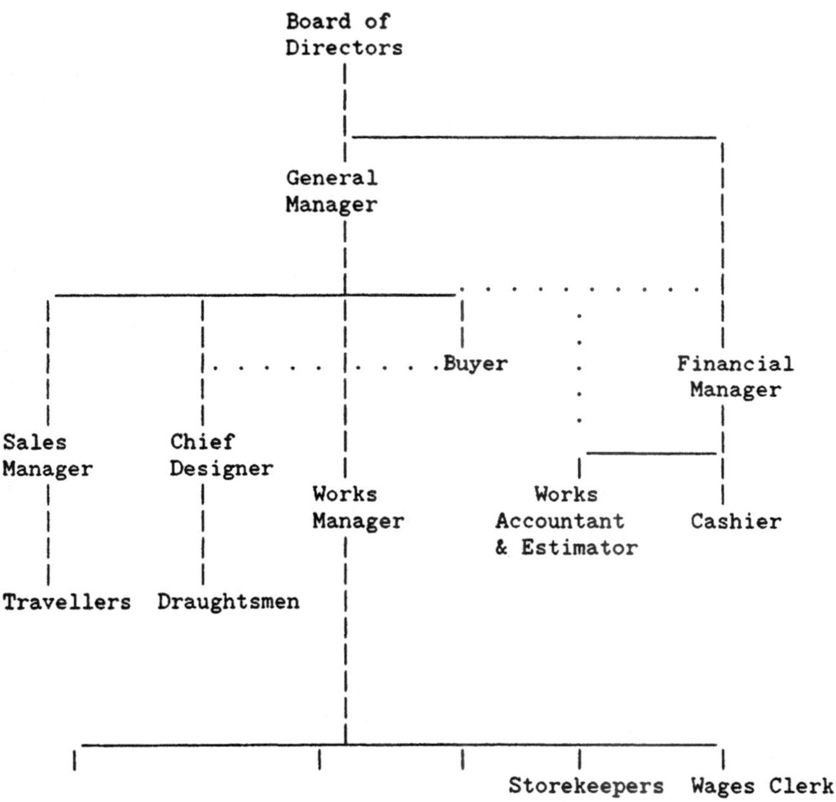

(not including assistants)

Source: Elbourne, 1914, p.31

It was noted that in order to simplify the diagram the offices of 'Works Accountant and Estimator' were combined, although it was quite usual for separate officers to act in the respective positions. Similarly the office of 'Financial Manager' represented a combination of those of 'Secretary and Accountant'. The dotted lines showed partial responsibility, hence despite the primary responsibility of the 'Works Accountant and Estimator' being to the 'Financial Manager' ("in view of the latter's responsibility for financial accounts with which the works accounts are interlocked, and on which the financial accounts are largely built"), there was also a secondary responsibility to the 'General Manager'. The reason for this responsibility being that "the Estimator, whether also the Works Accountant or a separate officer, should be invaluable in supplying the General Manager with the data necessary for dealing efficiently with the sales propositions on the one hand and production possibilities on the other" (ibid., pp.30-31). Elbourne notes that the "functions of the Works Accountant will be found to be very wide, and it is desirable that he should be qualified to bear an independent responsibility" (ibid., p.31). The nature of the responsibility is not only to obtain the costs of production, but also in administrating works additions, developments and experiments, the valuation of plant etcetera (ibid., p.226). He discussed the co-operation needed between the works accountant and the works manager:

> ... when the Cost Department as ordinarily constituted is, as it frequently is, an integral part of the Financial Department, the co-operation between the chief cost clerk (as he is probably called) and the works manager is unlikely to be very effective (ibid., p.228).

He viewed the role of the works accountant as a very important one, and wrote that:

> ... sometimes the duties of a Chief Cost Clerk approximate to those advocated for a Works Accountant, and there may be no material difference between the two beyond that of name. On the other hand, it is argued that the Works Accountant ought not to have been trained wholly as a clerk, but ought really to be an engineer who has fitted himself for works accounting duties. It is deliberately suggested that the opportunities attaching to such a position as this for estimating, organising, and administrative work in relation to works efficiency should make it both attractive in itself, as to status and remuneration, for a trained engineer with a bent for the commercial aspect of production, and also should afford an excellent training for even more responsible posts. Given the technical qualifications a works accountant might easily be able to act as an efficiency organiser (ibid., p.31).

Thus it is apparent that one of the unforseen consequences of the policies of the government during the war was a 'coming into the light' of cost clerks and accountants. Manufacturers, and perhaps even to some extent the general public, became aware of their importance. More people were trained in the work. A separate but related effect was an increasing awareness on the part of cost clerks and accountants of the significance of their own work. This awareness came to fruition in the formation of the ICWA directly after the war ended. Study of the formation and early development of this body suggests that the involvement of the chartered accountants with costing during the war gave the cost accountants working in industry a powerful professional model to copy. As one of the founders said: " ... we had in mind an Institute equal in status to the Chartered Accountants and throughout the early days, this ideal was always the predominating influence" (ICMA Archives, Russell 11). The coming together of individuals working with costing in industry into an organisation aspiring to be a professional *accounting* body is not a *necessary* historical development, for it appears that elsewhere in Europe this did not occur in the way in which it did in America (on France and Germany see Locke, 1984, pp.123-154; on Sweden, Jönsson, 1984).

Conclusion

The unprecedented scale of the First World War brought a profound transformation of British society, individuals from all walks of life became active citizens whose lives were shaped by orders from the state. Whilst before the war the state's dealings with suppliers of items required by the army and the navy had been based nominally (if not always actually) upon the notion of competitive tendering within a framework of free competition, during the war the tenets of free-trade were gradually left far behind. 'Cost', rather than market price, became the key both to deciding what manufacturers should be paid for items for which the government was the only customer, and a baseline through which profiteering was identified.

The regulations implicitly presupposed manufacturers to have a formal knowledge of the costs of their business activities. What was supposed to be visible to manufacturers was to be appropriated by the state in the interests of the British nation. Many manufacturers did not have this knowledge but it soon became apparent how important it was. Costs came to have a very real significance, in the sense that, rather than being a representation of past productive activity whose study could enable improvements in profits in the future, 'cost' became the actual *determinant* of profit in the case of many government contracts. Interestingly, it seems that one of the major reasons for the introduction of this legislation was pressure from unionists, particularly in the engineering sector. If they were going to give up their traditional working practices and accept 'dilution', they argued that their employers were going to have to give up their traditional right to maximise their profits at a time of shortage.

When the questions of profiteering were first raised, the possible solutions seemed to many to be quite simple: passing laws to limit the amount of profit made to standard amounts, or allowing manufacturers to make an amount of profit similar to that they were making before the war. As time passed the whole question 'What are profits? and at what point do they become unreasonable'? raised in *The Times* in March 1915, was revealed to be an extremely complex one (particularly where there was no market price for items). Questions of accounting, and in particular, of cost accounting, came under discussion by the government, manufacturers and educated public; they entered into a discursive domain beyond 'the obscure corners of great industrial enterprises'.

Eminent chartered and incorporated accountants became involved with costing through their work for the government, this brought them into greater contact with the elite of society, and probably enhanced the social standing of their profession. At the same time it served to emphasise to them the importance of cost accounting. The less eminent members of these bodies also came into contact with costing through their work, both direct and indirect, for the war ministries. The actual knowledge base of the profession began to change in response to this: far more sophisticated questions begun to appear on the subject in their examinations, the journal *The Accountant* included many articles on the subject. The portfolio of knowledge and techniques which the profession laid claim to as its field of responsibility before the war had only included cost accounting at a very minimal level, in response to the war its importance grew rapidly.

These events brought to the attention of the clerks and accountants working in industry the importance of their role, the product of their labours became the subject of concern by their employers and, in many cases, the visiting Ministry of Munitions' inspectors. The scene was set for the formation of a professional body for these employees, claiming for themselves the status and rewards of the members of the established and respected accounting bodies.

NOTES

(1) Interestingly, Trebilcock's investigation of the 'special relationship' of the cordite firms with the government, revealed that this had brought the question of 'costs' to attention at the turn of the century. The government used its factory at Waltham Abbey both as a pilot factory and as a price leader. If manufacturers quoted prices which seemed too high, the War Department set a price level based upon its own manufacturing experience. The trade protested that Waltham Abbey prices were incorrect, for they did not include rent, advertising and depreciation- charges which the private firm had to bear. Apparently, in 1902, a War Office Committee on the 'Organisation and Accounts of the Ordnance Factories', admitted that they had not achieved an accurate price for cordite in the last ten years (Trebilcock, 1966, p.373). Trebilcock comments that:

> Price control was the logical extension of a rigged tendering policy and the pivotal point of the government's command over its newly powerful suppliers. It may have lacked sophistication of detail, but, at the level of broad aims, it worked (ibid., pp.373-374).

(2) Their reticence about bringing in other suppliers was to some extent apparently justified; the first shells ordered from a wider list of suppliers by the Ministry of Munitions proved faulty, and brought the word 'dud' into common use (Taylor, 1970, p.50).

(3) The major interferences made at the beginning of the war included taking control of the railways, aiding banks and discount houses through guaranteeing approved commercial bills payable by the enemy and other insolvent debtors, and purchasing and importing sugar. A little later certain scarce supplies of raw materials needed for munitions manufacture were requisitioned or their export prohibited, for example TNT (Pigou, 1947, p.109).

(4) Conflict over these issues was particularly likely because in a number of centres for engineering production, for example Clydeside, the form of militancy had been influenced by the syndicalist movement, whose aims included the control by workers of the production process itself (Stevenson, 1984, p.67). Any *lessening* of workers' control would, it seemed, be angrily contested.

(5) The levy was difficult to administer for it left:

> ... a very large discretion to the Ministry of Munitions to fix standards in cases where the results of the trading in the last two pre-war years, which are the ordinary basis of pre-war

standards, afford no fair basis for comparison, and from the novel accountancy problems that had to be settled in connection with such matters as allowance for additional output, etcetera (*The Accountant*, 30 June 1917, p.597).

In 1917 it was reported that the amount of levy collected was "disappointingly small" (ibid.).

In September 1915 wider limitations on profits were introduced through the creation of an Excess Profits Duty (EPD). Originally introduced at a rate of 50%, it was raised to 80% in 1917. It was again based upon the excess of profits over a standard prewar profit figure. The duty applied to "all trades or businesses of any description", except farming, offices or employments, and: " ... any profession where the profits depend mainly on personal qualification, and in which the capital expenditure is comparatively small or non-existent" (*The Accountant*, 23 October 1915, pp.486-487). The rules were complex, and boosted the business of accountants (Jones, 1981, p.133). After the war the remark, at a social occasion, that the tax had been a "blessing in disguise" to the members of the Institute of Chartered Accountants resulted in laughter. It was commented that "many men who had never engaged an accountant before" had "had to call them in to deal with EPD" (*The Cost Accountant*, July 1921, p.25). According to Taylor it did not prevent profiteering, but it gave the government a useful additional source of income (Taylor, 1970, p.71).

(6) It is interesting to briefly examine his biography. He was a chartered accountant who received his early professional training in Liverpool, he became an associate of the ICAEW in 1891. He moved to America and, by the eve of the war, was the head of Barrow, Wade, Guthrie & Co., one of the largest professional practices in the United States. In addition he was also the senior partner of a London firm, Lever, Anyon, Honeyman & Spence (*The Accountant*, 24 February 1917, p.185; *The Times*, 12 November 1915, p.5). He returned to London from New York in 1915 to fill the post of Assistant Financial Secretary to the Ministry of Munitions (Jones, 1981, p.129). This seems to have been regarded as a successful appointment, at least at the time of the war (see, for instance *The Times*, 9 December 1917, p.10), although there is a suggestion in the official history that he was given too much work to be able to carry it all out successfully (Ministry of Munitions, unpublished, Vol.3, Pt.1, Ch.1, pp. 26-27).

In December 1916 he was promoted to Financial Secretary to the Treasury, the regard with which his work at the Ministry of Munitions was held is illustrated by the fact that this was a post normally held by a Member of Parliament, which he was not. In a debate on the matter in the House of Commons much opposition to the appointment of an outsider was expressed, one member declaring that "a more extraordinary blunder had never been committed than that of appointing to the post an official outside the House" (reported in *The Times*, 14 February 1917, p.10). In reply Bonar Law, the Chancellor of the Exchequer, noted how Lever was considered the "best man for the post" (ibid., p.12), his major job being to control expenditure (ibid., p.10). He became 'Sir Samuel Lever KCB', on reporting this honour *The Accountant* published an article praising his work, noting how he was "the first Chartered Accountant to obtain that coveted distinction" 24 February 1917, p.185). In 1918 he became Assistant Commissioner to the USA, in matters relating to finance (*The Times*, 26 February 1918, p.7).

(7) Here the Ministry of Munitions is discussed, however the DORA regulations concerning prices to be paid were also used in regulating the purchases of the War Office (all supplies for the army other than munitions) and the Admiralty (who dealt with their own munitions purchases as well as those of ships and other naval accessories).

The procedures used by the War Office to avoid "the payment of excessive prices" were summarised by the Director of Army Contracts, Mr Wintour, as falling into the following categories:

(1) Competitive tendering;
(2) examination of costings (where the requirements are not large compared with the total output of the industry);
(3) requisition of output; and
(4) control of raw materials.

He noted the effectiveness of method (2) by showing that:

> during the 12 months ended April 30 last the cost of contracts for hardware, horseshoes, brushes, and similar articles to the value of £8,500,000 was investigated and reductions were made amounting to £400,000 or 4.7% (from a paper compiled for the Committee of Public Accounts, reported in *The Times*, 29 June 1917, p.3).

This should be compared with the annual value of all War Office purchases of £350 million (as at June 1917). The impression generally given is that methods (3) and (4) were more important than (2) as far as the War Office was concerned. Methods (3) and (4) were applied, in particular to the wool, jute, flax and hemp trades. In the case of wool, in June 1916 the whole of the domestic wool clip was requisitioned and the wool supplied to the trade at fixed prices through authorised merchants acting as commission agents. In the following year the War Office purchased the whole of the Australasian wool clip and prohibited all private dealings in wool. In addition, the output of mills was requisitioned and paid for at prices built up from the fixed raw materials by adding a series of margins, assessed on the basis of costing estimates. Pigou notes how "in the end the manufacturer was virtually working for the government on a commission basis" (1947, p.113).

(8) The impression given by reports of the House of Commons debates given in *The Times* (they were reported verbatim), was that the armament firms had been forced to stop making large profits at the expense of the country. *The Accountant* gave a different version of events; commenting that Mr. Lever's department had saved the country millions of pounds, they wrote:

> ... but in the nature of things such momentous results could hardly be achieved without arousing some opposition. Munition contractors were naturally not particularly concerned in reducing prices; and, what is perhaps even more important, they had little or no idea how prices could be reduced, because- in varying degrees, but to some extent in all cases- they had no real idea what existing costs were. There are, indeed, more than grounds for suspicion that quite a large number of the biggest firms of contractors had no Cost Accounts worthy of the name; for when challenged to produce accounts in support of their assertion that the work "could not be done" at Mr. Lever's prices, they climbed down and accepted huge contracts at the reduced prices, rather than produce accounts in support of their own figures. It is not, of course, suggested that Government contractors were seeking to make undue profits at the expense of the country. The true facts would appear to be that, having no adequate Cost Accounts, they had no effective control over costs; and that the real triumph of Mr. Lever consisted in his being able to show them, by means of a proper accounting system, how economies could be effected and production cost reduced (*The Accountant*, 24 February 1917, p.186).

(9) For biographical details see note (6)

(10) It was reported that approximately 80 members of the ICAEW were involved with calculating the munitions levy of the controlled establishments alone (*The Accountant*, 25 May 1918, p.392).

(11) See note (5).

(12) It was during the war that the long fight of the incorporated society with the chartered accountants for equal privileges was, for the large part, ended. For instance, in the rules made by the Minister of Munitions in connexion with the Munitions of War Act, 1915, the word "audited" was defined as meaning "audited by a chartered or incorporated accountant, or by an accountant approved in

any particular case by the Board of Trade" (reported in *The Times*, 19 May 1916, p.15). In 1917 Webb & Webb wrote how "the 'Incorporated Accountant' is now usually coupled in official phraseology with the 'Chartered Accountant' of the older bodies" (Webb & Webb, 1917, p.30).

(13) In 1922 he was discharged from this work and obtained a position as an "Assistant Cost Accountant" and later as a "Cost and Works Accountant" at Morris Garages Ltd, where he became a member of the ICWA (ICMA Archives, Wood personal file).

(14) E.T. Elbourne qualified as a member of the Institute of Mechanical Engineers in 1896. In 1900 he visited the United States to study machine tools and factory organisation, he became absorbed in 'industrial administration'. He returned to England to take up the post of works organiser and accountant to Messrs. John Thornycroft & Co. Ltd., where he moved on to "high managerial appointment". His last appointment was as assistant general manager at Ponders End Shell Factory (from 1915). Although his book *Factory Administration and Accounts* was "accepted primarily as a practical treatise on administrative problems as they confront the administrator in his day-to-day work ... even in its early days it found ready acceptance as a 'text book' ... " (summarised from Urwick and Brech, 1949, pp.148-149).

CHAPTER 5

AFTER THE WAR: RECONSTRUCTION AND REALITY

> We have commenced a new chapter in the nation's history, a chapter headed "Peace". Are future generations to read therein the tale of hopes dispelled, of ideals shattered, of sacrifices in the great struggle through which we have passed all made in vain; or are they to find the awakening of a new industrial spirit, a new conception of the duties of employers and employed to the State of which both are members, the settlement of those grievances and misunderstandings which in the past have hindered progress and reform?
>
> M. Webster Jenkinson, 28 January 1919.

Reconstruction: The Vision

During the war great plans for 'Reconstruction' had been drawn up. Alfred D. Hall spoke for many when he wrote "few can fail to feel the force of inspiration and experience which is being born of the war, or to recognise the strength of the new hope with which the people are looking forward to the future" (quoted in Johnson 1968, pp.1-2). Many expected a new industrial and social order to come after the war and towards a vision of reconstruction the state sustained a continuous effort to plan for recovery, reconversion and a whole new era of reform (ibid., p.2). A relieving officer recalled how:

> World War I changed everything. It seemed to be a new concept of life- they came back with new ideas. ... After the war there was a song, 'How're you going to keep them down on the farm, after they've seen Paree?' They came back thinking 'this is the life' ... (quoted in Forman, 1978, p.26).

In these ambitious plans was embedded a vision of Capital and Labour working in harmony towards a newly efficient British state. Many in society seemed to share this aspiration: *The Statist*, an economic journal of "unimpeachable orthodoxy", wrote in early 1919, that the present order was "condemned by the pauperism it produced, the waste of manpower, unemployment, and the shameful standard of life of the working classes ... " (Mowat, 1955, p.21). At the close of the war, and briefly thereafter, it was possible to find even otherwise autocratic industrialists arguing in favour of such reforms as 'democratic management' (Child, 1969, p.47).

To aid in the bringing together of Capital and Labour to work for the good of Britain 'Whitley Councils' were to be set up for each industry composed of representatives of employers and workers. They were supposed to discuss everything "affecting the progress and well-being of the trade from the point of view of those engaged in it, as far as this is consonant with the general interest of the community" (quoted in Middlemas, 1979, p.137); this included improvement in management and the participation of workers in the operating of the business, as well as just wages and conditions (ibid.).

Reconstruction was to involve a new approach to management: one of the Ministry of Reconstruction's official publications was entitled "Scientific Business Management" and its opening words were: "The prosperity of an industry and of every man concerned in it is intimately bound up with the efficiency of management" (Urwick & Brech, 1949, vol II, pp.101-102). Six meetings of the Industrial Reconstruction Council were held to discuss 'scientific management', of which two were directly concerned with cost accounting. The first of these was entitled "The Worker's Interest in Costing (A Factor of Industrial Reconstruction)" and given by Webster Jenkinson (published in *The Accountant*, 8 March 1919, pp.185-195). He spoke of how the costing system was the "lantern which throws the limelight" on "obstacles to production efficiency" (ibid., p.186). If we as a nation were:

> ... to maintain our industrial supremacy, our object must be to obtain the highest percentage of efficiency out of our labour energy, and, consequently, it should be our hope to pay the highest wages in the world ... The firmly rooted idea that the lower the wage paid the worker the lower the cost of production and larger the profit is a weed in the field of manufacture to be ruthlessly destroyed (ibid., p.185).

He remarked how the "Whitley Report marks a new era in the science of British industrial organisation"; that as a "necessary corollary" of the "co-operation between employer and worker" the:

> ... efficiency data available to the management must also be at the disposal of the workers ... costs form a full scale contour map of a business ... all interested in the direction of the business must therefore, study the map in order that they may pick their way along the difficult path of industrial management" (ibid., p.185).

The second lecture involving costing was given by J.H. Boyd, Director, Costs and Efficiency Methods, Central Stores Department, Ministry of Munitions, and entitled "Costing in Relation to Scientific Management" (published in *The Accountant*, 12 July 1919, pp.33-40). He discussed the importance of scientific management in curing industrial unrest, declaring that:

> The relationship between manager and worker is a different thing to-day than it was several years ago, and it is yet in the state of evolution. Let us do all in our power to avoid this becoming revolution (ibid., p.40).

Costs he described as "the foundation on which scientific management must be built. They enter very largely into the whole structure, and finally they supply the roof" (ibid., p.33). Interestingly, he wrote of a tour which he had made of the country:

> ... there is a question as to the extent to which costs systems are being used in this country. That is a question which it is difficult to answer, because it would require more knowledge of what is going on in the country than I have got, but, as I have said, in that tour which I made I found that efficient costs systems were very very rare. I do know that good costs systems are in operation in this country in certain works, but I do not know that costs systems are in full operation throughout the whole of any particular industry. I feel, after the enquiries I made, that there is a very big necessity in this country for an awakening on this question of scientific management, of which costing is only one small part (ibid., p.40).

The vision of reconstructing Britain as an efficient and prosperous nation through the use of modern production and management methods was shared by many on the Left as well as in the Establishment. The origin of this seems to have been in the growth of interest by socialists in Britain, in the decade following 1910, in the structure of control within industry itself. Prior to that date criticism of capitalism had focused simply on the ownership of industry and the inequalities which had followed from it (Hyman, 1975, p.ix). Syndicalism made headway and the Socialist Labour Party became propagandists for an industrial unionism whose aim was to organise the workers in every factory into revolutionary industrial unions. Once socialism came workers would control industry through this union structure. These ideas were influential in the Shop Stewards Movement which, during the First World War, challenged the authority of the old craft based union structure. The idea of workers' control was prominent in the programme of the Guild Socialists, whose vision as outlined by G.D.H. Cole in 1917, was of increasingly effective trade unions gradually eroding established managerial perogatives, taking over the function of organising work (including appointing technical experts) and eventually squeezing employers' profit until nationalisation became inevitable. These ideas had a great impact in the Labour Movement at this time: amongst those attracted were militant shop stewards (ibid., pp.x-xiv). Writing on 'scientific management' in 1917 Cole wrote that "we must apply science; but we must not allow science to be a class monopoly" (p.20). Although he was opposed to the way in which scientific management involved the application of scientific principles to human beings he was not opposed to all aspects of it. On costing he wrote:

> The improvement of ... estimating of costs of production ... undoubtedly call for more 'science', and there can be no quarrel with any attempt to apply science purely in such spheres (ibid., p.4).

The Labour Party official programme adopted in 1918, which was given the title "Labour and the New Social Order", was written by Sidney Webb, a prominent member of the Fabian Society. It called for a new social order, based not on competitive struggle but on the 'socialisation of industry' and 'deliberately planned co-operation in production and distribution for the benefit of all who participate by hand or by brain' (Mowat, 1955, p.18). It is difficult to know to what extent Webb's views represented those of the party in general, but in his vision of the future there was an important place for management experts such as cost accountants. He wrote that the "function of management" was to be "a very exalted one"; however "this management, far from being autocratic" would "be dependent very largely on the reports of disinterested experts". The "efficiency of production" would increase greatly in future, "simply through the industry being carried on under the glare of a group of searchlights, playing on every process from different angles." He gave the cost expert as a specific example:

> Think, for instance, what it would mean to a particular factory to receive a report from an efficient outside costing expert, and to find out exactly what each component and every process was costing ... (1920, p.14).

Thus cost accounting was to play a role in the 'reconstructing' of Britain after the war. It was believed that the knowledge produced by costing systems would enable the efficient running, not only of individual organisations but the whole of Britain as a nation. Although the Left and the Establishment desired very different social ends, the means they expected to use had elements in common, including this explicit belief in the value of technical experts such as cost accountants.

Reconstruction Reality

The year of the formation of the Institute of Cost and Works Accountants (ICWA), 1919, was one of the most politically and economically turbulent in British history. By the summer of 1919 four out of every five men serving in the British army had been discharged and they were absorbed back into industry with surprising ease, much due to the rapid return of women employed during the war to 'the home' and a runaway boom (Taylor 1970, Chapter IV). At the end of the war conditions were tailor-made for such a boom in economic activity. There was a large volume of liquid or near liquid assets in the hands of the public and banks, a pent up demand for consumer goods which had been unavailable during the war, a large backlog of industrial investment to be made up and a serious shortage of houses (Aldcroft 1970, p.31). Demand rose rapidly, particularly after the removal of war-time controls in the spring of 1919, and 'reconstruction' began with a high level of government spending. Unfortunately productive capacity could not meet the expansion in demand and prices rose more rapidly than output (ibid., p.35). Concurrent with this there was industrial unrest. The insecurity of the government was made greater by the fear of a police strike: they had gone on strike in London in mid-1918 and did so again in several large cities in mid-1919. These were brief but unnerving incidents (Mowat, 1955, pp.38-39). When trouble broke out on the Clyde it seemed at first to herald the beginning of a revolution but it was quickly dealt with, as was other unrest that year (ibid., p.24).

Speaking in the House of Commons in August 1919, Lloyd George, the Prime Minister, identified profiteering as aggravating and inflaming the unrest (119 HC. Deb5s, Cols.657-658). The Government set up a committee to look into it and then, only a week later, ignored it and rushed through Parliament a hastily written Profiteering Act. It gave the Board of Trade power to "investigate prices, costs and profit" of articles "in common use by the public or being material, machinery or accessories used in the production thereof". If an investigation revealed profiteering had occured an order fixing a maximum price could be issued (reported in *The Incorporated Accountants' Journal* September 1919, p.233-234). The measurement of costs was a crucial part of the process of identifying profiteering; the problems of the work involved in doing this and the large numbers of government staff required to investigate were referred to a number of times in the debate over the Bill in Parliament (119 HC. Deb5s, Cols. 923-1026).

Writing of this period, the Executive Committee of the ICWA noted that as prices had risen "beyond living memory" costing had been "brought once more into the limelight". Although there had been few convictions, the prosecutions had kept "Cost and Works Accountants exceedingly busy for a considerable time" and cost accounting had been used as a "weapon in both camps" (*The Cost Accountant*, March 1922, p.179). Mr John Murray MP, speaking at the final meeting of the Central Committee under the Profiteering Acts, emphasised how "Ascertaining the 'Costings' in every business" was one of "our national needs in commerce" (reported in *The Cost Accountant*, June 1921, p.2). There was renewed public interest in costing. *The Times Trade Supplement* of 20th March 1920 reported how, in their zeal to "make out a case for 'exhortation' by the profiteers" the "political and partisan writers in the popular Press" invoked "methods of accounting that would make the most disreputable of financiers blush". In the same article a number of issues involving costing were discussed, such as whether or not stock should be allowed to be taken into account at replacement cost (reproduced in *The Certified Accountants' Journal*, April 1920).

In 1919 a passionate diatribe was published opposing the use of cost accounting in the campaign against profiteers: it was entitled "Profiteering: In Relation to Cost Accounting. A 20th Century Hoax" (Siday, 1919). Although it is hard to judge how widespread the feelings evinced by the author were, it is interesting to note the position taken. Siday pointed out the many possiblities for manipulation in the procedures used for allocating costs to different products, writing that: "cost accounting leaves the root cause and the main characteristics of profiteering untouched, and is of as much use in effecting a cure as astronomy" (ibid., p.13). In the conclusion he referred to the Profiteering Act as one of the "monstrosities of the War produced by Accountant Cuthberts"[1] and wondered what kind of country we had to "submit to measures which the average person can never hope to understand" (ibid., p.15). Indeed it appears that the Profiteering Act was not very effective, for although during the eighteen months of its existence 1800 profiteering committees were set up there were only 202 prosecutions, and they resulted in fines and costs amounting to a mere £2241 (Pigou, 1947, p.130).

By the end of 1919 the "cutting edge of revolution and of reconstruction alike had been blunted" (Mowat, 1955, p.25). The price-cost spiral, begun in 1919, became a "speculative ramp" (Aldcroft, 1970, p.35) but in April 1920 the end of the boom was signalled when the Bank Rate was raised to 7% and the Government decided on a policy of retrenchment in Public Expenditure (ibid., p.36). By the end of 1920 it had collapsed completely and *The Economist* called 1921 "one of the worst years of depression since the Industrial Revolution" (quoted in Taylor, 1970, pp.194-5). Unemployment more than doubled between December 1920 and March 1921 and in June 1921 it passed two million (ibid.); economic activity declined rapidly. In the Foreword to Howard Hazell's book *Costing for Manufacturers* (1921), Lord Leverhulme complained of the problems of manufacturers when "every item entering into costs of production has not only risen enormously" but is "fluctuating from day to day". It was "absolutely imperative" he wrote, "that today the manufacturer must discard all prewar methods of costing and adopt the most complete, thorough and most modern system that can be placed at his service" (p.5). Thus the depression which followed the boom brought with it yet more interest in costing as manufacturers looked for the most efficient way to rationalize their businesses. Roland Dunkerley (Works Accountant at Metropolitan Vickers Electrical Co., Ltd. [*1923 Yearbook*, ICMA Archives]), visiting the International Cost Convention held in Ohio in 1921 spoke of how:

> The call for quick re-adjustment of prices to meet emergency conditions, and the necessity to fix rock bottom figures in order to obtain business of any kind, forceably brought home to most manufacturers the necessity of cost systems from which information could readily and accurately be obtained (*The Cost Accountant*, January 1922, p.137).

Union activity and membership reached a peak in the immediate post-war period: trade unionism was described as "an infection going round the country like influenza" (quoted in Lockwood, 1958, p.185). In 1912 there were nearly three and a half million trade union members; in 1918, six and a half million and by 1920 eight and a third million. After 1920 numbers fell and the eight million mark was not reached again until 1943 (Pelling, 1976, pp.294-295). After a pre-war peak of nearly 41 million days lost through stoppages in 1912, in 1921 nearly 86 million days were lost- this dropped rapidly thereafter and has only ever been exceeded in 1926, the year of the General Strike[2] (Pelling, 1976, pp.294-295). Even stolid cabinet ministers were haunted by the spectre of Petrograd (Hyman, 1975, p.vii). In February 1922 the Chairman of the Federation of Master Printers, expressing the fears of many, commented:

> We, who are interested in manufacture, are faced with difficult, even dangerous conditions in the immediate future (*The Cost Accountant*, March 1922, p.189).

Some even spoke of how this threat from the unions could be alleviated by cost accounting: if workers were given the "actual facts of commerce" some peace would be obtained in the industrial unrest (J.M. Fells, *The Cost Accountant*, July 1922, p.27). Thus it seems that although the dream of a 'reconstruction' of Britain, which would bring with it national efficiency and of which cost accounting was an integral part, was largely unrealised and faded, the problems created by the boom followed by the slump continued to create interest in cost accounting. In the case of the Profiteering Act this interest stretched to the public domain in debate in the newspapers. Now the discussion will return to early 1919, when, in the heady days of the newly won peace, the ICWA was formed.

The Formation of the ICWA

On 8 March 1919 an "Institute of Cost Accountants, Limited" came into being. The Memorandum of Association gave the main objects of the new Institute as being to:

> ... provide an organisation for cost accountants, works accountants, estimating and cost clerks and others engaged in occupations requiring a mathematical and technical knowledge of industry in all its branches, embracing in such knowledge the cost of production, manufacture or sale of all articles produced, manufactured or sold (ICMA Archives).

W.E. Stacey, seemingly the prime mover in getting the new Institute started, appears to have been mainly interested in getting as many members as possible at a guinea per annum and charging an over-riding commission on all receipts (ICMA Archives, Russell 11). Given this, it is quite possible that he deliberately chose a title for the new Institute which was aimed at confusing its members with chartered accountants (Fellows would have become FCA's and Associates ACA's). Stacey, however, found himself joined in the venture by others who were more interested in making the Institute a 'professional' body than a money-making venture and he retired from the scene. One of those who joined, George Russell, writes how they:

> ... first altered the Memorandum and Articles to bring the Institute's activities more into line with an examining body, altering the entrance fees, subscriptions and planning its future policy. In this connection, we had in mind an Institute equal in status to the Chartered Accountants and throughout the early days, this ideal was always the predominating influence (ICMA Archives, Russell 11).

The new organisation needed publicity cheaply and quickly, a letter was sent to *The Times* (17 March 1919, p.18). In it it was noted that the Coal Controller appeared to have acted, in increasing the price of coal by 2s 6d a ton, without expert advice. Had he had the benefit of the advice of qualified cost accountants familiar with the work of collieries, he would doubtless have been placed in possession of the facts and figures to prove that the increase was unnecessary, and against the public interest. It was signed by Messrs Kilner, Kilner & Co. describing themselves as solicitors to the Institute of Cost

Accountants Ltd.[3] The accounting journals quickly picked up the entry of a newcomer onto their scene, and it seems that most of the ICWA's publicity in the accounting world in the early months came from the debate over the need for and the status of this new Institute. On publishing the details of this letter to *The Times*, *The Accountant* commented that they:

> ... should be interested to hear in due course who is connected with this movement, for upon that naturally depends its chances of success. That there is much scope for something of this kind goes without saying, for it is by no means everyone who describes himself as a "cost accountant" that is entitled to be taken seriously (29 March 1919).

Incorporated Accountants' Journal reported the apparent formation of the Institute in its April 1919 edition, writing that they:

> ... understood it has been formed with the object of protecting and assisting those members who are cost accountants largely connected with engineering. The first directors ... addresses are all in the suburbs of London, so we are not able to identify any of them with professional accountancy (April 1919).

Following the initial publicity a lively debate ensued in *The Accountant*. There was much questioning of the intentions and status of those involved. A correspondent calling himself "System" wrote that:

> From the time that the "Institute of Cost Accountants" came to our notice we have endeavoured to find out what cost experts are concerned, but we see that the Memorandum is subscribed by men of whom we have never heard, and all manner of works accountants, cost clerks, and the like will no doubt range themselves under its banner with a view to "trading" henceforth as "qualified" Cost Accountants (*The Accountant*, 10 May 1919, p.383).

Another correspondent called upon the promoters:

> ... publicly to establish their bona fides, and to demonstrate to those who have taken up the profession of Works Accountant as a livelihood that their interests are likely to be saved and protected by the Institute of Cost Accountants, Ltd (*The Accountant*, 17 May 1919, p.416).

The Institute insisted that it was not a "trading concern" and declared that:

> The war has brought out the great importance of this science with such emphasis that there is evidence of the professional accountant wishing to appropriate this branch to himself. We as an Institute, fully realise the importance of the professional accountant in the sphere which he has qualified for and satisfactorily fills but we also maintain that he should understand his limitations when approaching a type of work which calls not only for accountancy experience, but also demands practical knowledge which can only be obtained by close contact with actual factory conditions and detailed processes; and, in addition to this workshop organisation embracing machine efficiency, all of which is outside the scope of the commercial man (*The Accountant*, 17 May 1919).

With this letter they sent a type-written syllabus of the examinations as "a sufficient proof that the Council are alive to the high standard of efficiency required" (ibid.). The attitude to the new Institute can only be described as suspicious and in a leader on 7th June the editor of *The Accountant* wrote that they had been left "somewhat in the dark as to the true ultimate aims of the new combination" (*The Accountant*, 7 June 1919, pp.477-479).

Chartered and Incorporated Accountants

As discussed in Chapter 4, a 'profound metamorphosis' seems to have overtaken the chartered and incorporated accountants during the five years of hostilities (an editorial published in *The Accountant* in 1917 clearly demonstrates this change)[4]. Many of the younger members, articled clerks and staff had been to fight in the war and a considerable number of those who had not fought had become involved with costing, a subject many had previously thought beneath their dignity. To the younger members of the profession and the articled clerks who returned to professional practice after the war the world seemed to have changed but the accounting profession had not. The response of some was to join a "National Guild of Accountants' Clerks" whose aims included the establishment of a 'Whitley Council' for the profession, improving the salaries and status of members and establishing a pension scheme and an appointments bureau (*The Accountant*, 8 November 1919, p.388)[5]. A letter was sent to practising accountants making these points and meetings were organised, some being very well attended, the participants including young qualified accountants as well as clerks. The response of the employers and the ICAEW was not helpful however, the ICAEW responding to this move with a statement to the effect that "the Council are of opinion that the procedure of a Whitley Council is not applicable nor one which is appropriate to a profession such as that exercised by members of the Institute" (*The Accountant*, 3 January 1920, p.1). The response of employing accountants apparently varied from welcoming, to considering the business a joke and, by one of the largest employers in the profession, that if any member of staff "desired to join the Guild he must seek another situation" (*The Accountant*, 22 May 1920, pp.609-610). This lack of interest on the part of employers and the general downturn in the economy, which made jobs scarcer, were probably amongst the reasons why this Guild quickly disintegrated.

Meanwhile the Annual General Meeting of the ICAEW held in 1919 proved a stormy affair. The members appearing to have been divided into two camps, which can be christened 'reactionaries' and 'reformists'. Webster Jenkinson seems to have been the spokesman for the reformists. The reformists wanted changes in the Constitution of the Council and the method of election of its members, with the aim it seems of working for reforms in the system of training accountants, positive action to educate them in costing and efficiency matters and a reduction in the obstacles set in the path of those joining the profession in the form of the payment of premiums and long articles[6]. Webster Jenkinson had spoken in the preceding December on the issue of costing, declaring that if accountants could not "deliver the goods" a "new profession will spring up of works accountants and the existing profession would then practically be regarded as accomplished book-keepers and nothing more" (reported in *The Accountant*, 18 January 1919, p.46). At the AGM he spoke at length, causing laughter with the remark that "they say an army fights on its stomach; in the coming commercial struggle the British manufacturer has got to fight on his internal records". He follows this up by asking:

> Are we in a position to act as an accountants' service corps, and supply the trader with what he requires? I say without fear of contradiction that not 80% of our members know anything at all about internal office works, works costing and efficiency matters, and why should they? What has the Institute done to direct attention to this subject? What has it done to educate the members? ... I sometimes think the public generally have got an almost exaggerated opinion of the abilities of Chartered Accountants (*The Accountant*, 10 May 1919, pp.398-399).

Sir Gilbert Garnsey, who had been Controller of Munitions Accounts in the war, was greeted with shouts of "hear hear" when he asked the Council to bear in mind the "large number here who come prepared to take very drastic action" and he spoke of the problems of "restraining members feelings" (*The Accountant*, 10 May 1919, p.400). A compromise appears to have been effected between the generally reactionary Council and the reformists whereby a Committee of Enquiry was set up, but in the leader in the next issue of *The Accountant* it was commented that: "Everyone will realise that the movement that Mr. Webster Jenkinson voiced is far too widespread to be laid at rest by mere words, however tactfully chosen" (17 May 1919, pp.409-410).

The Costing Association

On the 28th March 1919 E. Miles Taylor, a chartered accountant with experience of costing who had worked in the United States for a period, had written to *The Accountant* and announced his intention to call a conference of those 'professional' accountants interested in costing. He wrote that in his opinion:

> Chartered Accountants are only now beginning to see the possibilities of cost-finding as a vital branch of the profession (*The Accountant*, 5 April 1919, p.277).

He went on to ask:

> ... how many men at the Admiralty, War Office, Ministry of Munitions- or the Coal Controllers! knew the first thing about it? ... Many of our leading manufacturers and distributors are keenly interested, and are looking to expert accountants for guidance. If we are not careful, however, the result of the crude experiments by outsiders will dampen enthusiam and seriously prejudice the movement in the eyes of the industrial community (ibid.).

It is clear from later correspondence that when he wrote of 'outsiders' attempting 'crude experiments' he was referring to the newly formed Institute of Cost Accountants Limited.

A 'Conference on Scientific Costing', organised by Miles Taylor was held on June 5th and 6th 1919. Opening the conference, the Chairman, Mr. Thomas Froude, announced that the conference would:

> ... consist of the reading of papers and endeavouring to find out from those present what was the opinion of persons interested in costing, as to its future. Should an Association be formed? If so who should be included? Should Works Accountants join with professional accountants, or should the latter carry on? (reported in *The Accountant*, 21 June 1919, p.529).

Following him, Miles Taylor gave the reason for the conference as being to:

> ... exchange views and get a grip on the principles that underlie costing as a science (ibid.).

Four sessions were held as follows:

1	Chairman	Mr Thomas Froude ACA of Taylor Froude & Co. (in the absense through pressure of business of Professor Lawrence Dicksee M.Com., FCA, who had promised to preside)
	Speaker	Miles Taylor FCA
	Subject	Practical Costing Methods
2	Chairman	Mr H.R. Cooper, Sopwith Aviation Co., Ltd.
	Speaker	Mr J.M. Fells FSAA
	Subject	Cost Accountancy: Its Evolution and Its Trend
3	Chairman	Mr G. Stanhope Pitt FSAA (Vice President of the Society of Incorporated Accountants).
	Speaker	Mr G.H.T. Allen, ACIS
	Subject	Costing in Relation to Selling
4	Chairman	Lieut.-Col J.Grimwood DSO, FSAA (War Office) Chief of the Army Costing Department
	Speaker	Mr Percy M. Taylor (in his absence read by Mr Thomas Frounde)
	Subject	Costing in Relation to the Public Services

The conference proceedings are reported verbatim in *The Accountant*: session 1, 21 June 1919, pp.529-534; session 2, 28 June 1919, pp.548-552, and sessions 3 and 4, 19 July 1919, pp.58-63.

Amongst those attending were several members of the ICWA but the majority of the participants seem to have been chartered and incorporated accountants with an interest in costing. It is interesting to note the presence, as chairmen, of both the chief of the Army Costing Department and the vice-president of the Society of Incorporated Accountants.

As at the Industrial Reconstruction Council Meetings, discussed earlier in this chapter, costing was presented as a tool to mediate between Capital and Labour. Miles Taylor remarking that costing would lead to the "greater efficiency of all parts of the community" (*The Accountant* 19 July 1919, p.60) and J.M. Fells that:

> ... there would in the future be something like compulsory disclosure of costing. Labour had to be considered in these matters, and the economic friction between Capital and Labour would inevitably lead to the disclosure of costs (ibid.).

There was much discussion of the future of cost accountancy, but no "crystallization" of the:

> ... somewhat diverse opinions to which this conference has testified as to the real function of cost and works accountants, and whether it was possible to draw a line of demarcation between the professional and the works accountants (*The Accountant*, 28 June 1919, p.548).

There was agreement, however, on the need for some form of standardisation of costing terminology (some calling it 'scientific nomenclature'), and it was agreed that a committee would be formed to discuss it. It was to have 12 members, 6 to be elected at the meeting and 2 each to be nominated by the ICAEW, the Society of Incorporated Accountants and Auditors and the ICWA. The committee failed to make progress, the reasons for this being the subject of some dispute, but it is clear that the Council of the ICAEW opposed the idea. After this abortive attempt to set up a joint committee some of the chartered and incorporated accountants interested in costing continued to meet and in August formed a Provisional Committee of the "Central Costing Association", as it was named. The proposal to form an Association did not commend itself to the governing body of either the Chartered or the Incorporated Institute[7], the Council of the ICAEW resolving that:

> ... the Costing Association, or any similar association, is unnecessary and undesirable, and that the Council deprecate the formation of such bodies (*The Accountant*, 19 June 1920, p.711).

In "deference to this view" no further steps were taken with the formation by those involved. The organising committee announced that they hoped that the Institute (of Chartered Accountants) and the Society "would take upon themselves individually, or preferably con-jointly, the services that the Costing Association thought it might usefully render to the profession"; namely acting as an educational centre for the distribution of literature and organising of meetings on the subject of scientific costing (*The Accountant*, 19 June 1920, pp.711-712).

Conclusion

At the ending of the war many believed that the national spirit which had emerged could be put to good use in reconstructing British society. Labour and Capital, working together, had won the military battles, and it seemed that the industrial 'battle' against foreign competition could be won in the same way. This was the context in which the discussions and actions of this period concerning cost accounting and cost accountants occured.

During the war cost accounting had been used as a tool of efficiency in the National Factories, and manufacturers had begun to follow this lead. In discussions of reconstruction it was often associated with scientific management, a link which I consider probably came through the war efforts of British chartered accountants who had had experience in the USA at some time, most notable of these being Samuel Lever. Not only the Establishment, but also socialists, supported costing as an apparently value-neutral technique for making production efficient- to the benefit of employers and employees.

The immediate post-war period brought profiteering (largely as a result of too much money chasing too few consumer goods), and this was identified as a major factor causing the unrest in the country. The Government attempted to stop the profiteers using legislation which relied upon investigations of costs, although this seems to have failed dismally, it meant that costing remained 'in the limelight'. It was in the midst of the dreams of reconstruction and the reality of unrest of 1919 that the question of who should properly take responsibility for the work of costing came into debate. On the one hand there was the attempted formation of an association comprised of chartered and incorporated accountants working in the field of costing; and on the other, the appearance of a new body, the 'Institute of Cost Accountants, Limited', claiming for its members working with costing in industry the status of professional accountants.

At the 1919 Annual General Meeting of the ICAEW the pressure for change, which had been building up during the war, came to a head. Reformists wanting, amongst other things, the Institute to take an active part in training members to meet the new demands from industry for help with installing and operating modern costing systems; ultimately achieved little. The ICAEW was to remain aloof from industry; the costing association which was in the process of being formed did not survive the displeasure of the Council. Despite this there was growing employment of its members in senior positions in industry.

The 'Institute of Cost Accountants, Limited', soon to become the ICWA, gradually, through the first months, began to define for itself what it considered the role and position of its members to be. In the early days the Council of the ICWA entered into a debate with critical chartered accountants through the letters column of *The Accountant*. This seems to have played a part in helping them to begin to define the cost accountant as an accountant with practical experience of manufacturing. A formulation which both *distinguished* them from chartered accountants, and *explained* their claim to similar status. The actions and reactions of the ICWA were shaped by the niche which they identified for themselves as an association of specialist professional accountants. It is these which will be explored in more detail in the next chapter.

NOTES

(1) According to the *Dictionary of Slang and Unconventional Language*, 'Cuthbert' dates from 1917 and refers to a "government employee or officer shirking military service" (Partridge, 1937).

(2) Since 1926 the maximum number of days lost has been only 29 million, this was in 1979 (HMSO, *Annual Abstract of Statistics*, 1985; Pelling, 1976, pp. 294-295).

(3) In full the letter read:

> <u>The Price of Coal</u>
>
> Sir, In examining the evidence given on this Commission one fact appears to stand out prominently, viz., that the increase of 2s 6d a ton on the selling price of coal was made without taking into account the cost of production, and the fact that the mines, taken together, were actually then working at a sufficient profit. Being under Government control the profitable mines should have been used to assist the unprofitable mines. The Coal Controller appears to have acted without expert advice, but had he had the benefit of the advice of qualified cost accountants, familiar with the work of collieries, he would doubtless have been placed in possession of facts and figures to prove that the increase was unnecessary and against public interest. The increase in the price of coal has lead to the present unrest in the coal-mining industry, and the consumer now knows he has been paying more than 2s 6d per ton too much for coal, a very material item to every user of coal.
>
> Yours obediently,
>
> KILNER,KILNER, AND CO.,
Solicitors for the Institute
of Cost Accountants (Limited).
30, Coleman Street EC2. March 14.

(4) The editor wrote:

> Hitherto, speaking in quite general terms, it seems to us that professional accountants have taken too narrow a view of both their opportunities and their responsibilities. In the past they have amply justified their existence as a profession by

> the improvements they have been able to effect in office administration and management. But so long as their mental horizon is bounded by the four walls of the office, there must always be a distinct limit to their possible utility. There is very considerable scope for expert organisation and systemisation outside the office of every business, and, to a very large extent, this constitutes what Mr. Derbyshire calls "a virgin field for accountants". Hitherto, one of the chief causes of inefficiency has been the complete divorce between the office, or "Accounts Department", of a business house and its operative departments, with the result that the former often devotes much time and expense towards the preparation of records which the latter do not require, and never use; while it does not always provide the operative departments with those records which they really need. There is abundant scope for development here by those accountants who will take the trouble to master the actual business methods employed in any particular house. The almost incredible success that will attend such work, when really thoroughly and ably done, has been abundantly demonstrated by Sir Samuel Lever KCB. In less sensational, but none the less in many important ways such success is open practically to every member of the profession who is able to appreciate the fact that accounts are of no use in themselves, apart from the facts and tendencies of which they are the record- that is to say, that accounting is not an end in itself, but merely a means to an end, that end being more efficient business management (*The Accountant*, 3 March 1917, p.211).

(5) It is particularly relevant to this study to note that even clerks were becoming organised at this period. Lockwood researched the history of five of the major clerical unions: the three of these dealing with clerks employed in commerce and industry (and not local or national government) show a peak in their membership levels around 1920- levels not to be achieved again until after the Second World War (1958, p.140). The Railway Clerks Association, founded in 1897, recruited rapidly during the war and by the end of the war over 60% of the clerks were members. In February 1919 they showed, for clerks, an unprecedented degree of solidarity and confidence when they organised a strike which was only averted by the yielding of the railway companies to their demands at the eleventh hour. Later that year they refused to blackleg in the National Union of Railwaymen's Strike despite the 'loyalty pay' offered to them (ibid., p.158). The Bank Officers Guild, founded in the last years of the war also recruited rapidly and by 1921 around half of the permanent bank-staff in England and Wales were members (ibid., pp.176-177). The National Union of Clerks had only 150 members in 1906 but by 1919-20 had 43,000 (only a small proportion of clerks although a large number in itself). In 1915 it was regarded as a landmark in the history of industrial relations when clerks striking at Nobel's Explosive Factory were supported in their action by the manual workers. In 1920 the union

was re-organised into virtually autonomous industrial guilds which were urged to co-operate with the manual workers in their respective industries (it was not a successful experiment and by 1926 the membership had fallen to around one-sixth of its 1919-20 level) (ibid., pp.162-165).

Interestingly a letter had appeared in *The Accountant* in April 1919 from the Assistant General Secretary of the National Union of Clerks suggesting that an Accountants' Clerks' Guild be formed in association with their union but I have found no further reference to any link between the two (26 April 1919, p.340).

(6) The war had disrupted the system of training, for many articled clerks in professional offices were called-up. This caused practical problems which encouraged the questioning of the whole system of premiums being paid for years of articled clerkship, even within the profession itself. As an instance of the problems, there is the case of the angry parent who wrote to *The Accountant* concerning his son's articles. He had apparently paid a premium of 250 guineas (almost £263), in January 1914, for his fourth son to be articled for 5 years to a member of a firm of chartered accountants in the City. The son had been called-up and had not completed the articles, however, the firm had refused to refund the premium saying that they had now to pay more than the normal rates to replace him (1 March 1919, p. 161). It is interesting that *The Accountant* published a letter from someone calling himself only 'Crusader', which read:

> ... institutions of a vigorous Empire should not be so much concerned regarding what a man has been as what he can do now. In engineering, military duties, aeronautics, etcetera, by sheer necessity, it has been proved that, with intensive study, long apprenticeships can be dispensed with ... If we are to equip our forces (in accountancy) we must remove barriers and provide opportunities for the development of talent ... experienced factory accountants should be admitted as members if such accountants could pass special examinations of the Institute (5 October 1918, p.181).

(7) It is interesting to note that the vice-president of the Incorporated Society, Mr. G. Stanhope-Pitt, spoke very positively of costing at the conference:

> ... justice has not been done to this all important question of costing, in the direction of which I believe the future of the accounting profession very largely lies (*The Accountant*, 19 July 1919, p.58).

Whether he was speaking in his own capacity, or whether this was the view of the Society (who later backed down once it was apparent that the the ICAEW would not support a costing association) is not clear.

CHAPTER 6

THE INSTITUTE OF COST AND WORKS ACCOUNTANTS

> In this connection, we had in mind an Institute equal in status to the Chartered Accountants and throughout the early days, this ideal was always the predominating influence.
>
> George Russell
> Founder member of the ICWA

Introduction

This chapter continues the discussion of the internal development of the ICWA which was begun in chapter 5. In essence this involves looking at the way in which they attempted to establish themselves as a professional accounting body. It was not just the question of being professionals which concerned the early members, but being *accounting* professionals. A process of attempted professionalisation does not occur in a social and political vacuum, and one of the most distinctive features of the ICWA was the way in which they tried to model their occupational closure along the lines of the ICAEW. During this process the founder members felt their way towards defining what techniques and knowledge a cost accountant should have, and exactly what their position was viz a viz others working in related jobs in the factory, in particular, on the one hand, engineers, and on the other, cost clerks. This was an ongoing process, and as the founder members began to, in a sense, *define* themselves, this very definition itself brought in a certain type of new member. These, in turn, played their part in the process of *definition*. In this chapter the discussion is limited to the internal aspects of the professionalisation attempt; in the next it will be broadened in order to relate some of these aspects to the wider social and political context.

The Organisation of the ICWA

As is often the case with organisations, the newly formed ICWA seemed to be kept operating during the first few years through the determined efforts of a group of dedicated individuals. Organising the affairs of the Institute was noted by Charles Lewton to have taken up almost the whole of his, Claude Todman, Dick Ryall and George Russell's spare time [ICMA Archives (hereafter IA), Lewton 14][1].

The problems of obtaining premises and administrative assistance proved difficult for the organisation had little money. By the end of the first three months they were in their third registered office and they had appointed their third Secretary, Martin Blair. Lewton describes how:

> In those days we were very hard up and I well recall Moran's attendance at his first Council meeting (in July 1920), held in Blair's office, which was very small and had little furniture. When Moran came in some of us were seated upon desks. There were not enough chairs. A bad impression I'm afraid (IA, Lewton 12).

The founders of the Institute were striving to make it a professional body however, so impressions were perceived to be important. In September 1920 they moved 'office' to 38 Grosvenor Gardens, NW1. This was also the office of Todman Ryall & Co. Ltd., a company set up, as the name suggests, by two of the most active members of the Institute. The firm appears from an advertisment to have sold dynamos and motors. A close relationship seems to have existed between the the ICWA and Todman Ryall & Co. Ltd. up until 1923, when it appears that they stopped trading. Ryall became the Honorary Secretary of the Institute and his secretary, Miss Myers, became Secretary. This marked the end of an era in the Institute's history, for most of the early activists had by then dropped out. Ryall, who seems to have dominated the affairs of the Institute in the early period, left after rows within the Council and Executive. Following the move to 6 Duke Street, St.James, in September 1923, the organisation of the Institute was restructured, the procedures for running the Institute's affairs were made more formal and, it appears, more democratic.

The membership of the Institute grew gradually. By the end of 1919, 37 members had been admitted; in 1920, 181 were admitted, in 1921, 164; in 1922, 111; in 1923, 113; in 1924, 73; and in 1925, 89 (IA, Register of Members). At the time the *1923 Year Book* (IA) was prepared (spring, 1923) there were a total of 526 members. The topographical listing gave 501 of these as practising in Britain and 23 overseas (2 members in the alphabetical list were missed out of the topographical section). The British members were fairly widely spread over the country, with concentrations in the major industrial towns, as would be expected:

London	122
Manchester	57
Birmingham	39
Glasgow	22
Sheffield	18
Leeds	14
Coventry	11
Bristol	8
Newcastle on Tyne	7
Derby	5
Runcorn	5
Sunderland	5
York	5
	318
Less than 5 members	183
Total in UK	501

The Council decided that if the ICWA was to become a professional body whose members had the status of 'professional' accountants they had to be selective in their choice of members. They had to be able to counter the claims of those like 'System', quoted earlier, that all manner of cost clerks and the like would be trading as 'qualified' cost accountants (*The Accountant*, 10 May 1919, p.383). There were three basic ways of dealing with this, firstly to get already established and influential cost accountants to join and help with the work of the Institute; secondly, to be very careful in selecting those initial members to be admitted without examination; thirdly, to bring in comprehensive and suitably difficult examinations.

Influential Cost Accountants

Established cost accountants had to be persuaded to join the ICWA. They had to be convinced of the seriousness of the Institute's aims, and the advantages which a professional body would bring to the occupation. One of the early members of the Council recalled going to visit A.E. Goodwin, Secretary of the Master Printers' Federation in order to put forward the "merits and claims of the Institute, ... it was necessary to convince these gentlemen that we were not an association of Cost Clerks" (IA, Lewton 1 & 14). J.D.C. Mackay, the principal of the School of Accountancy contacted them. Lewton writes how he and Ryall "dined with him in London", and that the "measure of our success with him can be judged by the fact that, a few days later, we received from him an application to join the Institute" (IA, Lewton 1)[2]. In February 1920 J.M. Fells, one of the joint authors of the by then classic book *Factory Accounts*, joined. Amongst the active members were, as I noted earlier, a number holding quite senior positions in industry, and in the case of Reginald Townsend, the Civil Service. By 1923 he was Advisor on Costs to the Director-General of Factories, at the War Office Royal Ordnance Factories.

During the years up to the 1924 reorganisation it seems to have been the practice to co-opt onto the Council any moderately important person who could be persuaded to join. There were a total of 24 people who were Council members at various times during this period but 14 of them attended less than 10 meetings. For instance, A.H. Gledhill of

Gledhill-Brook Time Recorders became a member but only managed to attend 2 meetings, and H.G. Jenkins, the prolific writer on industrial administration, only 6 meetings. In contrast, of the 55 meetings held in total, Ryall attended 54, Russell 48, and Todman 40 (IA).

Selecting Members

The Council of the newly formed ICWA were faced with distinguishing 'suitable' members from the vast mass of cost clerks and others working in industry. George Russell wrote:

> ... we were 'deluged' with applications from cost accountants, cost clerks and many other sections of the industrial community. Works managers, estimators, all seemed to feel the need of a body which would cater for an entirely works outlook upon costing instead of the hitherto professional auditor's view (IA, Russell 11).

Somehow a basic core of people had to be selected from established senior cost clerks and accountants, people who would not expect to have to sit examinations, and indeed would probably show no further interest in the ICWA if asked to do so.

When Stacey and Kilner drew up their original scheme for the formation of the Institute it seems that they had no intention of trying to distinguish cost clerks from cost accountants and would simply admit anyone who cared to pay a guinea per annum (IA, Russell 11). Such a subscription was clearly totally inadequate for an examining body (ibid.), and on March 18th it was decided to revise it as follows:

	Fellows	Associates	Students
Entrance Fee	3 guineas	2 guineas	1 guinea
Annual Subscription	2 guineas	1 guinea	$^{1}/_{2}$ guinea

Source: IA, Council Minute Book (hereafter, CMB), 18 March 1919.

Members admitted were to be divided into two categories, namely associates and fellows. Associates had to satisfy the Council of their "general experience in cost accountancy". Fellows should have held the "position of chief cost accountant (works or factory) on the staff of a manufacturing concern for a period of at least three years", or have "held some position which is considered by the Council as equivalent thereto". Although those admitted fellows were to have "passed the final examination", and those as associates were to have "passed the Institute examination", the Council allowed themselves the discretion of being able to admit a person to membership without examination, provided that they considered them eligible to be so treated (IA, CMB, 18 March 1919).

The first design of application form, for the 'Institute of Cost Accountants Limited', included amongst the personal details it requested the nature of the applicants present position (with full particulars), examinations passed (if any), and the applicant was asked to "state fully past experience and nature of such" (IA, Bryce personal file). The names and addresses of three persons to whom the Council could apply for references were requested, and it appears that these referees were asked if the candidate had "practical experience" and was a "fit and proper person" (ibid.). The first members were admitted provisionally on the basis of the form and formally entered in the Register of Members (IA) when satisfactory references were provided.

As time went on the application form became more sophisticated and by May 1921 (probably also earlier) a form was in use which asked questions which attempted to delve more deeply into the applicant's experience and knowledge. He[3] was asked to state what costing experience he had and "this statement of the candidate's practical experience" was to "show concisely the work upon which he is engaged and the degree of personal responsibility involved in his present employment". Under "particulars of past experience" the candidate was to indicate the work upon which he was previously engaged and also "particulars of any technical knowledge and workshop experience". Details of education, examinations passed, membership of other societies and the size of the business he was employed in were also requested (IA, Tebby personal file). References were taken up for each applicant and the referees were asked a carefully worded set of questions regarding the candidate, including one asking: "Has the applicant to your *definite* knowledge an understanding of the following subjects: (a) Mathematics? (b) Book-keeping and Accounts? (c)

Economics?" and another asking: "Has the applicant to your *definite* knowledge had practical experience in the following subjects: (a) Cost and Works Accounting? (b) Workshop Practice? (c) Factory Organisation?" The referee had to answer simply "Yes" or "No" to each of these (IA, Tebby personal file). This "practical experience" was considered very important, since it was this, after all, which distinguished cost accountants from financial accountants. The level of education suggested by a knowledge of mathematics and economics, on the other hand, was to distinguish the cost accountant from the ordinary clerk.

The Institute frequently proclaimed how selective they were. At the first Annual General Meeting in 1920 Ryall noted that over 60% of the applicants were being rejected (*The Accountant*, 3 July 1920, p.18). By April 1923 they had 606 members, but Russell wrote that:

> ... the membership could, without difficulty, have been made up to 3000 or more, but by the strictness with which these applications were overhauled, the type of persons admitted were of an extremely high standard (IA, Russell 11).

The truth of such claims is of course hard to judge, but it does appear from surviving personal files that quite a lot of care was taken- in some cases prospective members even being interviewed in an attempt to judge their suitability.

Out of these dual processes of selection and self-selection the ICWA was emerging as an organisation representing a diverse group of people with two things in common: they had some involvement with costing and desired to be formally associated with it through becoming members of the newly formed ICWA. Taking as an example the year from June 1921 to May 1922, an analysis of the titles of the jobs held by those admitted reveals a fascinating variety. Out of 139 members admitted during this period, 6 did so through the route of passing the examinations (it took some time to get a system of examinations set up), the rest mainly through scrutiny of application forms and references. Of the 139, 60 had titles such as 'cost accountant', 'works accountant', 'chief cost accountant' or the like; 14 were described as 'secretary', 'secretary and accountant', or something similar; 13 were 'chief cost clerks'; the other 52 had a huge variety of titles, from 'estimator', 'assistant manager' and 'factory manager' to a 'liquidator' an 'investigator of costs (Admiralty)', a 'flour-mill accountant' and 'The General Secretary of the Guild of Calico Printers, Bleachers, Dyers and Finishers' Foremen' (analysis prepared from lists in *The Cost Accountant*). Following on from this analysis a more exhaustive one was made of all of the 501 British members listed in the topographical section of the *1923 Year Book* (IA). This listing gave the job title and place of employment of all members. Categorising such a wide range of titles was difficult, but no apology is given for the large number of categories, for it was felt that to use less would misrepresent the variety which existed.

(1)	'cost accountant', 'works accountant', 'chief cost accountant' etcetera	180
(2)	'accountant', 'chief accountant', 'superintendent of accounts branch' etcetera	47
(3)	'secretary' or 'assistant secretary'	43
(4)	'secretary' combined with some other title eg. 'secretary and accountant', 'secretary and general manager [excluding those in (13)]	37
(5)	including the word 'cost' in job title, but wider than those in (1), eg. 'costs and statistical officer'	31
(6)	'chief cost clerk', 'cost clerk' or similar	29
(7)	'cost consultant' (independent)	25
(8)	managers other than those covered under (2) or (4), eg. 'commercial manager'	23
(9)	'director', 'managing director' etcetera	15
(10)	government (not local authority) employee	10
(11)	'estimator', or 'estimating' in job title	9
(12)	appear to be working for an accounting partnership	8
(13)	'secretary' combined with some title conveying the idea of involvement with costs, eg. 'secretary and cost controller'	6
(14)	'clerk', other than some title indicating cost clerk	6
(15)	lecturers	5
(16)	other	27
		501

It can be seen that 180, or 36% of the membership had the title 'cost accountant' or something quite similar. If those with a slightly wider job title are included [category (5)], this goes up to 42%. Another 6% were chief cost clerks or the like, and 1% combined the title of 'secretary' with something to do with costs. With the addition of 3% in the other categories where cost was mentioned [for example the cost inspectors working for the Calico Printers Association were included under (16)], all in all a total of 263, or just over half of the membership were working in industry and had a job title which directly linked them with costing. In addition 5%, 25, of the membership were independent cost consultants, most of these (15) operated from London, 3 operated from Manchester. This leaves a goodly proportion of the membership, around 43%, whose job description does not automatically link them with cost accounting at all. There are two possible explanations for their acceptance as members; firstly that the ICWA did not stick rigidly to their policy of only admitting individuals with experience of cost accounting; secondly, that costing was not a clearly defined occupation and (probably in smaller companies in particular), the person who had historically acquired responsibility for cost accounting was not necessarily called 'the cost accountant'. There can never be a certain answer to this question, both factors are probably involved, perhaps the second more than the first. The Institute were certainly choosey over who they admitted, only 3 'cost clerks' were members, the clerks in category (6) were largely 'chief cost clerks'. On the other hand if a person of the status of 'secretary and accountant' to a moderate sized company applied it seems likely that they would have been admitted if their job description and referees comments indicated some experience of costing. How much real experience they had had would have been almost impossible to judge.

An interesting feature[4] of the analysis of members' jobs is the number of members it reveals whose titles include the word 'secretary' (categories (3), (4) and (6)]. Many of these were members of the Chartered Institute of Secretaries. Of the total membership of 526, 103 were members of other professional bodies: 57 were fellows or associates of the Chartered Institute of Secretaries (mostly associates), 24 were chartered accountants (10 of these Scottish), 19 were incorporated accountants, 7 had engineering qualifications, only two had degrees.

It is worthwhile making a slight diversion at this point to examine the issue of students and training contracts- known as 'articles'. Service under articles, as Stacey writes, "was and remains the sina qua non of obtaining an accountancy qualification with all the chartered bodies" (1954, p.21). It is not surprising then, that the ICWA, brought in the idea of service under articles. It is hard to imagine how they envisaged the principal-pupil relation could possibly be sustained within an industrial setting, where both principal and pupil were employees. The bye-laws, however, contained detailed regulations regarding articled clerks, such as bye-law 54 which read:

"No member shall have in his service at the same period more than two articled clerks... " (IA, *1923 Year Book*, p.57). Articles were registered with the Institute and were recorded in the Executive Committee Minute Book (hereafter, ECB), the earliest being between A.S. Lees and L.Endall (IA, ECB 35, 13 January 1921). Some parents approached the Institute desiring articles for their sons (IA, ECB 57, 11 May 1921). However, no great number of them seem to have been registered and it does not appear that they were compulsory for students. This is hardly surprising as the Institute's members were spread thinly over the country and in many cases there would have been no member employed at the same company as the student. Indeed, none of the retired members whom I interviewed remembered anything about such a scheme. For example, although the Works Secretary, L.V. Kenwood, at Fort Dunlop in Birmingham was a fellow of the Institute, Mr Badgery, who worked there at the time he was a student member in the early 1920s, was not in any way his 'pupil' (Interview, Badgery). It may have been possible to set up a scheme of articled pupillage involving the independent 'cost consultants', but, as I have already noted they formed only 5% of the membership.

Stacey suggests that the use of this system by the ICWA is a matter of "considerable curiosity" and a "classic case of perpetuating the shibboleths of outworn tradition" (1954, p.100). What Stacey has missed, however, is the importance to the Institute's claim (at least in their own perceptions) to be a body of 'professional accountants' of such "tradition". This was one of the trappings which accompanied the claim. Accounting institutes, except the newer (and very much lesser) ones, had articled pupillage as one of their preconditions for membership, therefore the ICWA simply had to have it.

Examinations

The future of the Institute was seen to lie in establishing a system of examinations which would act as credentials for cost clerks to move into higher positions in the organisation. Summers Hunter described how there was, in large commercial offices, works and factories a:

> ... large body of clerks many of whom are engaged on the ascertainment of Costs, and in preparing data for the use of management... but they are clerks and clerks only. They start as office boys and they finish as clerks, head clerks, or senior clerks ... and there is an end of it.

He emphasized that things could be different, there was:

> ... no reason at all why these in an office such as I have tried to picture to you, should not be men of education and standing, and men deserving of a status such as they have not to-day [Inauguration meeting, North East Coast and District Branch of the ICWA, (reported in *The Cost Accountant*, November 1922, p.178)].

For their own credibility as a professional body it was important to the Institute that they got an examination system operating quickly. After an abortive attempt to hold examinations in June 1920, the first were held in December 1920. It is not clear how many sat the examination, but it was reported that 3 passed and 11 were given permission to sit again the subjects in which they failed (IA, CMB 69, 2 June 1920; ECB 41, 10 February 1921). The proportion of members gaining entry through the examination route, rather than through direct entry, gradually rose. Of the 139 members admitted in the year June 1921 to May 1922, only 6, or 4% of those had passed an examination. Of the 526 members listed in the *1923 Year Book* (IA) around 14% had done so through the examination route.

The examinations were found difficult by the students. Many had to work long hours and it seems that they probably had little chance to study for them (a number of the retired members whom I interviewed commented on the problems they faced). In October 1922 Mr Mackay, speaking on behalf of the Institute as Honorary Secretary of the Scottish Branch, said that up to that point in time only 48% of the candidates who had sat the examinations had passed them (*The Cost Accountant*, December 1922, p.229). Of the students registering with the Institute, most failed ever to become members. In 1919, 3 students registered, none of these qualified; in 1920, 53 students registered, 23 qualified; in 1921, 103 students were registered, only 26 qualified. All in all, in the period up to the end of 1925 over 600 students had registered, but it appears that only 28% ever qualified as members. Many dropped out appearing never even to have sat the examinations[5].

The constant dilemma between reducing the standard and increasing the membership, or retaining a moderately small but hopefully well qualified membership, seems to have been resolved in favour of the latter (IA, Stanley Berger). In justifying the process of closure of the professional body the Institute used the idea of the importance of their position in industry. The responsibility which their members were to bear in industry apparently made the passing of tough examinations essential, and the passing of those examinations indicated the suitability of that person for promotion to a high position. Thus the system of credentialling members and the claims for the social necessity of the techniques were linked in a circular relationship with one another.

The ICWA as a Professional Body

The early members of the ICWA modelled their attempt to close the occupation 'cost and works accountant', and create a new profession, around the attributes which they perceived professionals to have; in particular those of the ICAEW. Despite their position as employees, they perceived themselves as professional advisors, writing that:

> The principle aim of the Institute is to provide for the business community the professional cost accountant who can be considered quite as worthy of the confidences of the business community as the legal profession and Chartered Accountants are at present (*The Cost Accountant*, December 1922, p.217).

When the toast of 'kindred' or 'allied' institutes was made at the Second Annual Dinner, Howard Hazell (a vice-president of the ICWA), described them as the Institutes of Chartered Accountants and Secretaries, and "others who by their antiquity have acquired an authority and profundity of wisdom to which we can lay no claim. We are probably most closely allied to the Chartered Accountants" (*The Cost Accountant*, July 1921, pp.24-25). Curiously, however, at the Third Annual Dinner, the ICWA asked Captain H. Riall Sankey, President of the Institute of Mechanical Engineers, to propose the toast of 'kindred institutes'. He said:

> I am puzzled to know what the kindred societies are. If you say they are the Chartered Accountants, or the Institute of Secretaries, then I have no business to respond, but I would like to take a much larger view and say that the kindred societies are, for example, institutes like the Mechanical Engineers. If you say that, then the number is legion... (*The Cost Accountant*, March 1922, p.197).

A year later things had still not got any clearer it seems, for Howard Hazell, asked to make this toast again, rose to say that he "was not certain what constituted a kindred Institute to the Institute of Cost and Works Accountants"[6]. This confusion is indicative of the contradictions implicit in the ICWA's desire to model itself upon the independent professions whilst the majority of its members were employees engaged largely in office work. It is an issue which will be returned to in the next chapter when some wider aspects of the relationship between cost accounting and society are considered.

Distinguishing Cost Accountants from Cost Clerks and Engineers

The development of the ICWA brought into being a discourse about the role of the cost accountant in the factory. In particular the differences between the cost accountant, the cost clerk and the engineer, were discussed. As was noted in chapter 6, much of the debate over the status of this new professional body, which took place in *The Accountant* in 1919, was concerned with the issue of whether or not cost accountants were really just clerks, not *professional* accountants. The ICWA had felt obliged to try to distinguish cost clerks from cost accountants, in a letter to *The Accountant* published in May 1919, they wrote that "as an Audit Clerk is presumably in a preliminary stage to a professional accountant, so also a Cost Clerk is in the same relation to a Cost or Works Accountant" (17 March 1919, p.416).

The question of 'cost clerks' viz a viz 'cost accountants' was at the root of a discussion in 1922 and 1923, over the failure of candidates to pass the Institute's examinations. In an editorial in the October 1922 edition of *The Cost Accountant* this failure was discussed at length. The author wrote:

> Generally speaking, it might seem that the right type of student has not yet been attracted by this profession. In our opinion, cost accountancy is the most mistaken of all professions, as in many directions it is considered that any person who can accomplish a simple calculation is sufficiently competent to carry out those duties connected with Scientific Costing, and he is often looked upon as the "clerk" on the Works side. One has therefore not far to seek a solution to why so many candidates fail in the Institute Examinations. The profession offers, at the present time, far greater prospects than any other profession; and for the youth who has had and exceedingly good Secondary or better still, Public School education, there are unlimited opportunities (*The Cost Accountant*, October 1922, pp.129-130).

In the report on the 1923 examination similar points were made, the Examination Committee reporting that they were "afraid that the wrong type of candidate is coming forward ... "; candidates should be of such a:

> ... degree of education and experience as will enable them to uphold their important positions with dignity and ability...

Cost accountancy had suffered in the past:

> ... partly through the arbitrary selection of individuals to carry out an imperfectly understood function, partly through the lack of importance which had been attached to this profession, and which is expressed in the very low salaries which have been received ... (*The Cost Accountant*, October 1923, p.158).

The problems which the cost accountant faced now and would face to a greater degree in the future meant a need for "really well trained well educated men" and presupposed:

> ... an intelligence of a higher order than has been considered necessary in the past as the equipment of the "cost clerk". The Examination Committee have therefore set, and are continuing set, a high standard in their examinations and the syllabus (*The Cost Accountant*, October 1923, p.158).

The failure of candidates at the examinations, and the associated failure of students ever to become members was generally taken by the Institute as an indication of inadequate knowledge, intelligence, or preparation, on the part of the students. As one might expect there were few instances of the failure being blamed on the difficulty or inappropriateness of the examinations, or on the inadequacy of the courses and books available to them.

The relationship with engineers came up in the consideration of 'workshop experience'; something the Institute placed emphasis on the members having had. Some took this as far as wanting cost accountants to train as engineers for a period. In a lecture to the Birmingham Branch of the ICWA entitled "Workshop Experience and its value to the Cost Accountant", F. Beale-Grover expressed the view that students should begin with "engineering shop experience" and at "least two years of real work- five would be better"; the aspirant should apply himself "as assiduously as if he intended to be an engineer". He should "handle tools: hammer and chisel ... "; parents should not object to "the dirty condition he will get into" if "while getting dirty on the outside ... he stores his mind with knowledge and gains experience which no books can give, and knowledge is always power". Workshop experience was compared to the practical experience doctors had to gain through dissecting bodies and working in hospitals (*The Cost Accountant*, September 1923, pp.131- 134). It is interesting to note the apologetic tone with which the 'dirtiness' is mentioned- there is an implicit suggestion that it is merely a stage which the recruit must pass through, before reaching the clean office desk so often given greater status in Britain than the factory floor.

In an editorial in the October 1922 issue of *The Cost Accountant*, the link between engineering and costing was examined. The author gave the object as being "to correct the wrong impression which exists in some directions, regarding the Costing Profession, and to indicate the type of person who is best suited to this work". He described the "Costing

Profession" as in effect a combination of that of the engineer and that of the accountant, as he put it, such a person was an an "engineer-accountant". As a profession it offered to the youth with a "liking for Engineering, continual association with the technical side of the business ... " (p. 129). This editorial caused much controversy and the November correspondence column recorded "considerable exceptions" to this definition of a cost accountant as an "engineer-accountant". The author had to explain that he had not meant to imply that the "most suitable approach to Costing was to be gained through a thorough apprenticeship in engineering ... ". He said that he had been trying to make the point that "technical knowledge" was important for grappling with the "higher branches" of the work such as "the relationship of design to cost, or the presentation of a statement showing the relative cost efficiency of rival process methods ... " (*The Cost Accountant*, November 1922, p.165).

The need, which those organising the affairs of the Institute, perceived for members to have had 'workshop experience', was translated into an examination paper entitled 'workshop knowledge'. George Todman (the engineer on the Institute Executive) explained the rationality behind this examination:

> ... the Cost Accountant, to be of any use, must be in the position of the technical man and give results which he can vouch for as accurate because he does not need to rely of information supplied from outside which he is not in a position to prove (*The Cost Accountant*, July 1921, p.37).

The questions asked on this paper attempted to test both the candidates general workshop knowledge and his knowledge of the trade in which he was involved. Questions such as: "What do you understand by Tool Steel? Give its nature, properties and applications", were combined with ones such as: "Describe technically any process or part of a process of manufacture with which you are familiar" [IA, workshop knowledge paper, Intermediate Examination, December 1922, (*1923 Year Book* (IA), p.171)]. Mr Mann, who became an associate member of the ICWA in 1925, described the difficulties this examination caused by virtue of the stress it laid on the engineering trades, and because it "gave scope for practically anything". He wrote of how the candidates sympathised with each other after having sat this paper, and in particular with the indignant clerk from Rowntrees who asked how a man engaged in costing in the chocolate manufacture trade could possibly answer a question concerning the causes of faults in castings? Mr Mann noted that the relevant examiners report referred to the fact that only one of the candidates knew anything at all about Parsons turbines. He suspected the candidate was actually himself. He had happened, by pure chance, to read about them in an advertisment for an encyclopaedia sent to his father the week before the examination. He was thus enabled to answer a question obviously quite outside the knowledge of the average examinee (personal correspondance).

In the opinion of the Beale-Grover it was "theoretical students" who had trouble with this paper. He insisted that this knowledge was important, and that it was the "hub upon which the wheel turns" (an interesting mechanical metaphor), when a man applied for a position as a cost accountant "the practical training is the factor which carries a great weight in his favour" (*The Cost Accountant*, September 1923, p.133).

Whether an examination on 'workshop knowledge' could really test 'practical experience' is a moot point and one which the Institute seems to have appreciated. The subject of "qualified cost clerks" came up at a number of Executive meetings in 1921. The point at issue seems to have been what the Institute would do if mere 'cost clerks' passed the examinations- individuals who had proved their knowledge to be adequate but with little work experience other than processing and copying figures. The idea of making the entire preliminary examination (at that time consisting of mathematics, mechanical knowledge, the writing of an English essay, book-keeping and an optional modern language) a "technical examination" was proposed, but ultimately rejected. Whilst the practical experience of the aspirant cost clerk was at the discretion of his employer, the Institute could scarcely refuse to admit clerks who were trying to better themselves by passing the examinations. The problem was clearly illustrated in the case of H.S. Sperry. He passed the Intermediate Examination in June 1922, and was thus eligible to be considered for associate membership. On his application form, however, the answers given to the questions asked of the referees concerning 'practical experience' seem to have been answered in a rather unsatisfactory way. They were, it will be recalled:

> Has the applicant to your *definite* knowledge had *practical experience* in the following subjects?
> (a) Cost and Works Accounting
> (b) Workshop practice?
> (c) Factory Organisation?

Two of the three referees gave no answer to parts (b) and (c), his current employer answered 'No' to these questions. He was employed as a 'chief cost clerk', he wrote that:

> ... my only technical knowledge and workshop experience has been gained in my employers' works where my duties take me constantly to the shops and as a cadet pilot during the latter part of the war (IA, Sperry, personal file).

This experience must have been considered adequate for he was admitted as an associate.

Conclusion

The Institute of Cost and Works Accountants was engaged on what can be termed [following Larson (1977)] a 'project' of professionalisation, with the aim of achieving the same status and monetary rewards as the chartered accountants who in turn had been influenced by the legal profession in their own process of professionalisation (Macdonald, 1984). They looked forward, as one member wrote in 1922:

> ... to the day when every large firm will employ its own Cost Accountant and every small firm will be able to find a consultant cost accountant of unimpeachable integrity and first-rate ability and employ them with the same regularity as they now employ Chartered Accountants to audit their accounts (*The Cost Accountant*, December 1922, p.235).

It was an ambitious project inevitably tempered by the practicalities of the situation in which they found themselves. For example, whilst that most essential item, examinations, were set up, many members continued to be admitted on the basis of their application form and references; by 1923 only 14% of the current members had entered through the examination route. Training contracts (articles) were registered between members and students, however, the crucial issue of how such a system could operate in a situation where both were employed by a third party, seems to have been ignored.

Dingwall writes of how the appearance of an occupation may involve not only the splitting off of a group of specialised members within an existing occupation (fission), but also the bringing together of individuals who had not previously been associated, under a common label (fusion) (1983, p.619). The formation of the ICWA seems to have involved 'fusion' to a far greater extent than 'fission'. When the ICWA was first formed the founder members apparently found themselves 'deluged' with applications from many sectors of the industrial community, including works managers and estimators. Through an ongoing process of selection of members and refinement of the entry requirements, accompanied by *self-selection* on the part of those applying (presumably deciding that joining would be of benefit to them), the ICWA gradually took on a more definite shape as an association. An analysis of the members included in the *1923 Year Book* (IA), revealed that the job titles of many of them (43%), did not automatically link them with costing at all. Whilst it is difficult to interpret this finding in any definite way, I would suggest that this was due to the fact that in many works cost accounting itself was carried out by individuals with other responsibilities (for example, being 'Secretary'). The occupational specialisation 'cost accountant' was perhaps not yet recognised by all employers, particularly the smaller ones. One point is clear, the appearance of the ICWA certainly did not result from a 'fission' of existing bodies of accountants, for only 8% were members of the chartered or incorporated bodies. Interestingly, more (11%) were members of the Chartered Institute of Secretaries. On a personal level, my interviews with retired members indicated that (with the exception of those working in very large businesses where cost accounting was well established) becoming students or members of the ICWA helped them to understand what a cost accountant *was* in terms of role and status.

In the process of the Institute's growth, a definition of the role of a 'cost and works accountant' and the knowledge and technical skills involved, occured. This can be illustrated by the change in the questions asked of the referees of candidates applying for membership. In 1919, referees were simply asked if the candidate had 'practical experience' and was a 'fit and proper person'. By 1921, they were being asked very specific questions about the candidates experience and knowledge. In asking if candidates had a knowledge of mathematics, economics and book-keeping & accounts, the ICWA were both addressing the question of the knowledge of the individual candidate *and* setting forth a public statement to candidates and employers of what knowledge it was that a cost and works accountant should possess (employers were usually asked to be referees). Similarly, the questions asked concerning practical experience both addressed that of the individual applicant *and* set forth a statement that a cost and works accountant was somebody who had had not only suitable accounting experience, but also understood 'workshop practice' and 'factory organisation' from a practical point of view.

To the cost accountants whom I interviewed, who joined the ICWA as members or as students in the 1920s, getting involved with the Institute became part of their own ambition for social advancement. They did not come from families with the resources to support them whilst they trained to become chartered or incorporated accountants. They learnt commercial skills such as book-keeping at evening-classes and they studied for the Institute's examinations through postal courses, which they had to pay for. Many had to work long hours and most of their spare time had to be taken up with study for the examinations if they were to succeed. They were personally striving to be better than the mere 'clerk'. Given this, it is ironic that the Institute wrote in *The Cost Accountant* that for "the youth who has an exceedingly good Secondary, or better still *Public School* education (ie. in the British context a private one), there are unlimited opportunities" in the profession (October 1922, p.129-130). Few of their members had been educated in public schools; the evidence I have suggests that they came from lower middle class and upper working class backgrounds. They believed in personal betterment through hard work and diligent study. In Britain, however, a country where a public school education in the Classics was to be envied, and to be a 'gentleman' an ideal (Wiener, 1981), it is perhaps not surprising to find such statements as part of the rhetoric of a group of people aspiring to be 'professional'.

NOTES

(1) It is interesting to briefly examine the biographical details of the most active members:

Dick Ryall:

When first involved with the ICWA was working for A.W. Lyon. & Co. Ltd. as a cost accountant (IA, Lewton 14; *1923 Year Book*).
In 1920 set up in business with Claude Todman (see above). After leaving Todman Ryall described himself as a 'consulting cost accountant' (IA, *1923 Year Book*).

Claude Todman:

When first in contact with the Institute was working as an electrical engineer at A.W.Lyon & Co. Ltd. (IA, Lewton 14). He was an associate member of the Institute of Electrical Engineers and the Institute of Mechanical Engineers.
In 1923 he was described as a managing director of Todman Ryall (IA, *1923 Year Book*).

George Russell:

A member of the London Association of Accountants. At the end of the war he was working as an accountant at Gwynnes Ltd, a firm which appears to have been involved in the manufacture of aircraft (IA, Lewton 1). By 1923 he was holding the post of chief works accountant at this company (IA, *1923 Year Book*).

Albert Williamson:

In 1923 he was Secretary and Organiser to the Federation of Master Printers Costing Committee (IA, *1923 Year Book*).

Bill Hudspith:

In 1919 he was working for Muntz Metal Co., in Birmingham. By 1923 was chief accountant at Crosse & Blackwell in Burton on Trent (IA, CMB 25, 9 September 1919; *1923 Year Book*).

Donald Moran:

Chief cost accountant at Peek Frean & Co. Ltd., in 1923 (IA, *1923 Year Book*).

R.H. Wilson:

A chartered accountant; in 1923 was costs manager at Huntley and Palmers Ltd (IA, *1923 Year Book*).

Reginald Townsend:

A chartered accountant; he was working at the Royal Arsenals in 1919. By 1923 had been promoted to the position of Advisor on Costs to Director-General of Factories, at the War Office, Royal Ordnance Factories (IA, Lewton 1; *1923 Year Book*).

Roland Dunkerley:

In 1919 he was working at Messrs Hans Renold Ltd in in Manchester. By 1923 he had moved to be Works Accountant at Metropolitan Vickers Electrical Co. Ltd. (IA, 9 September 1919; *1923 Year Book*).

C.W. Charlesworth:

He was working as Commercial Secretary to the County Borough of Wolverhampton Electricity Supply Department in 1923 (IA, *1923 Year Book*).

(2) It seems from later events that at least part of his interest was caused by a desire for his accountancy school to become official tutors for the ICWA exams. He did not obtain this objective.

(3) 'He' is used in this passage in accordance with the wording on the form. Women were not excluded from membership, however the *1923 Year Book* (IA) contains the names of only two women, out of a total membership of 526.

(4) Another feature worth noting is that of the 10 government employees all but 2 worked in London, several worked for the War Office. The 5 lecturers included 3 from The School of Accountancy and 1 from Metropolitan College; these institutions offered courses by post for students of the ICWA (the main source of instruction for the examinations).

(5) The analyses of members and examination pass rates in this and the previous paragraph, were prepared from the examination results given in the ECB, CMB and *The Cost Accountant*; the Register of Members and the Register of Students (IA).

(6) Interestingly, he notes how he turned to a guide to the commerce and industry of London entitled "Kelly's Business Directory", only to discover that the ICWA was classified with funeral workers, teachers of dancing, a gramophone society, the Stage Society, and even the "Advertising Clubs of the World". A classification with which, hardly surprisingly, he disagreed (*The Cost Accountant*, August 1924, p.78).

CHAPTER 7

COST ACCOUNTING AND SOCIETY

> It is evident that Cost and Works Accountants have a vast amount of work before them. The field of their labours comprises the whole industrial world ...
>
> The Executive of the ICWA, March 1922.

Introduction

The focus of the previous chapter was very much 'inwards'- upon the ICWA's attempt to establish themselves as a professional accounting association, and the process of definition of the role of the cost accountant that this began to bring with it. There is a necessity now, however, to broaden the discussion to look at some issues concerning the relationship of this aspirant professional body and the techniques it desired to monopolise, to their wider social, political and industrial context.

The first aspect to be examined is the way in which the status of 'the truth' was claimed for cost accounting, and how this entered into the ICWA's presentation to the world of the role and status of the cost accountant. The second is the support which the ICWA received from prominent industrialists- this was a social approbation which seems to have been very important to the ICWA's acceptance (if limited), as a reputable organisation. The reasons for it are difficult to fathom, but interesting connections can be made with the general social and industrial context. The third aspect looked at is that of the division of labour within the bureaucracy of the office, one of whose products in Britain was professional associations, such as the the ICWA, for those working in the office. Fourthly, the reactions of the chartered accountants to cost accountancy is examined, and fifthly, and finally, the general relationship between the use of cost accounting and the position in society of the members of the ICWA, is related to the industrial context of Britain in the early 1920s.

Depoliticising Cost Accounting: The 'True Facts', Science and Standardisation

During these years of the 'coming into the light' of cost accounting and its progressive institutionalisation and professionalisation, a discourse was developing around it which claimed for it the status of 'science' and that it gave 'the facts'. Concomitantly cost accountants were being presented as the professional collectors and processors of these facts.

The first edition of the book *Factory Accounts* by Garcke and Fells, published in 1887 (and discussed in Chapter 3), contained a wide variety of subject matter. From such topics as the "law of fire and boiler insurance", the "rating of factories" and a "summary of Factory and Workshop Acts" to the "conflict of Capital and Labour" and details of financial schemes for the co-operative partnership of employers and employed. However by the time of the seventh edition of the book, published in 1922, the contents had become much more narrowly restricted to ones of a type which would not be considered inappropriate in a costing text today. In the Foreword it was stated:

> ... and while hitherto it has seemed appropriate to make some references to economic and social questions in relation to the remuneration of labour and allocation of profits, we are of the opinion that those questions have now become of such importance, and they are so interwoven with social and political conditions and considerations, that they do not admit of being dealt with except at greater length than would be practicable, and in a more controversial spirit than would be desirable in a technical work (1922, p.iv).

Such a change illustrates two processes; firstly, the coming into being of a subject matter with defined boundaries to its content - it had become clearer precisely what factory accounting *was* to be and how it was to differ from other aspects of management such as the remuneration of labour; secondly, a process of depoliticisation whereby the 'technical' was clearly distinguished from the 'political'.

From the vantage point of 'the technical' the ICWA could comment on current industrial problems. When J.R. Clynes, President of the National Federation of General Workers (and soon to narrowly lose the Labour Party Leadership election to Ramsey MacDonald), accused employers of taking advantage of the workers' difficult position to enforce wage reductions which were not justified, the Editor wrote that:

> While it is not the desire of this Magazine to take sides between Labour and Capital, we cannot but feel that, at a time when the capture of the world's markets depends on cheap production, the Labour representatives are sadly mistaken in giving utterence to remarks which tend to conceal the economic necessity for wage reductions (*The Cost Accountant*, August 1922, pp.102-103).

A suggestion had been put forward that a law should be passed that would make it a requirement that Public Companies ballot their shareholders before presenting a demand for a reduction of the wages of their employees. The ICWA commented:

> The object of the proposal is obviously delay, and an appeal to popular prejudice rather than fact, which alone can govern the division of the surplus between Cost and Selling price. the coming of Scientific Costing to each industry would be, we feel certain, the biggest step forward yet made towards the removal of the distrust which complicates the relations of Capital and Labour (*The Cost Accountant*, September, 1922, p.112).

Thus the claim to be presenting the "economic facts of life" (Garcke & Fells, 1922, p.v) and the "true cost" (*The Cost Accountant*, March 1922, p.179) enabled the Institute not only to comment from a technical perspective on current problems but also to suggest that the problems *themselves* could disappear if the rationality of cost accounting was applied to them.

The political realm of rights and justice was not to be part of the discourse of cost accounting- a discourse in which only the technical was legitimate. Even to invite a political speaker to address an Institute meeting was not considered legitimate. When the same J.R. Clynes was invited to the Manchester meeting the Executive were furious and the Secretary was instructed to inform the Secretary of the Manchester Branch that he was not considered "a suitable speaker or chairman" and to enquire whether the "branch would like a professional lecturer instead of a somewhat ornamental one" (IA, EMB 224-225, 12 October 1923). They suggested that:

> ... the following gentlemen be approached viz Sir Ed. Stockton, Mr Austin Hopkinson, Sir Chas Macara, Mr Lee (or another Director of Messrs Tootal Broadhurst), Mr McConnell (Chairman of Fine Spinners), Mr Loris Mather (Chairman, Messrs Mather & Platt) and that if the Branch Committee has not the time to interview one or more of these gentlemen a representative will be sent from Head Office for the purpose (ibid.).

Furthermore, when a lecture was given by a "trade union member of the Institute" entitled "The Inter-relation of Economics and Costing" the Magazine Committee refused to publish it in *The Cost Accountant* (it was usual to publish lectures) on account of its "strong political tone", which "surprised" them, and commented that: "The article is of such a character that the conditions under which it was delivered seems to warrant enquiry" (IA, EMB 239, 14 November 1923).

The raison d'être of the ICWA was, by the beginning of 1922, being described as the advance of *scientific* costing. At the Institute's first conference held in February of that year, the topic for discussion was 'The Necessity for Scientific Costing'. The Executive told, in their paper to the conference, how the urgent need during the war for securing from all available resources the maximum output of war material at a minimum of cost had led to businessmen recognising "the necessity for Scientific Costing" (*The Cost Accountant*, March 1922, p.179). The implicit comparison was to the unsystematic methods largely prevalent before the war and still existing in many industries. In an Editorial in *The Cost Accountant*, "scientific knowledge" was described as "knowledge reduced to system" and something which "progressed from generalisation to generalisation". The editors reflected that:

> ... costing is hailed as a science, and we believe costing, per se, is scientific. But where are its generalisations; in fact is there any single generalisation proved to be true and accepted by all? Undoubtedly the absence of accepted definition is due to the infancy of the science ... (January 1922, p.135).

Research work was the necessary means to achieve a "theory of scientific costs" (ibid.). The problem was seen as one of establishing accepted definitions of costing terms and the members of the Institute were requested to include "the study and definition of Costing terms" in their 1922 New Year resolutions (ibid., p.136). The origins of this use of the word 'scientific' cannot be known with any certainty but it is probable that scientific management was a major influence in creating this form of discussion, through its appearance in the 'reconstruction' plans discussed earlier. In the Editorial mentioned above, the "theory of scientific management" was described as "of recent growth" and that here "knowledge" had been "reduced to system" and it had been "possible to assign specific meanings to words such a Planning, Progress, Schedule time, Standard task, Time and Motion Study, Fatigue, Welfare Work etcetera ...". Costing was "included in the scheme of organisation" but adequate consideration did "not appear to have been given to the word ... " (ibid., p.135).

However not everyone at the Institute's conference was happy with the use by the Executive of the phrase 'scientific costing'. Mr. Stelling FCWA, a cost consultant, complained that "we have no definition" and remarked:

> I personally feel rather afraid that if we adopt that phrase we shall be open to the same amount of criticism, misunderstanding, and misrepresentation that the early exponents of scientific management were subjected to, and I suggest standardised costing would be more suitable to use than this phrase scientific costing, which I feel cannot define myself (*The Cost Accountant*, March 1922, p.187).

This issue of standardised costing which Mr Stelling raises was one which created much discussion in the ICWA at this period. At its simplest, when people referred to 'standardisation' they were referring to the standardisation of costing terminology. Often, however, what was being discussed was what is more generally known now as 'uniform costing', but then sometimes called 'trade costing'. This involves standardisation for whole industries. The Executive gave the example of the printing industry and wrote that it should proceed along the lines of:

> (1) Definition of terms
> (2) Classification of expenses
> (3) Application of agreed principles
> (4) Adoption of uniform method
>
> This would facilitate an exact comparison of costs and estimates, items by item, between the various units in industry with the object of treating and removing differences as to selling prices (*The Cost Accountant*, March 1922, p.181).

In an Editorial entitled 'Standard Costing' accompanying the publishing of a verbatim report of the conference, the Editors remarked that it was necessary "for Trade Associations to apply the fundamental principles of costing in the establishment of standardised costing in their respective industries". Emphasis must be "given to the phrase fundamental principles" for it is by these that "true progress will be made ...". There are "certain great truths that are applicable to costing in all trades ..." (*The Cost Accountant*, March 1922, p.175).

Both 'scientific' costing in general and 'standardised' costing as just described, were seen as having a contribution to play in the solution of current industrial problems. At the conference it was suggested that costing data today "should be used in combating pernicious propaganda among the industrial classes" (ibid., p.186). If "the true facts" were shown to the employees "in a way they can appreciate and understand in their own light", in particular the problem of eliminating waste, they would be:

> ... honest enough to come along with us and say, "we are with you. We will do our part in helping you to get your costs down" ... they will come together, either through their shop stewards or some other organisation, and determine to bring it down (ibid., p.190).

The workers had to be shown the "overhead expenses which have actually to be carried by the men on their backs, on their wages, before the product can be sold ..." (ibid.). Standardised costing for an industry would not only benefit that industry, it was declared, but it "was essential from a public point of view" that such systems were developed for as many industries as possible as they would enable "adjustments between sections of the community to be made in equity". A "brighter day" would dawn for the community when they could:

> ... turn with confidence to a statement of costs conceived on true principles, and presented in a form which leaves no doubt of the significance of each item. The workman will lose his distrust, and with that gone, many of our present difficulties will likewise disappear ... (*The Cost Accountant*, March 1922, p.175).

Hazell wrote that if all industries had such schemes they would be doing " a service to their trade and a service to their country" (*The Cost Accountant*, March 1922, p.188). These examples, which are typical of the form of arguments used, illustrate a point made earlier, that not only was this accounting being regarded as simply a technical matter but also something which could help to solve the problems themselves.

These were some of the benefits the Institute claimed for the use of standardised costing in industry. The benefits to the recently formed Institute itself of this proposed 'standardisation' should not be ignored however. Taking first the benefits of standardising costing terminology, Larson writes of the benefits to the project of professionalisation undertaken by the members and supporters of a new professional body of a knowledge base which is standardised (1977, Chap. 4). If costing terminology was standardised in a way laid down by the ICWA it would greatly enhance the legitimacy of the Institute's position; in particular its claims to be the only professional accounting body which properly catered for cost accountants. In this way it could even possibly help the ICWA in the process of 'closing' the occupation to outsiders; of making the members of the ICWA the only ones acceptable for the carrying out of certain jobs- even ultimately the only ones allowed by law to carry out these tasks. This is a process by which, as Max Weber describes, organised groups of individuals come to monopolise particular economic opportunities (Weber, 1978, pp.339-343). It could also bring together the members of the Institute, who came from diverse backgrounds and had very different work experiences, under a single banner and give them a sense of unity and common purpose as they introduced this standard terminology into the costing systems in the businesses in which they worked. These potential benefits did not go unnoticed. In a Editorial in the journal it was noted that:

> By a 'standard' is implied that 'which is authoritatively established by rule', and it is on this basis that this Institute can make its claim, both as regards its own prestige and the imperative necessity of costing to the commerce of the Empire (*The Cost Accountant*, March 1922, p. 174).

The benefits to the social standing of members could be extended if standardised costing systems, as well as terminology, were widely introduced in industry; in particular if wages disputes in each industry came to be regularly settled by reference to costs in that industry. In this regard the Executive wrote:

> The personal reputation of the Cost Accountant who acts as a Statistical Officer to any particular industry may well be an important factor in retaining the confidence of both sides in such disputes. The possibility of such a condition of affairs opens up a prospect in which the profession of Cost and Works Accountant may become one of considerable dignity as well as of

inestimable value to the community generally (*The Cost Accountant*, March 1922, p.181-182).

Within the ICWA the spirit of reconstruction was clearly visible in the first few years as they proselytized the benefits of scientific and standardised costing systems. Systems which would give 'the whole truth' about production and would help to make Britain an efficient nation. The country was being brought to a standstill by strikes, and there was a sudden trade depression. It was cost accounting which would bring 'the economic facts of life' to bear on these political and industrial problems. If workers in depressed trades could be brought to understand the parlous nature of their industries' position surely they would accept wage cuts without further trouble. As Dickens' Victorian schoolmaster, Mr Gradgrind said, "facts alone are wanted in life" (1854, p.1) and the particular facts required by Britons were apparently cost accounting facts.

Influential Industrialists

The early activists in the Institute perceived it as important to obtain influential support for their project. On September 9th, 1919, they resolved that Lord Weir should become the first President, and in the event of his refusal Sir Robert Hadfield and Lord Leverhulme were to be invited (IA, CMB 24, 9 September 1919). It appears that Lord Weir accepted the position in October, however in November they wrote back to him "inviting him to reconsider his decision to accept the presidency, with a request that he would receive a deputation"[1] (IA, CMB 29, 7 October 1919; CMB 32, 4 November 1919). On December 2nd it was reported that Lord Leverhulme had accepted the position (IA, CMB 25, 2 December 1919).

By December 2nd they had invited, and obtained the support of, both as honorary members and as vice-presidents; Sir Robert Hadfield D.Sc., FRS., Sir Charles Wright Macara, Sir Herbert Austin KBE, Sir Gerald Muntz and Neville Gwynne. These men, particularly Hadfield, Macara and Austin, were prominent industrialists whose names frequently appeared in the Press[2]. Later others, such as Seebohm Rowntree, joined them. They actively supported the new body and the meetings which they chaired, or spoke at, provided a way of attracting new members, a forum for new members to meet one another and a means of bringing to the attention of businessmen the importance of costing. What they seem to have shared at this period was enthusiastic support for reconstruction and a belief that cost accounting was an important element in the efficient organisation of production, albeit in their own very idiosyncratic ways.

Lord Leverhulme was the most active: H.G. Jenkins may not have been overstating when he declared that "Lord Leverhulme's position in Industry has guaranteed us support ... " (*The Cost Accountant*, December 1922, pp.216-217). Sir Harry Brittain KBE., MP., remarked: "I cannot imagine any society at the head of which is Lord Leverhulme failing to get what it attempts to achieve" (*The Cost Accountant*, April 1923, p.389), and Mr. H.W. Allingham that:

> In fact, I think that for a young Institute just starting in its life, to have been successful in persuading so well-known a man as Lord Leverhulme to take on the position that he did when the Institute was unknown, when its capabilities were unknown, was a feather in the Institute's cap (*The Cost Accountant*, July 1921, p.28).

There was a "crowded attendance" when he gave an address in the Memorial Hall in central Manchester under the auspices of the ICWA. He entitled it "Human Factor Influences on Costs" and it was received with "loud cheers". The Lord Mayor attended to introduce "our greatest business man" and amongst those present were the President of the Manchester Chamber of Commerce, the President of the Manchester Engineering Trades Employers Federation and the President of the Manchester Society of Chartered Accountants (*The Cost Accountant*, December 1922, p.212).

The question of why these industrialists were so enthusiastic in their support of the ICWA in these early years is one which can never be answered with certainty but it is interesting to consider some of the circumstances surrounding it. There were a number of current problems which industrialists faced which the further development of costing could appear to be able help them with. Firstly, in the period directly after the war when prices were fluctuating wildly industrialists could imagine a sophisticated costing system being able to help them with production and pricing decisions. Secondly, in the recession which began in late 1920 many companies found it hard to remain profitable, even to stay in business. A highly developed costing system could be seen as enabling a company to locate precisely where in the business profits and losses were being made and hence rationalise operations successfully.

Thirdly, there was continuing government interference with the pricing of goods. The latter point had caused Lord Leverhulme great problems. Lever Bros. had such control of the soap industry that it was said that they could fix prices to suit themselves. In 1920, in response, the Government set up a sub-committee of the Standing Committee on Trusts to look into the matter under the chairmanship of Sir William Beveridge. Leverhulme conducted his own defence, emphasising the complexity of calculating costs and profits in a time when all prices were fluctuating and explaining the necessity of using up stocks bought at heavy costs. The Committee however were bound by their terms of reference to examine the short term only and ordered that the soap be reduced in price, best household soap to be reduced from 11d to 4d per pound (Wilson 1954, Vol.1, p.248).

Fourthly, there is the interest which they must surely have had in their accountants and clerks being professionals- members of a social group which supported owners and managers- not unionists. Many cost accountants had access to priviledged and confidential information, and it could cause great problems for manufacturers if this information was leaked indiscriminantly to the trade unions. Goodrich writes of how, amongst workers, there was a desire to know what profits employers were making but as a trade union leader had said to him, the employers would discuss anything with them "except perhaps costing and profits". Goodrich described it as a "keenly felt frontier of control" (1920, p.249). Speaking at the ICWA Annual Dinner in January 1921, Sir Herbert Austin gave a speech in which he gave two points of advice to the new Institute, the first of them being that:

> I really do hope that the Institute will keep away from its operations and from its work any trade union influence of any kind whatever: that you will endeavour to make your Institute not an Institute which collectively is out simply to benefit the members as a body ... that you will not allow yourselves, because you call yourselves 'Works Accountants', you will not allow your Institute to be subject to any influences of that character (*The Cost Accountant*, July 1921, pp.22-23).

As noted earlier this was a period when the unions had more members than ever before. Manufacturers were worrying over the possibility that their ownership and control of industry would be removed from them either suddenly and forceably, or through gradual change of the type which the Guild Socialists supported. Lockwood's research into the history of five of the major clerical unions indicated that the three of these dealing with clerks employed in commerce and industry (and not local or national government) show a peak in their membership levels around 1920- levels not to be achieved again until after the Second World War (1958, p.140). The unionisation of clerks was a threat that manufacturers could not ignore- for it brought into question the whole structure of authority in their businesses-especially if there was co-operation between the workers on the shop floor and those in the office. Although some employers would appear, at this period, to have supported the notion of sharing information with the workers as part of 'joint control', Child, in his study of British management thought, suggests that they were paying little more than lip-service to it (1969, pp.47-48).

It is interesting to note that the first real wave of industrial trouble which Lord Leverhulme experienced at Port Sunlight (his famous industrial 'village' where housing and other social facilities were provided as well as work) came just after the war and was due to disputes involving clerks. One of these disputes concerning office staff went to arbitration but another caused a strike: some of the clerks working at Port Sunlight were members of the National Warehouse and General Workers Union, others members of the Liverpool Shipping Guild. The Union members came out on strike because their right to negotiate on behalf of all clerks was not accepted by Lord Leverhulme or the Guild (Jolly, 1976, pp.178-179).

The Division of Labour in the Office

The 1921 census revealed another huge jump in the growth of clerks. Whereas in 1911 there were 477,535 "commercial and business clerks" (1911 Census, Summary Tables, p.274); by 1921 there were 997,729 under a wider category XXV111, "Clerks and Draughtsmen (not civil service or local authority)". The sub-headings under this were as follows:

<u>XXV111</u>

930 Company Secretaries and Registrars
931 Heads and Managers of Commercial Office Departments
932 Draughtsmen
933 Costing and Estimating Clerks

There were 19,433 'costing and estimating clerks', and 17,268 'heads and managers of commercial office departments'. The majority, namely 924,883, were in the category 'other clerks'(1921 Census, Occupational Tables, p.21).

It thus appears that there was a big increase in the number of clerks from 1911 to 1921, although the changing census classifications make comparisons uncertain. What is certain is that by 1921 the existence of a specialised occupation of costing or estimating clerk was *officially* recognised[3]. An analysis, by industry, of these 'costing and estimating clerks' revealed that most worked in engineering and basic manufacturing industry (this is given in full in the Appendix). Albeit indirectly, these statistics give some indication of the growth of bureaucracy in organisations and, as part of this, growth in the creation of cost accounting systems. The introduction of a "more scientific classification of both occupations and industries" (ibid., Industry Tables, p.3), in 1921, had brought official recognition of the division of labour which had occured in the office.

As the number of clerks grew, the work of the office was reorganised and divided up into tasks in a systematic manner. Separate departments were created for the various different functions identified. In other words, the work was socially rationalized; this generally occured before machinery was introduced on a large scale (Mills, 1956, p.192). One of the results of the process of division of labour, which has occured in the office as well as the factory, is the creation of a hierarchy of status and of remuneration. It was no longer a question of there being a few clerks assisting the owner with the administration. This division of labour led gradually to the demotion of the occupational category 'clerk', as specialists such as 'office manager' and 'cost accountant' emerged. On the Registrar-General's scale of social classes, of which there were five at this time (the criteria for these being levels of training and skill, education, professional qualifications, whether work is manual or non-manual and, to some extent, the assumed social status and accompanying lifestyle of those in the occupation), clerks were allocated to the highest class, class I, in 1911; in 1921 they were demoted to social class II, and in 1931 they fell again- to be placed in class III where they now remain (Hakim, 1980, p.566).

In the second two decades of this century a distinct managerial stratum was developing. The new categories in the 1921 census are one pointer to this. Another is the foundation of specialized institutes aimed at a specifically managerial membership. Each concerned with one or more of the various aspects of industrial administration (Child,

1969, p.15). The foundation of the more prominent management institutes was as follows:

1911 Sales Managers' Association

1913 Welfare Workers Association (This was at first strictly speaking not a 'management' institute; after the First World War, however, it became increasingly identified with management and in 1931 adopted the title 'Institute of Labour Management'.)

1915 Office Managers' Association

1919 Institute of Cost and Works Accountants

1920 Institute of Industrial Administration

1931 Works Managers' Association

Source: Child, 1969, p.16

The increasing division of labour in the office encouraged the employment of women. They could be paid less than men and the deskilled tasks which they were given could be taught to them quickly. The employment of women as clerks was accelerated by the war, they were urged to take over their brother's or husband's job whilst he was away fighting (*The Times*, 30 October 1915, p.5). In July 1914 there were 33,000 women clerks working in industry, by 1918 there were 102,000 (Stevenson, 1984, p.83). Despite the return of many of them to the home after the war some did stay in clerical employment, particularly in the lower grades (ibid. p.114).

Analysis of the 1921 census figures for 'costing and estimating' clerks revealed that 17% of them were women (*The Cost Accountant*, September 1925, p.94). Less than 0.4% of the members of the ICWA were women, precisely 2 out of the 526 listed in the *1923 Year Book* (IA). This suggests that the emergence of the ICWA was not only a part of the social stratification of the division of labour in the office but at the same time a gender based stratification was occuring. Women were beginning to perform many of the poorly paid and repetitive office tasks, whilst men were finding that the acquisition of educational credentials was necessary for their advancement within the hierarchy of the office.

The Chartered Accountants and Costing

Although the year following the end of the war had been a difficult one for the old hierarchy at the ICAEW, it was soon forgotten. The Council made small 'not very adventurous' changes in its procedures, cost accounting officially became part of the examination syllabus (it was examined in the Final under the heading 'Advanced Bookkeeping and Accountancy, including Costing and Taxation (Two Papers)' (reported in *The Accountant*, 9 October 1920, pp.370-371). The movement for reform was virtually 'laid to rest' as the feverish atmosphere of 1919 dissipated. The 1920 Annual General Meeting was a very tame affair in comparison (reported in *The Accountant*, 8 May 1920, pp.540-550), and by 1921 the usual topics, such as 'grants to students' societies', returned to dominate the proceedings (reported in *The Accountant*, 7 May 1921, pp.568-578).

The columns of *The Accountant* continued to contain articles on cost accounting, but it was a trickle compared to the flood at the end of the War. Articles as potentially revolutionary (in accounting circles) as "The Workers Interest in Costing" (discussed earlier) seemed an enigma by 1922. Correspondence in *The Accountant* continued the debate over the status of the members of the ICWA, a common attitude expressed being that:

> In most cases the "cost accountant" is the pre-war "works book-keeper" or "works cashier", and it is my contention that because this official is honoured with a new title he is not, as he claims, endowed with the sole right of advising businessmen on costing" (*The Accountant*, 5 August 1922, p.209).

Others thought the existence of such a debate unfortunate. E.T. Elbourne (whose book was discussed in Chapter 4) felt that the administrator, the cost accountant and the financial accountant should co-operate to fulfil the needs of industry and their efforts should not be viewed as competitive. He wrote: "we do not want to see imported into this sphere the trade union problem of "demarcation", with its many acrimonious disputes" (*The Accountant*, July 22 1922, p.151). At the official level opposition continued. The ICAEW successfully prevented the ICWA from obtaining the prestige of a Royal Charter, arguing that "such persons are not employed in professional work but in the service of traders" (*The Accountant*, 5 May 1923, p.683); such persons were the "technicians of industry" suggested The

Incorporated Accountants at their 1923 Autumnal Conference (reported in *The Cost Accountant*, November 1923, p.181).

Chartered and incorporated accountants interested in costing were to have to work independently, without a great deal of institutional support from their respective professional bodies. Some were extremely successful, such as Webster Jenkinson, who reorganised the ailing Vickers company (Scott, 1962, pp.156-159), and D'Arcy Cooper, who took over the chairmanship of Lever Bros. from the first Lord Leverhulme (Wilson, 1954, Vol.2, p.297). Not, however, until the post 1945 era was an accountant employed in industry, as opposed to being self-employed, permitted to sit on the governing board of the ICAEW (Locke, 1984, p.123). Ironically, given their attitude to the ICWA, it was these professional bodies that the ICWA desired to imitate-even to the extent of attempting to find out how they arranged the tables at their Annual Dinners in order to do the right thing themselves.

Returning to 'business as usual'

The acute industrial unrest which followed the war died away without bringing the reconstruction of society or the rationalisation of industry; by 1922 the government's reconstruction programme was almost totally forgotten (Johnson, 1968, p.3; Mowat, 1955, p.43). The old idea that reducing taxation would solve Britain's economic problems resurfaced. Public economy became an important consideration and an anti-waste campaign was begun against 'squandermania' and 'Dilly' and 'Dally', the two mythical idle civil servants (Taylor, 1970, p.240). It was largely to be left to businessmen to 'reconstruct' Britain[4].

By the end of 1920 many workers were worse off, in terms of real wages, than they had been before the war. One result of this was that the attention of the trade unions was turned away from the long-range objectives of nationalisation and workers' control and towards short-range demands for wage increases (Mowat, 1955, pp.27-28). Concomitantly, there was no longer discussion of the management techniques, such as cost accounting, which the workers would use to organise industry in their own interest. The year 1920 marked the end of an era for the Labour Movement. As Hyman remarks, Sidney and Beatrice Webb could scarcely have been more mistaken when they wrote that 1920 marked the opening of a new chapter in British trade unionism, when the movement was stronger than it had ever been before and seething with new ideas and far-reaching aspirations (1975, p.xviii).

In the 1920s there was a wave of mergers and a drive towards the 'rationalization' of industry was introduced from Germany around 1924 (Pollard, 1962, p.97). Hannah describes this as British firms 'catching up' with a structure of industry created in the United States before the First World War (1983, p.96). This was not a universal phenomenon in Britain however, for there remained a comparatively low level of investment in new machinery and in educating the workers in new skills[5]; capital was invested abroad rather than at home (see Gamble, 1981; Locke, 1984; Pollard, 1962). Many businessmen were 'restorationists', yearning for the return of pre-war conditions (Littler, 1982, p.101). It seems, with hindsight, that to keep up with her competitors Britain needed to have engineered a major switch to new industries, industries requiring different skills and materials. The steps which were taken towards this were, however, mostly done without planning, hesitantly, clumsily and expensively (Pollard, 1962, p.93).

This situation was reflected in cost accountancy[6], for although it seems probable that the 'rationalization' movement brought with it some increase in the extent and intensity of usage of cost accounting systems there were great variations between industries and between firms within industries. The Balfour Committee on Industry and Trade, set up in 1924, commented on business costing systems in its final report as follows:

> The evidence we have received shows that, although the position is undoubtedly improving, it is by no means satisfactory, even in some of our largest and most important industries. The costing systems of some firms no doubt leave nothing to be desired; but in other cases there appears to be inadequate knowledge of costs, due, as one of our witnesses said, "to indifference, or more often ignorance, of scientific methods of costing, which are generally looked upon at best as a necessary evil". Further, there is little uniformity of principle throughout the costing systems within a given industry (Cmnd. 3282, 1929, pp.225-226).

This uneven development was reflected in the experiences of cost accountants whom I interviewed who had been working at this time. For those who worked in the expanding sectors of the economy or in those old sectors being 'rationalized' there were prospects for self-advancement as cost accounting systems became more sophisticated. Some moved beyond being concerned with just cost accounting as they became more successful. For those who worked in declining sectors, there were fewer opportunities, their employers did not appreciate their skills and resources were not provided for improving the cost accounting systems.

Conclusion

This chapter has ranged widely in its discussion of the relationship between cost accounting, the social organisation of its practitioners and the social context of Britain in the 1920s. It was socially, economically and politically a turbulent period. The patriotic atmosphere of 'one nation' which had come into being during the war was becoming day by day less tangible in the waves of industrial unrest, but at the same time many were clinging to its spirit as the way out of the country's difficulties. The latter was the case with the ICWA, they recognised, in the dreams of reconstruction, a very honoured role for themselves as mediators between Capital and Labour- cost accountants were to be purveyors of 'facts' to the nation. These 'facts' were to be just that, no political impurities were to taint their virgin whiteness- or so it seemed. The cost accountant was to be a man above the vagiaries of politics, a 'technical' and 'scientific' man, working simply to the benefit of the British people. This 'one nation' philosophy surfaced within the discussions of costing itself, standard terminology and uniform costing were presented as the solution to ensuring that British industry *as a whole* was competitive on the world market by ensuring maximum efficiency.

Whilst the ICWA was publically proclaiming their apolitical stance, internally they were quick to disassociate themselves from anything which might link them with socialism. Their rather hysterical reaction to the invitation which the Manchester branch made to J.R. Clynes to speak, is an interesting case of this. As an aspiring professional association eager for the continued support of prominent industrialists, it is not hard to understand their support for Capital, rather than Labour. Although evidence is scanty, it seems quite likely that one of the reasons that industrialists were so happy to support the ICWA was that they had an interest in their cost accountants and clerks being 'professionals'. The possibility of the unionisation of office workers, and of their collaboration with union members on the shopfloor must have struck fear into the hearts of manufacturers.

Whilst, as was noted in the previous chapter, the ICWA liked to link itself with the ICAEW; Child places it in a different context, namely as one of a group of management institutes which were formed in the two decades from 1911 to 1931. The people joining the ICWA were, it seems, by and large, successful clerks who had gained for themselves a responsible position in the administration of work in the factory. In this, they had much in common with those 'sales managers', 'office managers' and 'industrial administrators' who were presumably joining the associations which Child lists as being formed. It seems curious that, in all my study of the records of the ICWA I never once came across a reference to any of these bodies. On the other hand, perhaps it is *not* surprising: the ICWA was anxious to distance itself from other employees and to associate itself firmly with more independent professionals- bankers, accountants, and solicitors, as they said.

Overall, the situation in the 1920s in Britain, which Mowat describes as an "uneasy relationship between stability ... and change" (1955, p.202), was mirrored in cost accounting. It is a bureaucratic control system, part of the largely twentieth century concept of the organisation of work which involves taking its control away from those who do it. Yet despite the modernity of the craft, its practitioners associated themselves into a professional body which was nineteenth century in its social intent.

NOTES

(1) The reason for this change is not recorded, perhaps it was because they felt that his standing and popularity as an industrialist was greater than Lord Weir's, on the other hand perhaps Lord Leverhulme showed greater interest. Lord Weir does not appear to have been too offended by this move, for he did accept a vice-presidency in 1921 (IA, ECB 84, 10 October 1921).

(2) On Leverhulme see Jolly (1976); on Weir, see Reader (1968, 110-112); on Hadfield, Tweedale (1985); on Rowntree, Child (1969, pp.44-51) and on Austin, Church (1984). There are verbatim reports of their speeches in *The Cost Accountant*.

(3) The association of costing and estimating clerks together is interesting. It recalls the association made in Elbourne's book *Factory Administration and Accounts* (1914), between the works accountant and the estimator. It is thus curious that only 9 of the job titles of members as listed in the *1923 Year Book* (IA) contained the word 'estimate' or 'estimator'.

It is interesting to look at the Industry Tables in the census to examine in which industries, and in what proportion to other clerks, the costing and estimating clerks were employed. An analysis by industry is given in the Appendix to this thesis. As an indication of the relative proportions of the members of the occupations analysed under the heading 'clerks and draughtsmen (not civil service or local authority)' the analyses for three of the industry classifications are given overleaf:

Classification of occupation under XXV111	Steel Works and steel rolling mills	Manufacture of textile machinery and accessories	Production of newspapers and periodicals
930 Company Secretaries and Registrars	106	66	128
931 Heads and Managers of Commercial Office Departments	203	37	118
932 Draughtsmen	741	435	-
933 Costing and Estimating Clerks	639	206	114
939 Other Clerks	6401	1899	7774

Source: 1921 Census, Industry Tables (pp. 40,53,128)

It appears that there was no category covering 'accountants' working in industry. It seems likely that they were included under 931 or 933.

(4) Despite this two measures past by parliament in 1919 and 1920 did have a lasting impact, although not forseen at the time. The first was the provision by the government of substantial subsidies for the building of 'homes fit for heroes'- as they had been referred to in the campaign promises (Mowat, 1955, pp.43-45). The second was the provision of state aid to protect unemployed workers from the consequences of industrial fluctuations, it was intended originally as self-financing insurance but the continuing high level of unemployment wrecked its solvency (ibid., pp.45-46).

(5) Despite the initial belief that the slump of 1921 was a temporary set-back and the result of post-war adjustments (Pollard, 1962, p.92-99), it soon became apparent that Britain's position in the world- military, financial and industrial- was one of reducing importance. This is shown, for instance, by the fact that Britain's share of world export trade in manufactured goods fell from 27.5% in 1911/1913, to 23.8% in 1921/1925 (Pollard, 1962, p.188). Perhaps the

greatest weakness was the fact that the country was producing most in the areas in which world demand was going down.

(6) It is worth mentioning at this point the "army costing experiment" as it became known. Set up in 1919 it aimed to establish in the Army:

> ... a set of accounts on commercial income and expenditure principles with the ultimate aim of arriving at the true annual cost of each Army Unit and establishment, in detail and under all items, cash and accrued receipts and payments, services rendered and received, capital charges, &c (Walkland & Hicks, 1960, pp.51-52).

A new corps of Military Accountants was raised to organise the system. Eventually, in 1925, the system experiment was ended there was a return to cash accounting. The War Office, Treasury and the Comptroller and Auditor General being unanimous in their evidence to the Public Accounts Committee in 1925 that the extra cost of the new accounts exceeded the savings. Even if the system had been fully developed, they argued "the factor of military efficiency was not susceptible either in general or in detail of being represented in money terms"(quoted in ibid., p.55).

CHAPTER 8

CONCLUSION

> What we call the beginning is often the end
> And to make an end is to make a beginning.
> The end is where we start from.
>
> T.S. Eliot

Underlying the writing of this thesis has been the belief that it is important to question the dominant view of accounting in society, a view whereby it is regarded as a purely technical matter outside the realm of the social. First, in the theory chapter, the nature of cost and management accounting as as social practice was explored and some ideas were developed of how it could be studied. These ideas provided the basis for the second part of the thesis, a case study of cost accounting in Britain in the period 1914 to 1925. The aspect of cost accounting focused upon was the emergence, in the context of a 'coming into the light' of cost accounting during the First World War, of a new association, the Institute of Cost and Works Accountants. This body claimed for those working with costing in industry, a professional position analogous to that of chartered accountants. The events surrounding this provided a fascinating context in which to examine cost accounting as a social practice: a practice not simply shaped by its context, but itself playing a constitutive role in creating that context.

Methodologically, this work was inspired by Michel Foucault's genealogical history, *Discipline and Punish*. The principle features of this are, firstly, its basic understanding of our society as a 'society of normalisation'- one in which disciplinary institutions and techniques play a central role in maintaining the social order; secondly, a notion that these institutions and techniques are involved in the creation of 'truth' ie. that their techniques produce a knowledge which is widely accepted in society; and thirdly, that the way to understand how this came to be is to make a very detailed study of the emergence and development of these techniques. The latter involves looking not just at the major events and interpreting them in the light of what we know now, but at the small shifts in ways of conceptualising things; at the great plans which came to nought- in other words exploring the rich "singularity of events outside of any monotonous finality" (Foucault, 1977, p.139). Whilst maintaining this basic perspective the analysis moved through a critique of certain aspects of Foucault's work (most notably his lack of consideration of the power of human agents) to a consideration of the role, albeit restricted by social conditions, of practitioners of disciplinary techniques in creating and defining their own work. The grouping of practitioners of particular techniques into professional bodies, integrated into the powerful elites in society, encourages the furthering of the knowledge and practice of those techniques. Such a perspective can help to explain why work in different social and cultural milieu is disciplined in different ways.

The Professionalisation of Cost and Management Accounting

The case study presented in the latter part of the thesis, that of cost accounting in the period 1914-1925, was primarily concerned with the growth of interest in cost accounting during the First World War, and the events surrounding the subsequent formation of an association claiming professional status for those practising the techniques in organisations.

By the eve of the First World War cost accounting systems had apparently been introduced into many of the larger works in Britain, however some systems were very inadequate and in smaller works costing tended to be very much a 'rule of thumb' affair. Despite the development of a discourse about the techniques- in the form of textbooks and articles in trade journals, there does not seem to have been a clearly defined occupation 'cost accountant'. There were, on the one hand, specialist 'cost clerks' emerging out of the division of labour in the factory, and on the other, various 'consultants' (some of them professional engineers and accountants, many others not formally qualified) involved with their design and installation.

The elite of accountants, the members of the ICAEW, had widened their sphere of professional knowledge to include cost accounting, but at rather a minimal level, for neither the questions on it in their examinations, nor the articles appearing in *The Accountant* were very sophisticated. There seems to have been some differences of opinion amongst the members as to the importance of this new field 'cost accounting'; a few were very keen, the rest either indifferent or even hostile. The latter views perhaps associated with the tentative nature of the acceptance in society of chartered accountants as professional people. Too much association with industry could damage their claim to be like the respected members of the older, 'gentlemanly' professions such as the law.

Such a context was to change, however. As part of the monumental transformation of society which occured during the war cost accounting was brought to the attention of manufacturers and into the realm of public discussion. The bringing of cost accountants and cost accounting 'into the light' came as a virtually unanticipated consequence of the war-time legislation that was passed with the intention of helping to prevent profiteering (the cause of much working-class discontent), and to provide a basis for setting the prices of contracts for items for which there was no clearly identifiable market price. It came as part of an uneasy resolution between the desire to keep 'business as usual' and to set up a command type economy to cope with the massive problems of production of armaments and distribution of scarce resources, including food, at a time of war.

The government, manufacturers, and even some members of the public became more *aware* of cost accounting. Those 'tucked away in their factory fastnesses' who were involved with costing in industry suddenly attained a new importance in the eyes of manufacturers; for the facts which they created now had a very real effect upon the profits of business- they were no longer simply 'mere' representations of activity. Revenue became actually *dependent* upon the measurement of costs. In addition, the relaxation of union working practices and mass production of armaments in itself encouraged the spread of 'rational' techniques of management, such as cost accounting.

Whilst the practitioners of cost accounting were 'coming into the light' in the factory, eminent chartered accountants were becoming involved with it through their work in the war ministries. Chartered and incorporated accountants were identified by the government as individuals who could deal with the horrendous accounting problems caused by the legislation that they had passed. Essentially their role became to *police* many of the economic aspects of centralised control. Recognising their importance, the government made a large number them (depending on age and marital status) exempt from service when conscription was introduced in 1916. These events had the dual effect of increasing the status of accountants, and making cost accounting a much more respectable activity within the profession (it became more clearly part of the portfolio of activities which these professional accountants considered their field of knowledge and practice). The examinations of the ICAEW begun to include sophisticated questions on cost accounting. Before the war only a passing knowledge of the subject would seem to have been necessary in order to qualify as a chartered accountant. By 1918 a much more thorough understanding was required- for included in the examinations were complex numerical questions on the subject, and in addition ones concerning the performance of 'cost audits'. Detailed articles on cost accounting became common in *The Accountant*. The knowledge base of the profession itself changed as a result of the war. Their work in the spheres of bankruptcy, audit and accountancy prior to the war had brought some general recognition of the importance of accountants to the life of the country; their war-work greatly increased this, one sign of it being the civil honours which they received, something for which their work had not previously been considered of suitably deserving merit. They had come into much closer contact with the privileged elites of British society and benefited accordingly.

The events of the war set the stage for the emergence, directly after the war ended, of two organisations for the practitioners of cost accounting; the one aimed at chartered and incorporated accountants, the other at those clerks and accountants actually operating those systems in factories. They appeared at a time when the country was in a state of economic and social turmoil. Towards the close of the war many believed that the spirit which had emerged of 'one nation', of Labour and Capital working together for the good of everyone in the country, could be maintained. Britain could win the trade war as she was winning the military battles, cost accounting was to be an important 'weapon' in winning this fight. Although socialists such as Sidney Webb, and industrialists such as Lord Leverhulme, had very different *ends* in view as to the future of British society, the *means* which they envisaged using were similar in that they wanted the rationalisation of production- including therein the furthering of the use of cost accounting. In the plans for reconstruction cost accounting appeared as a technique of some importance. Seeing it another way, in the formation and discussion of these plans another arena emerged for cost accounting discourse, an arena whose characteristics helped to shape the content of this discourse.

Despite these developments the attempt to bring together chartered and incorporated accountants in a costing association failed, the traditionalists within the ICAEW managed to restrain almost all efforts towards, as the reformists saw it, 'modernisation'. In the eyes of those desiring change the Institute appeared 'old fashioned'- its system of payment of premiums for articles seemed set to ensure that those with talent, but no money, were excluded; its elderly hierarchy was too absorbed in the old established areas of practice to understand the enormous opportunities which awaited them if they would only get more involved with industry. The reformists saw involvement with cost accounting as the future road to success for accountants, who might otherwise degenerate into being an organisation of mere book-keepers. However, the Institute largely succeeded in ignoring all the demands for change. It made no moves to try to educate its members in cost accounting, except that its presence in the examination syllabus was formalised. It did not interfere with the 'premium' system in operation with regard to articles. It dealt with the claims of the National Guild of Accountants' Clerks for (amongst other things) a Whitley Council scheme for those clerks and accountants who were employees in professional offices, simply by declaring them 'inappropriate' and ignoring their demands. Nevertheless, despite the attitude of the ICAEW, there was a growth in the employment of accountants in senior positions in industry from the early 1920s (Armstrong, 1985).

It was at this time that a specialist organisation for those practising costing in organisations came into being, namely the ICWA. This body had an inauspicious start as an association originated, so it seems, largely with the aim of making money for its creator. However, it was soon taken over by individuals who had a vision of organising cost accountants into a professional association. This body claimed for itself a place amongst the established professional accounting associations. The members of any aspiring profession do not operate in a social vacuum- they only know what a profession *is* through the concrete examples which they see around them in society. These examples set a frame of reference through which they begin to define their role. In the case of the ICWA it was the ICAEW which acted as the main reference point as to what a professional association did and how 'professionals' should behave.

The war had brought chartered and incorporated accountants greater social recognition and status. It had set the seal on the legitimacy of *accounting* as a socially recognised profession. Given this, it is not surprising that what appeared to them as an attempt by those working with costing in industry to exploit this advance, caused the chartered and incorporated accountants annoyance. They considered that the ICWA was encroaching upon their 'territory' of knowledge and practice. If a manufacturer required advice on the installation or operation of a cost accounting system, then the qualified accountant operating from his professional office was equipped to do the job. According to the ICAEW, the ICWA members claim to be professional accountants was inappropriate, for they were the 'technicians' of industry.

The scene was being set for professional rivalry within accounting over this work 'cost accounting'. The ICWA had set the terms of this debate by claiming to be a professional accounting body- a rather awkward claim for a body whose members were mostly employees to make. As employees they were in a very different relationship to their 'clients' (if one can refer to their employers in these terms) than the members of the ICAEW, most of whom worked, independently from their clients, in professional offices. Despite this, the whole question of the relevance and applicability of the traditions of chartered accountants never appears to have been considered by the ICWA, at least such discussion was never even vaguely hinted at in the Minute Books, or in the public discussions recorded verbatim in *The*

Cost Accountant. In their own self-definition they seem to have dealt with this by *defining* themselves as skilled accountants with *practical* workshop knowledge. They were basically accountants, the thing which both made them different to chartered accountants, and in the field of costing actually superior, was this technical experience and knowledge. The attempt of this group, consisting mostly of individuals working in offices in factories, to model their occupational association upon the practices of the older professions led to strange anomalies. For instance, protocol appeared to decree that professions had to have articled clerks. Despite the obvious difficulties which would occur in a situation such as that the ICWA were in, where a third party, the employer, was directly in control of both the principal and the clerk, articles were registered. Indeed, in their application for a Royal Charter the regulations controlling the articled clerk-principal relationship were laid out in great detail, including ones regulating the number of articled clerks a principal could have.

The whole process of professionalisation was instrumental in creating the role 'cost and works accountant', both for individuals who joined (this came through clearly in a number of my interviews with members who had been working during the period) and, more generally, in organisations and society. This process of definition encouraged three related forms of standardisation to come to cost accounting, as it had done to accounting in the late nineteenth century after the formation of the ICAEW. Firstly, there was the the beginning of 'standardisation' of practitioners, in the sense that conditions were set for entry to the Institute, including experience, education, and (of gradually growing importance) examinations. Secondly, came the start, albeit small, of standardisation of knowledge. Cost accounting began to be more clearly distinguishable from other related fields of knowledge; both the Institute's journal, and the examinations, were important in this process. Related to this came a third form of standardisation, inevitably extremely slow, of the practice itself. Again examinations and the journal both encouraged this.

The standardisation of practitioners, knowledge and practice was furthered by the fact that the ICWA created *physical* opportunities for discourse on the subject of cost accountancy. In the early years the public meetings which they held in London, and in other major cities in Britain, provided a forum for discussion which was not merely internal to the ICWA. Well-known industrialists, local dignitaries, and members of other professional bodies were gathered to hear lectures, and to talk about various aspects of cost accounting. These discussions were often as much concerned with the role of the cost accountant in industry and society as with the technical details of knowledge and practice. Probably with more influence internally amongst members, than externally, was the monthly journal entitled "The Cost Accountant", begun in 1921. This provided a forum for the presentation and discussion of ideas concerning the subject, mainly technical, but inevitably also regarding the role and status of the cost accountant. The "Notes and Commments" column provided as space for the Institute to bring to the attention of members matters they considered concerned them. Through editorials they gave a perspective on current events from a cost accountant's point of view. The correspondence column giving an opportunity for feedback from members. The role of the cost and works accountant in organisations and in society was made clearer to members and students through this discourse, at the same time there was probably some impact upon the wider business community too.

The ICWA did not only create physical spaces for discourse, but also an intellectual one. This occured through the choice of subjects included in the journal, for discussion at meetings and in the examinations. Taking the examinations as an example, whilst the 'workshop knowledge' examination paper was clearly not a cost accounting paper, its presence indicated that this domain of knowledge was *associated* with cost accounting. This, and the other ancillary papers, created an intellectual boundary around the subject matter. There was cost accounting at the core, but it was a cost accounting placed in the context of these associated subjects. Thus it occupied an *intellectual space* between book-keeping and accounts, general business methods and organisation, economics, mathematics, workshop knowledge and certain law subjects (for instance the Factory Acts): these being the subjects other than costing questioned at the Intermediate and Final examinations in 1923 (IA, *1923 Year Book*). This definition of an intellectual space in which cost accounting knowledge was to grow and develop reflected the characteristics of the niche which the ICWA were defining for themselves in the professional and business world as an association of accountants with practical experience who could act as valuable advisors to businessmen.

One of the consequences of the coming into being of an association of practitioners is the appearance of a physical and intellectual space for discourse about the area to occur. The physical settings provided for discussion are clear to see, less clear, but nonetheless important is the intellectual space created as the knowledge base of the profession is defined in relation to other other subjects.

The early members of the ICWA made their own history in the sense that they pursued a policy of exclusionary closure based upon the model provided by chartered accountants; however, their actions were inevitably shaped by the social context in which they occured. They actively sought and exploited opportunities for furthering their cause, at the same time the range of opportunities which presented themselves were a function of the historical moment.

Given that the ideal of 'public service' was a central element in the professional ideology which had developed in England (Duman, 1979, p.114), the successful presentation by the ICWA of a claim to be working for the public good could facilitate their claim to be a profession. 'Reconstruction' was a moment very conducive to this, for it was a time when the members of such an occupation who were largely employees, could claim to be working in the public service. Making British industry efficient was being seen from a national, not only a firm oriented, perspective. It was pointed out that if all companies in an industry had accurate uniform costing systems then the comparisons of costs thus enabled would mean that the least efficient firms would be made aware of their situation. Accidental undercutting of the prices of efficient firms, by inefficient ones with inadequate cost accounting systems, was a situation which was bad for the nation, not just for particular manufacturers. At the same time disputes within firms between Capital and Labour concerning wages were to be settled by reference to costs. Figures of costs would simply reveal the maximum an employer could afford to pay his workers and there could be no arguing with *the facts*. The profession of cost and works accountant could become one of considerable dignity if cost accountants became the arbitrators in disputes between Capital and Labour.

However, as the ambitious plans of reconstruction were forgotten in the depression of the early 1920s, and the threat of a workers' revolution receded, these ideas of the ICWA faded out of their discussions. The ideas no longer had much credibility in the wider society and thus the opportunity of the Institute to exploit them on behalf of their members was no longer there. They would seem to be interesting evidence, though, of the subtle links between a profession and its context: in this case between the adoption of a professional ideology associated with the independent professions, the context of of the 'one nation' spirit of reconstruction and an area of planned practice which would bring to these cost accountants a role independent from their employers.

Cost and Management Accounting in Society

This work has raised many issues beyond those discussed in the preceding section. One of the most fascinating of these is the question of the "conditions of possibility" for cost accounting to emerge. This disciplinary technique, which enables very diverse activities in an organisation to be compared, contrasted, aggregated and analysed through their translation into the common terminology of money, emerged in factories during the nineteenth century. This emergence seems to have been associated with, amongst other things, the beginning of the separation of ownership from control, businesses becoming larger in size, the rise of labour as an organised force, and pressure from competition between manufacturers. Within the factories of the early industrial revolution the old feudal notions of work prevailed, labour was used extensively, and the amount of work performed was governed by custom. This was gradually replaced, during the nineteenth century, by the understanding that labour was a commodity, a factor of production to be bought and sold like any other. It was in this context that the activities of workers became the subject of more detailed management, and the *cost* of labour an object for analysis.

In the discussion of the development of cost accounting prior to 1914 it was noted how the early cost accounting systems in use at, for instance, the works of Boulton & Watt and Wedgwood, did not spread quickly to other factories. This was due, it was suggested to there being only a very limited discourse about them. The methods were largely the design of the family owners of the businesses, they came into being gradually rather than suddenly, as part of a pre-designed plan, there were no sophisticated books on the subject, or journals dealing with the issues; lastly, costs were considered to be a trade secret. Later, in the latter part of the nineteenth century, when the organisation of business had become a subject for wide debate through the publication of textbooks, trade journals and associations, there were *physical places* for discourse to occur. Accounting entered into the *text*. The growing concern with the structure and operation of business opened up, in a sense, an intellectual 'space' for discourse about systems for 'discovering' and controlling costs; accompanying this came a physical space in the sense of trade associations and journals. When pre-existing professional groups, in particular engineers and accountants, took an interest in it, the knowledge and practice began to be shaped by their interests and concerns.

By the eve of the First World War some chartered accountants had become extremely interested in this area, and it was they (and a smaller number of incorporated accountants) who took senior positions in the war ministries dealing with it. Through their involvement with cost accounting during the war they had an impact on the practice of cost accounting. Through the articles that appeared in *The Accountant* they influenced the knowledge of cost accounting. It was their power and position which was perhaps one of the factors leading to *costing* in Britain becoming closely connected with the practice of *accounting*. Another factor was maybe the lack (despite a flurry of interest in the period of reconstruction) of an established scientific management movement to provide an alternative physical and intellectual space for its discussion. The establishment of an association for those working with cost accounting in industry as a professional *accounting* body further confirmed the link between accounting and costing.

Most of the discussion up to this point in the conclusion has been based upon the understanding that cost and management accounting knowledge and practice reflects issues and ideas current in the wider society. Such relationships are not uni-directional however, for cost and management accounting plays a constitutive role in creating that society. These systems produce a widely accepted 'truth' about life which influences peoples' perceptions of the world and their actions within it.

This constitutive role can be seen in operation in the period researched in this thesis, for during the First World War the compromises engendered by the maintenance of a basically capitalist economy through a period of close government control led to cost accounting becoming important. As the state attempted to find means to operationalise the draconion powers it had taken to control industry, the 'economic facts of life' which these cost accounting systems produced took on a significance beyond the boundaries of the business organisation. The using of costs as a means for determining revenue, and as a means of identifying profiteering, increased the reification of them. They became the apparently underlying *reality* which could be used as a base for calculating a substitute for market price.

Another instance of this constitutive role is to be seen in the relationship between cost accounting and the idea of 'reconstruction' developed during, and in the period immediately following, the war. Britain was to win the trade war by becoming an efficient nation: a notion of efficiency crucially dependent upon the assumption that the widespread use of costing systems would enable the rationalisation of production. In the nationalistic vision of an efficient reconstructed Britain, can be seen the concept of an efficient business enterprise writ large- an 'enterprise' in which contented workers manufacture good quality saleable products for the world market in the most cost effective way possible. The perception of this solution, and indeed, the problem to which it was directed, were dependent upon a prior understanding of costs *as* measurable facts. In other words the language and concepts of accounting shaped the understanding and proposed solution of Britain's problems as a nation.

Accounting and the State

The relationship between accounting and the state is a fascinating one, and it is worthwhile bringing together some of the points raised at various points in this thesis, although their detailed exploration remains for further work.

From the very beginning of the profession in England and Wales, the institutions of the state have been involved. The bankruptcy and companies legislation of the mid-nineteenth century, introduced to mediate the relationship between those investing in businesses and those who run them, and between business and the general public; was strongly connected with the appearance of an accounting profession. They emerged as specialists in creating and presenting the economic 'facts' of the life of a business or an individual- making 'visible' to agents of the state, in a clear form, the nature of those transactions. The audit legislation, introduced during the latter part of the nineteenth century, extended this role. The auditor began to be seen as a guarantor of the economic 'facts' coming from a business or individual. Whilst presenting themselves, and being presented by others as independent professionals they were dependent upon the institutions of the state- indirectly or directly- for their work[1]. As I have discussed in Chapter 4, the enormous expansion of the state's sphere of control during the First World War brought much prestige, and business, to chartered and incorporated accountants. One unintended consequence of the actions of the government during the war with regards to taxation, was to lead to the formal legal acceptance of accounting as one of the professions.

Whilst on the surface of it the relationship between cost and management accountants and the state is less direct (dealing as they do, with the internal accounts of enterprises), this thesis has clearly shown that at certain times in history there have been important links. The arms industry prior to the First World War witnessed this, for the Government used the costs of manufacture at their national factories to pressurise their contractors In the First World War this relationship became more complex as 'costs' became the facts determining not only the prices which manufacturers received for the munitions of war, but through profiteering legislation many of the essentials of life.

The state in 1918 was a very different thing to what it was in 1914. Cost accounting itself facilitated this expansion of the state, for the systems which were set up in national factories, and which manufacturers were developing, provided a knowledge about production which the state used. This form of knowledge was very appropriate to a setting in which, despite the state control of industry, the basic capitalist system of manufacture remained intact.

Further research on the relationship between accounting and the continuing growth of the state is needed. Such a study would be in sympathy with that recently suggested by researchers interested in the state (Evans et al, 1985); they emphasise the importance of detailed historical and comparative study to understanding the intertwining of the state with societal structures. Research on the relationship between accounting and the state could play a significant role in such explanations, for accounting not only provides an important facilitative device in mediating the relationships between business organisations and the state; it provides a whole way of perceiving the relationship.

Implications and Further Work

Although the present study only examined cost accounting in its social context in one short period of time, the research has more general implications for research and practice in accounting. One of the most important points to be brought out is that the practice, knowledge and social organisation of accounting exist neither independently from each other, or from the social context in which they occur. Accounting must be understood as a social phenomenon intimately linked to the society in which it exists, and in order to study its present, it is necessary to study its past. Although this work does not cover the period up to the present, it sheds light on some aspects of the current state of the knowledge and practice of cost and management accounting in Britain. Perhaps more significantly though, it sets an agenda for further research in accounting, an agenda for extending our understanding of accounting in society.

The emphasis placed here on the importance of 'history' is an unusual one, for historical research in accounting has tended to be ignored in academia in favour of the furthering of current knowledge and practice. In arguing that the accounting of the past is the "food of antiquarians", not worth the effort of the serious historian, and has little of worth to tell us, Lister puts a common point of view in a manner perhaps a little more extreme than most (1983, p. 68). It is likely that his attitude has been conditioned by the traditional histories of accounting, which, focusing upon the technical and procedural aspects alone, appear only to illustrate how accounting has gradually got better. Coupled with this are the histories of professional associations which seem only to celebrate their growth and success.

My work here goes some way towards illustrating how inadequate such traditional history is. For instance, the profound effect which the social upheaval of the First World War in Britain had on cost accountants and cost accounting in this country is largely ignored by writers such as Edwards (1937), Solomons (1952) and Garner (1954), all of whose texts are considered classics in the field. Part of the problem with their work stems from a general lack of contextual awareness, a lack which leads, for example, to events in the US and in

Britain being juxtaposed in a historically insensitive manner. History like this, which focuses upon the technical alone, itself furthers the conception of accounting as 'merely' concerned with the collection of economic facts. It helps to conceal the essentially social nature of the activity.

On the other hand, the histories of professional associations tend to studiously ignore the technical aspects of the craft which their members practice. They ignore the subtle linkages between the social position of practitioners and the knowledge which they claim jurisdiction over, linkages which have been illustrated in this thesis. The existence of a professional association provides both a place and an intellectual focus for debate about the knowledge and practice. A debate which influences the actual content of that knowledge and practice. 'Professionalisation' is a complex social phenomenon involving the linkage of a body of people with a body of knowledge and techniques. The relationship between the people and the practices must be understood in their social context. It is hoped that in this context this study of accounting has a contribution to make, not only to the field of accounting, but also to the sociology of the professions. The latter being a field which, according to Saks (1983), has suffered from the lack of adequate empirical research. In bringing in the knowledge base of the profession as a factor to be considered when examining a process of professionalisation the work done here has gone beyond most in this field.

In the field of academic research in accounting an interest in the history of accounting has surfaced under the rubric of 'positive' research. 'Positive' research is directed towards explaining why certain accounting practices in society exist, and does so by assuming a world made up of rational actors maximising their own self-interest. In the case of the appearance in the accounting literature of theories concerning the nature of depreciation, Watts & Zimmerman 'explain' them as a simple result of the regulation of the rates of profit allowed to be made by rail companies (1979, pp.290-293). They analyse accounting theories "as economic goods, produced in response to the demand for theories" (ibid., p. 273). From this perspective, theories of depreciation arose as the result of a demand for theories rationalising depreciation as an expense (ibid., p.293). This work of what has become known as the 'Rochester School' essentially uses the principles of economics to 'explain' the existence of accounting in its present form, and indeed aims to predict how it will change (1980, p.107). Although interesting critiques have been produced of this approach (see Christenson, 1983; Tinker et al, 1982), I would suggest that the most fruitful way of criticising this School is through theoretically informed historical research of the form carried out in this thesis.

The knowledge and practice of accounting undergo changes, these changes are intertwined with important social changes. It is in such a context that further research on accounting in Britain, of the form of that done in this thesis, could make an important contribution to furthering our understanding of the relationship between accounting and the society in which it is practised. Another, and perhaps an even more valuable contribution, could come from studies of this nature comparing accounting in different countries. By the study of the similarities and differences in practices between one country and another, new understandings can emerge of the roles of accounting in organisations and society. In Britain accounting plays a prominent role in industry, as Armstrong writes, there is a "comparative pre-eminence of accountants in British management hierarchies" and an "emphasis on financial modes of control within British companies" (1985, p.1). It is interesting to speculate about a possible link between the presence of a large number of professional accountants working in senior positions in industry and this emphasis on financial modes of control. Additionally it would be interesting to examine whether these factors are related to the value placed in Britain on the knowledge and practice of *professionals* as opposed to bureaucrats. International comparative research could provide fascinating insights into this question. Work already done in this area suggests that in Continental Europe professional accountants have neither been produced in such relatively large numbers, nor moved into such senior positions in industry. At the same time there is less emphasis in those countries on financial modes of control (Hopwood, 1985; Horowitz, 1980).

To end on a reflexive note, looking at accounting now, one of the most distinctive differences from the period considered in this thesis is the presence of accounting academics. During this century accounting has become the subject of academic work- knowledge about accounting is now being created and refined in universities, business schools and other such institutions. This was a phenomenon only just beginning in Britain in the period 1914 to 1925. The complex relationship between the practice of accounting, its knowledge, and the social organisation of the work has been made yet more so by the institutionalisation of accounting as an academic subject. The importance of this linkage must be revealed by detailed historical study.

Conclusion

In this thesis there has been a detailed examination of the complex interplay between knowledge, techniques, institutions and occupational claims at one period in the history of accounting. It is through such genealogical history that accounting can begun to be understood as a fundamentally social activity, not merely a technical one. Hopefully it has illustrated that those who seek to understand the present role of accountants and accounting in organisations and society would do well to examine its past. Additionally, that those who seek to understand the history of accounting ignore the complex relationship between the social and organisational context and the knowledge and practice of the subject at their peril.

NOTE

(1) It is worth noting that the state itself sanctions the activities of the accounting profession by the giving of royal charters. Although there has never been the restriction of practice to a list of state registered individuals (as has been the case with some other professions, such as medicine), restrictions have gradually come into force concerning who can carry out the accounting and auditing work required by law. Certain professional bodies, sanctioned by the state, effectively carry out what is 'registration' in all but name, for only their members are allowed to perform this work.

APPENDIX

COSTING AND ESTIMATING CLERKS

Industry	No.
Coal Mines	282
Coal, Iron and Steel Companies	59
Manufacture of Earthenware, China, Porcelain, etc.	44
" Glass (not Bottles)	77
" Alkalis & Heavy Acids	98
" Dyes	85
" Drugs & Fine Chemicals	69
" Paints & Colours	71
" Vegetable Oils, etc.	64
" Soaps, Candles, etc.	151
" Pig Iron (Blast Furnaces)	84
Steel Works & Rolling Mills	639
Iron Foundries	138
Brass, etc., Foundries	71
Manufacture of Tubes (Iron or Steel)	123
" Stationery Engines & Power Transmission Plant	258
" Steam Locos, Road and Rail, and Railway Plant	247
Agricultural Engineering	154
Textile Machinery, etc.	206
Heating and Ventilating Engineering	92
Machine Tools	157
Other Engineering (not Marine or Electric)	1931
Manufacture of Generators, Motors, Transformers, Switchgear	1266
" Cables, Wire, Flex	493
Electric Wiring and Contracting	83
Other Electrical Manufactures	498
Building Rolling Stock for Railways and Tramways	284
Manufacture of Self-Propelled Vehicles (not Steam) and Cycles	1123
" Carriages, Coach and Motor Bodies	99
" Cycle & Motor Accessories	78
Shipbuilding and Repairing and Marine Engineering	1032
Manufacture of Boilers & Tanks	136
" Bolts, Nuts, Rivets	

& Screws	66
Constructional Engineering, Bridge and Girder Work	192
Sheet Metals Working (not Brass and excluding fine Brass, fine Brass, Cannisters, etc.), Stamping and Piercing	76
Manufacture of Stoves, Grates, Ranges	71
Other Metal Industries	184
Cotton Weaving	154
Textile Bleaching, Printing, Dyeing, Finishing	154
Tailoring (including Waterproof and Leather Coating)	194
Manufacture of Boots, Shoes & Slippers (not rubber)	211
Cocoa and Chocolate Manufacture	138
Manufacture of Tobacco, Cigars, Cigarettes, Snuff	104
Saw Mills & Joinery Works	125
Cabinet and Furniture Making and Upholstery	123
Manufacture of House & Shop Fittings	113
Paper & Board Making	65
Manufacture of Paper Bags, Envelopes, Stationery	126
Production of Newspapers, Periodicals	114
Job & General Letter Press Printing	602
Building and Contracting	995
Manufacture of Tyres & Other Rubber Goods	176
" of Scientific Instruments & Other Apparatus	100
Gas Works	168
Electricity Supply	99
Railway Transport Service (excluding those employed in Railway Companies' Works, Docks, Shipping Services, Hotels and Catering Departments)	179
Cartage & Hauling Contracting	99
Shipping Services (excluding those employed in Shipping and Railway Companies' Repair Yards and Marine Engineering Shops)	91
Harbours, Docks, Piers & Lighthouses	60
Dealing in Drysaltry, Oils, Colours (Wholesale)	77
" Metals, Metal Goods and Tools (Wholesale)	128
" Textiles and Clothing	

(Wholesale)	81
" Furniture	110
General & Export Trading and non-Textile Packing	131
Departmental Stores, General Shops, etc.	173
TOTAL	15671[1]

Source: *The Cost Accountant*, September 1925, p.94

NOTE

(1) The total number shown in this analysis is 15,671; the actual total, noted in the text of chapter 8, and in the totals in the census was 19,422. It appears that the person who prepared the table missed out industries where there were very few cost and estimating clerks employed. A number of checks to the analysis were made, and because these showed the table to have been accurately prepared, it was not considered worth repeating the exercise.

BIBLIOGRAPHY

Abrams, P., History, Sociology, Historical Sociology, *Past and Present* (1980) pp.3-16.

Adams, R.J.Q., *Arms and the Wizard: Lloyd George and the Ministry of Munitions 1915-1916* (London: Cassell, 1978).

Addison, C., *Four and a Half Years: A Personal Diary from June 1914 to January 1919* (London: Hutchinson, 1934).

American Accounting Association, *The American Accounting Association: Its First 50 Years* (Sarasota, FL: AAA, 1966).

Aldcroft, D.H., *The Inter-War Economy: Britain, 1919-1939* (London: Batsford, 1970).

Anderson, G., *Victorian Clerks* (Manchester: Manchester University Press, 1976).

Anglo-American Council on Productivity, *Management Accounting: Report of a Specialist Team which visited the United States of America in 1950* (London: Anglo-American Council on Productivity, 1950).

Arendt, H., *The Human Condition* (Chicago: University of Chicago Press, 1958).

Armstrong, P., The Rise of Accounting Controls in British Capitalist Enterprises. Paper presented to the Interdisciplinary Perspectives on Accounting Conference, Manchester, July 1985.

Bahmueller, C. F., *The National Charity Company: Jeremy Bentham's Silent Revolution* (Berkeley, CA: University of California Press, 1981).

Banyard, C. W., *The Institute of Cost and Management Accountants: A History* (London, ICMA, 1985).

Baritz, L., *The Servants of Power: A History of the Use of Social Science in American Industry* (Westport, Connecticut: Greenwood Press, 1974).

Bentham, J., *Works of Jeremy Bentham* ed. Bowring (Edinburgh: William Tait, 1843).

Bentham, J., *Correspondence* Vols 1-6, eds., Sprigge, T.L.S., Christie, I.R., (London: Athlone Press, 1968-).

Berg, M., *The Machinery Question and the Making of Political Economy, 1815-1848* (Cambridge: Cambridge University Press, 1980).

Blau, P. M., *The Dynamics of Bureaucracy* (Chicago, IL: University of Chicago Press, 1955).

Braverman, H., *Labour and Monopoly Capital* (London: Monthly Review Press, 1974).

Brown, R., *A History of Accounting and Accountants* (London: Frank Cass, 1968; originally London: Frank Cass, 1905).

Burchell, S., Clubb, C., Hopwood, A., Hughes, J. & Nahapiet, J., The Roles of Accounting in Organisations and Society, *Accounting, Organisations and Society* (1980) pp.5-27.

Burns., J. H., Dreams and Destinations: Jeremy Bentham in 1828, *The Bentham Newsletter* (1978) pp. 21-30.

Cain, M., The General Practice Lawyer and the Client: Towards a Radical Conception, in Dingwall, R. & Lewis, P. (eds.) *The Sociology of the Professions* (London: Macmillan, 1983) pp. 106-130.

Chandler, A.D., *Strategy and Structure: Chapters on the History of the Industrial Enterprise* (Cambridge, MA: MIT Press, 1962).

Chandler, A.D., *The Visible Hand: The Managerial Revolution in American Business* (Cambridge, MA: Harvard University Press, 1977).

Chandler, A.D. & Daems, H., Administrative Coordination, Allocation and Monitoring: A Comparative Analysis of the Emergence of Accounting and Organisation in the USA and Europe, *Accounting, Organisations and Society* (1979) pp.3-20.

Chatfield, M., *A History of Accounting Thought* (New York: Robert E. Krieger, 1977).

Child, J., *British Management Thought* (Hemel Hempstead: George Allen and Unwin, 1969).

Christenson, C.J., The Methodology of Positive Accounting, *Accounting Review*, (1983) pp.1-22

Church, R.A., Herbert Austin, in Jeremy, D.J. (ed.), *Dictionary of Business Bibliography* (Sevenoaks: Butterworths, 1984).

Clawson, D., *Bureaucracy and the Labour Process: The Transformation of US industry 1860-1920* (New York: Monthly Review Press, 1980).

Cole, G.D.H., Scientific Management, in Cole, G.D.H. (ed.) *Some Problems of Urban and Rural Industry* (Oxford: Ruskin College, 1917).

Collingwood R.G., *Autobiography* (Oxford: Oxford University Press, 1970; originally Oxford: Oxford University Press, 1939).

Cooper, E., 57 Years in an Accountants Office, *The Accountant* (22 October 1921) pp.553-563.

Delgado, A., *The Enormous File: A Social History of the Office* (London: J. Murray, 1979).

Dev, S., *Accounting and the LSE Tradition* (London School of Economics, 1980).

Dickens, C., *Hard Times* (London: J. M. Dent, 1979), originally published in weekly parts in 1854.

Dingwall, R., Accomplishing Profession, *Sociological Review* (1976) pp. 331-349.

Dingwall, R., "In the Beginning was the Work .... " Reflections on the Genesis of Occupations, *Sociological Review* (1983) pp.605-624.

Duman, D., The Creation and Diffusion of a Professional Ideology in Nineteenth Century England, *Sociological Review* (1979) pp. 113-138.

Dunkerley, R., *A Historical Review of the Institute and the Profession* (London: ICWA, 1946).

Edey, H.C., Panitpakdi, P., British Company Accounting and the Law 1844-1900, in Littleton, A.C. & Yamey,B.S. (eds.), *Studies in the History of Accounting* (Homewood, Illinois: Richard D. Irwin, 1956) pp.356-379.

Edwards, R.S., Some Notes on the Early Literature and Development of Cost Accounting in Great Britain, *The Accountant* (1937) pp.193-195; 225-231; 253-255; 283-287; 313-316; 343-344.

Elbourne, E.T., *Factory Administration and Accounts* (London: Longmans, 1914).

Epstein, M.J., *The Effect of Scientific Management on the Development of the Standard Cost System* (New York: Arno Press, 1978).

Esland, G., Professions and Professionalism, in Esland, G., & Salaman G. (eds.) *The Politics of Work and Occupations* (Milton Keynes: Open University Press, 1980) pp. 213-250.

Evans, P. B., Rueschemeyer, D. & Skocpol, T., On the Road to a More Adequate Understanding of the State, in Evans, P.B., Rueschemeyer, D. & Skocpol, T. (eds.) *Bringing the State Back In* (Cambridge: Cambridge University Press, 1985) pp. 347-366.

Evans, R., Regulation and Production, *Lotus International*, Vol 12 (September 1976) pp. 6-14.

Forman, C., *Industrial Town: Self-Portrait of St Helens in the 1920s* (Newton Abbot: David & Charles, 1978).

Foucault, M., *Madness and Civilization: A History of Insanity in the Age of Reason* (London: Tavistock, 1967).

Foucault, M., Orders of Discourse, *Social Science Information* (April 1971) pp.7-30.

Foucault, M., *The Archeology of Knowledge* (London: Tavistock, 1972).

Foucault, M., *The Birth of the Clinic* (London: Tavistock, 1973).

Foucault, M., *Discipline and Punish: The Birth of the Prison* (Harmondsworth: Penguin, 1977a).

Foucault, M., *Language, Counter-Memory, Practice* (Ithaca, NY: Cornell University Press, 1977b).

Foucault, M., *The History of Sexuality* Vol 1 (New York: Robert Hurley, 1978).

Foucault, M., Questions of Method: an interview with Michael Foucault, *Ideology and Consciousness* (Spring 1981) pp. 3-14.

Foucault, M., *Power/Knowledge* (Brighton: Harvester Press, 1980).

Freidson, E., Medical Personnel, in Sills, D.L. (ed.) *International Encyclopedia of the Social Sciences* (New York: Macmillan, 1968).

Freidson, E., *The Profession of Medicine: A Study in the Sociology of Applied Knowledge* (New York: Dodd Mead & Co., 1970).

Gamble, A., *Britain in Decline* (London: Macmillan, 1981).

Gandal, K. & Kotkin, S., Governing Work and Social Life in the USA and USSR, *History of the Present* (February, 1985) pp. 4-14.

Garcke, E., & Fells, J.M., *Factory Accounts* (London: Crosby, Lockwood, 1st edn. 1887; 7th edn. 1922).

Garner, S.P., *Evolution of Cost Accounting to 1925* (Alabama, AL: University of Alabama Press, 1954).

Garner, S.P., Highlights in the Development of Cost Accounting, in Chatfield, M. (ed.), *Contemporary Studies in the Evolution of Accounting Thought* (Belmont, CA: Dickenson, 1968) pp.210-221.

Garrett, A.A., *History of The Society of Incorporated Accountants 1885-1957* (Oxford: Oxford University Press, 1961).

Gaskell, E., *North and South* (Harmondsworth: Penguin, 1970), originally published in 1854-5.

Giordano, A.G., *Concise Dictionary of Business Terminology* (Englewood Cliffs, NJ: Prentice-Hall, 1981).

Godelier, M., Language and History: Work and its Representations: A Research Proposal, *History Workshop Journal* (Autumn 1980), pp.164-174.

Goldstein, J., Foucault among the Sociologists: the "Disciplines" and the History of the Professions, *History and Theory* (1984) pp. 170-192.

Goodrich, C.L., *The Frontier of Control* (London: Pluto Press, 1975; originally London: G.Bell 1920).

Gordon, C., Afterword, in Foucault, M., *Power and Knowledge* (Brighton: Harvester, 1980) pp.229-259.

Gould, S.J., *The Mismeasure of Man* (New York: W.W. Norton, 1981).

Gross, D., Space, Time and Modern Culture, *Telos* (Winter, 1981-82) pp. 59-78.

Haber, S., *Efficiency and Uplift* (Chicago, IL: The University of Chicago Press, 1964).

Hacking, I., How should we do the History of Statistics? *Ideology and Consciousness* (Spring 1981) pp.15-26.

Hakim, C., Census Reports as Documentary Evidence: The Census Commentaries 1801-1951, *Sociological Review* (1980) pp.551-580.

Hannah, L., *The Rise of the Corporate Economy* 2nd edn (London: Methuen, 1983).

Hazell, W.H., *Costing for Manufacturers* (London: Nisbet, 1921).

Held, D. & Krieger, J., Theories of the State: Some Competing Claims, in Bornstein, S., Held,D. & Krieger, J. (eds.) *The State in Capitalist Europe* (London: George, Allen and Unwin, 1984) pp.1-20.

Hindess, B., Power, Interests and the Outcome of Struggles, *Sociology* (1982) pp.498-511.

Hobsbawm, E.J., *Labouring Men* (London: Weidenfeld and Nicholson, 1968).

Hobsbawm, E.J., *Industry and Empire* (Harmondsworth: Pelican, 1969).

Hobsbawm, E.J., *The Age of Capital 1848-1875* (Tunbridge Wells: Abacus, 1977).

Hopwood, A. G., The Development of 'Worrying' about Management Accounting, in Clark, K.B., Hayes, R.H. & Lorentz, C. (eds.) *The Uneasy Alliance: Managing the Productivity-Technology Dilemma* (Boston, MA: Harvard Business School Press, 1985).

Hopwood, A.G., The Archeology of Accounting Systems, *Accounting, Organisations and Society* (1986).

Horngren, C.T., *Introduction to Management Accounting* 6th edn. (Englewood Cliffs, NJ: Prentice-Hall, 1984).

Horowitz, J.H., *Top Management Control in Europe* (London: Macmillan, 1980).

Hoskin, K. & Macve, R., Accounting and the Examination: A Genealogy of Disciplinary Power, *Accounting Organisations and Society* (1986).

Hyman, R., *Forward* to Goodrich (1975), *op.cit.*, pp.vii-xli.

Ignatieff, M., State, Civil Society, and Total Institutions: A Critique of Recent Social Histories of Punishment, in Morris, N., & Tonny, M. (eds.) *Crime and Justice: An Annual Review of Research* (Chicago, IL: University of Chicago Press, 1981) pp. 153-192.

Institute of Chartered Accountants in England and Wales, *The History of the Institute of Chartered Accountants in England and Wales & its Founder Bodies 1870-1965* (London, ICAEW, 1966).

Institute of Cost and Works Accountants, 1919-1969: Portrait of a Profession, *Management Accounting* (1969) pp.91-95.

Irvine, J., Miles, I. & Evans, J. (eds.) *Demystifying Social Statistics* (London: Pluto Press, 1979).

Jeal, E.F., Some Reflections on the Evolution of the Practice of Accountancy in Great Britain, *The Accountant* (10 April 1937) pp.521-529.

Jenks, L.H., Early Phases of the Management Movement, *Administrative Science Quarterly* (1960/61) pp.421-447.

Johnson, H.T., Early Cost Accounting for Internal Management Control: Lyman Mills in the 1850s, *Business History Review* (1972) pp.466-474.

Johnson, H.T., The Role of Accounting History in the Study of the Modern Business Enterprise, *The Accounting Review* (1975) pp.444-450.

Johnson, H.T., Towards a New Understanding of Nineteenth Century Cost Accounting, *The Accounting Review* (1981) pp.510-518.

Johnson, H.T., The State of the Art of Management Accounting Research: History, In Bromwich, M. & Hopwood, A.G., (eds.) *Research and Current Issues in Management Accounting* (London: Pitman, 1986).

Johnson, P.B., *Land Fit for Heroes: The Planning of British Reconstruction 1916-1919* (Chicago, IL: University of Chicago Press, 1968).

Johnson, T., Work and Power, in Esland, G. & Salaman, G. (eds.) *The Politics of Work and Occupations* (Milton Keynes: Open University Press, 1980) pp. 335-371.

Jolly, W.P., *Lord Leverhulme: A Biography* (London: Constable, 1976).

Jones, E.F., Some Accountancy Problems of Yesterday and Today, *The Incorporated Accountants' Journal* (1937) pp.182-188.

Jones, K., & Williamson, K., The Birth of the Schoolroom, *Ideology and Consciousness* (Autumn 1979) pp.59-110.

Jönsson, S., Mental Standardisation and Industrial Development. Paper presented to the European Accounting Association Conference, Brussels, April 1985.

Kaplan, R.S., The Evolution of Management Accounting, *The Accounting Review* (1984) pp.390-418.

Kitchen, J., & Parker.R.H., *Accounting Thought and Education: Six English Pioneers* (London: ICAEW, 1980).

Landes, D.S., *The Unbound Prometheus* (Cambridge: Cambridge University Press, 1969).

Larson, M.S., *The Rise of Professionalism: A Sociological Analysis* (Berkeley, C.A: University of California Press, 1977).

Lister, R.J., Accounting as History, *International Journal of Accounting Education and Research* (1983) pp.49-68.

Littler, C.R., *The Development of the Labour Process in Capitalist Societies* (London: Heinemann, 1982).

Lloyd, E.M.H., *Experiments in State Control at the War Office and the Ministry of Food* (Oxford: Clarendon Press, 1924).

Locke, R., *The End of Practical Man* (Greenwich, CT: JAI Press, 1984).

Lockwood, D., *The Blackcoated Worker: A Study in Class Consciousness* (Hemel Hempstead: Unwin University Books, 1958).

Lukes, S., *Individualism* (Oxford: Blackwell, 1977).

Macdonald, K.M., Professional Formation: the Case of the Scottish Accountants, *British Journal of Sociology* (1984) pp.174-189.

McKendrick, N., Josiah Wedgwood and Factory Discipline, *The Historical Journal* (1961) pp.30-55.

Mackensie, J. & Mackensie, N., *The First Fabians* (London: Weidendeld and Nicholson, 1977).

Marglin, S., What do Bosses Do? The Origins and functions of Hierarchy in Capitalist Production, in Gorz, A. (ed.), *The Division of Labour: the*

Labour Process and Class Struggle in Modern Capitalism (Hassocks: Harvester Press, 1976) pp.43-89.

Markus, T.A., *Order and Space in Society* (Edinburgh: Mainstream, 1982).

Marriner, S., The Ministry of Munitions 1915-1919 and the Government Accounting Procedures, *Accounting and Business Research: Special Accounting History Issue* (1980) pp.130-142.

Merkle, J.A., *Management and Ideology: The Legacy of the International Scientific Management Movement* (Berkeley, C.A: University of California Press, 1980).

Middlemas, K., *Politics in Industrial Society, The Experience of the British System Since 1911* (London: Andre Deutsche, 1979).

Mills, C. Wright, *White Collar* (New York: Oxford University Press, 1956).

Ministry of Munitions, unpublished official history (8 Vols) British Library ref. BS28/12.

Ministry of Munitions Journal, British Library ref. BS28/8.

Mowat, C.L., *Britain Between the Wars, 1918-1940* (London: Methuen, 1955).

Nelson, D., Scientific Management, Systematic Management, and Labour, 1880-1915, *Business History Review* (1974) pp.479-500.

Nelson, D., *Frederick W. Taylor and the Rise of Scientific Management* (Madison, WI: University of Wisconsin Press, 1980).

Nietzsche, F., *On the Genealogy of Morals* (New York: Random House, 1969).

Parkin. F., *Marxism and Class Theory. A Bourgeois Critique* (London: Tavistock, 1979).

Partridge, E., *Dictionary of Slang and Unconventional Language* (Henley: George Routledge, 1937).

Pelling., H. *A History of British Trade Unionism* 3rd edn. (Harmondsworth: Penguin, 1976).

Pigou, A.C., *Aspects of British Economic History 1918-1925* (Macmillan, 1947).

Pollard, S., *The Development of the British Economy 1914-1950* (London: Edward Arnold, 1962).

Pollard, S., Factory Discipline in the Industrial Revolution, *Economic History Review* (1963) pp.254-271.

Pollard, S., *The Genesis of Modern Management* (Harmondsworth: Penguin, 1968).

Pollins, H., Aspects of Railway Accounting Before 1868, in Littleton, A.C. & Yamey, B.S. (eds.) *Studies in the History of Accounting* (Homewood, IL: Irwin, 1956) pp.332-355.

Portwood, D., & Fielding, A., Priviledge & the Professions, *Sociological Review* (1981) pp.749-773.

Rawlinson, E.B., Some Notes on Cost Accounts, *The Incorporated Accountants' Journal* (July 1911) pp.264-268.

Reader, W.J., *Architect of Air Power. The Life of the First Viscount Weir of Eastwood 1877-1959* (Glasgow: Collins, 1968).

Renold, C., Management Accounts, *The Cost Accountant* (September 1950) pp.108-129.

Rider, J., Cost Accounts, *The Incorporated Accountants' Journal* (May 1904) pp.178-187.

Roll, E., *An Early Experiment in Industrial Organisation: Being a History of the Firm of Boulton & Watt, 1775-1805* (London: Longmans, 1930).

Rose, N., The Psychological Complex: Mental Measurement and Social Administration, *Ideology and Consciousness* (Spring 1979) pp. 5-68.

Rueschemeyer, D., Professional Autonomy and the Social Control of Expertise, in Dingwall, R. & Lewis, p. (eds.) *The Sociology of the Professions* (London: Macmillan, 1983) pp.38-58.

Saks, M., Removing the blinkers? A Critique of Recent Contributions to the Sociology of the Professions, *Sociological Review* (1983) pp. 1-21.

Scott, J.D., *Vickers: A History* (London: Weidenfeld and Nicholson, 1962).

Siday, G.A., *Profiteering: In Relation to Cost Accounting. A 20th Century Hoax* (London: E.J. Larby, 1919).

Solomons, D., The Historical Development of Costing, in *Studies in Cost Analysis*, Solomons, D. (ed.) (London: Sweet and Maxwell, 1952) pp. 1-52.

Sowell, E.M., *The Evolution of the Theories and Techniques of Standard Costs* (Alabama: University of Alabama Press, 1973).

Stacey, N.H.A., *English Accountancy, A Study in Social and Economic History, 1800-1954* (London: Gee, 1954).

Steiner, G., *Heidegger* (London: Fontana, 1978).

Steintrager, J.J., *Bentham* (George Allen & Unwin, 1977).

Stevenson, J., *British Society 1914-45* (London: Allen Lane, 1984).

Stone, W.E., An Early English Cotton Mill Cost Accounting System: Charlton Mills 1810-1899, *Accounting and Business Research* (1973) pp.71-78.

Sutherland, G., The Magic of Measurement: Mental Testing and English Education 1900-1940, *Transactions of the Royal Historical Society, 5th Series* (1977) pp.135-153.

Taylor, A.J.P., *English History 1914-1945* (Harmondsworth: Pelican, 1970).

Taylor, F.W., *Scientific Management* (New York: Harper and Row, 1964; originally 1911).

Thompson, E.P., Time, Work Discipline and Industrial Capitalism, *Past and Present* (1967) pp.56-57.

Thompson, E.P., *The Making of the English Working Class* (Harmondsworth: Pelican, 1968).

Tinker, A.M., Merino, B. & Neimark, M.D., The Normative Origins of Positive Theories: Ideology and Accounting Thought, *Accounting Organisations and Society* (1982) pp. 167-200.

Trebilcock, R.C., A 'Special Relationship'- Government, Rearmament, and the Cordite Firms, *Economic History Review* (1966) pp. 364-379.

Trevelyan, G.M., *Illustrated English Social History*, Vol 4 (Harmondsworth: Pelican, 1964).

Tweedale, G., Sir Robert Hadfield, in Jeremy, D.J., (ed.), *Dictionary of Business Bibliography* (Sevenoaks: Butterworths, 1984).

Ure, A., *The Philosophy of Manufacturers: Or, an Exposition of the Scientific, Moral, and Commercial Economy of the Factory System of Great Britain* (London: Charles Knight, 1835).

Urwick, L., & Brech, E.F.L., *The Making of Scientific Management* 2 Vols, (London: Management Publications Trust, 1949).

Walkland, S.A. & Hicks, I., Cost Accounting in British Government, *Public Administration* (1960) pp. 49-59.

Watts, R.L. & Zimmerman, J.L., The Demand for and Supply of Accounting Theories: The Market for Excuses, *Accounting Review* (1979) pp.273-305.

Watts, R.L., & Zimmerman, J.L., Positive Research in Accounting, in Nair, R.D. & Williams, T.H. (eds.), *Perspectives on Research* (Wisconsin: University of Wisconsin Graduate School of Business) pp.107-128.

Webb, B., & Webb, S., What is to be Learnt from the Professional Associations of Brainworkers as to the sphere of Control by Vocational Organisations? Fabian Report published in *New Statesman* (1917) as additional pages: 21 April 1917, pp.1-24; 28 April 1917, pp.25-48.

Webb, S., *The Root of Labour Unrest: An Address to Employers and Managers*, Fabian Tract No. 196 (London: Fabian Society, 1920).

Weber, M., *Economy and Society*, eds., Roth, G., & Wittich, C., (Berkeley, CA: University of California Press, 1978).

Weeks, J., Foucault for Historians, *History Workshop Journal* (Autumn 1982) pp.106-119.

Wells, M.C., *Accounting for Common Costs* (Champaign, IL: Center for International Education and Research in Accounting, University of Illinois, 1978).

Wheeler, S., *On Record* (New York: Russell Sage Foundation, 1969).

Wheldon, H.J., *Cost Accounting and Costing Methods* (London: Macdonald and Evans, 1932).

Wiener, M.J., *English Culture and the Decline of the Industrial Spirit, 1850-1980* (Cambridge: Cambridge University Press, 1981).

Williams, O.A., *Life in a Railway Factory* (London: Duckworth, 1915).

Williams, R., *Keywords* (London: Fontana, 1983).

Wilson, C., *The History of Unilever: A Study in Economic Growth and Social Change* (London: Cassell, 1954).

Woolgar, S., Laboratory Studies: A Comment on the State of the Art, *Social Studies in Science* (1982) pp.483-498.

Printed in Great Britain
by Amazon

59991882R00185